SOUTH NORFOLK
VIRGINIA
1661–2005

SOUTH NORFOLK
VIRGINIA
1661–2005

A DEFINITIVE HISTORY
VOLUME ONE

RAYMOND L. HARPER

Charleston · London

History
PRESS

Published by The History Press
18 Percy Street
Charleston, SC 29403
866.223.5778
www.historypress.net

Front cover image: This photograph of the South Norfolk Volunteer Fire Department was taken in 1916 on the grounds of the South Norfolk Grammar School on B Street. *Photo courtesy of Ben Newberry.*
Back cover image: Members of the South Norfolk Assembly of God met in this converted garage at the intersection of Bainbridge Boulevard and Poindexter Street in 1930 with their pastor, J.M. Oliver. The church later became the Bethel Assembly of God, and is now located at the corner of Decatur and Grady Streets. *Photo courtesy of Ray White.*

First published 2005

Manufactured in the United Kingdom

ISBN 1.59629.065.X

Library of Congress Cataloging-in-Publication Data

Harper, Raymond L.
    South Norfolk, Virginia (1661-2005) : a definitive history / by
Raymond L. Harper.
        p. ; cm.
    Includes bibliographical references and indexes.
    ISBN 1-59629-065-X (v. 1 : alk. paper) -- ISBN 1-59629-066-8
(v. 2 : alk. paper)
        1. South Norfolk (Chesapeake, Va.)--History. 2. Chesapeake
(Va.)--History.   I. Title.
    F234.C49H374 2005
    975.5'523--dc22
                        2005023473

CONTENTS

PREFACE

T HE *HISTORY OF SOUTH NORFOLK (1661–1963)* was first published without images in
October 1994. The following year, it was revised and approximately 170 photographs
were included. That edition was available until 1999. At that time, *Images of America—
South Norfolk* was published by Arcadia Publishing of Charleston, South Carolina, and
was reprinted in January 2002. The *Images of America* volume is mostly pictorial and tells
the story of South Norfolk in pictures and captions. The 1995 edition of *History of South
Norfolk (1661–1963)* has continued to be in demand and requests for copies are received
almost weekly.

During the years since *History of South Norfolk (1661–1963)* was published, I have acquired
many additional photographs of the wonderful, old city of South Norfolk and would like
to share them with former citizens and those who have chosen to reside in the present
borough of South Norfolk. With that in mind, a decision was made to produce a rewrite
of the original *History of South Norfolk (1661–1963)*. This revised history contains more
information and photographs, and includes text and images of events occurring since 1963.
This edition surpasses the original in knowledge and physical size. In order to include most
of the available material, it was necessary to divide the images and text into two volumes.
The process of working the material into two volumes was difficult. In most cases, there is
more material than can be used, and decisions had to be made as to what to include and
what not to include. The question then arises as to where the material should be placed,
in volume 1 or volume 2. I hope the reader approves of my choices and accepts this work
cheerfully as it is presented.

Most of the older citizens who contributed information and pictures used in the
original history have since died. Among them are Linwood L. Briggs Jr., age eighty-
two; Fannie Virginia Butt, age seventy-three; Rosa Whorton Funk, age ninety-nine;
Louise Garrison (age unknown); Iola Bateman Harper, age ninety-two; Lee Henley,
age eighty-five; Vernell Holloman, age ninety-one; Edwin Jones, age seventy-nine;
Anne Davis Kristiansen (age unknown); Richard F. (Billy) Morgan, age eighty-nine;
Alton W. Overton, age ninety-eight; Frank L. Portlock Jr., age ninety-four; Robert
Pride (age unknown); Eloise Smith (age unknown); Ann Grimes Tregembo, age
seventy-one; Jack Twine, age eighty-two; Jessie Wilder (age unknown) and Kathleen
Wilson, age ninety-five.

In addition to those listed above, there are many others that have given freely of their time and allowed me to make copies of their old photographs of historical importance. I would especially like to thank the following who have been of assistance to me throughout my writing years: Francene King Barber, Richmond County Museum; Ed Beard, retired professional football player and coach; William Benton, fellow author; Irwin M. Berent; Waverly Berkley III; Eloise Wilson Bondurant; Eleanor Rae Newberry Briggs, who provided photographs and notes from the collection of her father Lennon H. Newberry; Amelia Burton; Jimmie and Mike Creekmore, proprietors of Creekmore Hardware; Vincent Curtis; Jack Dabney; J. James Davis Jr.; Quinton C. Davis III; Pat Everton; Hardy Forbes; Mildred Gay; John Ben Gibson III; Lil Hart, retired clerk of the Chesapeake Circuit Court; the Reverend Gregory Hensley, pastor of the Southside Baptist Church; Kaye Herndon; Charles Hackworth, Hackworth Reprographics Inc.; Edna Doughtie Holloman; Robert Hitchens; the staff of the Kirn Memorial Library—City of Norfolk, Virginia; Jimmie Johnson; Dr. Raymond T. Jones, vice president of Public Radio Service WHRO; Kenneth Kimmons; Myrtle Lambert; Suzy Loonan; Mildred Miles; Carl G. Newbern; Sheriff John Newhart; Shirley Paxson; Hazel Rhodes; Deborah Rountree; John Rudis; members of the Chesapeake Fire Department; Annie Pierce Sawyer; Gloria Perry Scarano; James and Virgie Scott; Stuart Smith, Chesapeake Police Department, retired; D.R. Smithson; Richard Spratley; Frankie Sweetwood; Don Tatem, owner of Industrial Hardware; Lou Trzinski; Belle Warden; Edna Weaver; Ray White; Richard Womack; Lois Wood; Jerome Yavner; and Stanley Zedd.

I would like to dedicate these books to my wife of fifty-six years, Emma Rock Harper; our two daughters, Shari and Karen; our son-in-law, John Rudis; and our three grandchildren, Alexa Raye, Colby John and Collin Steven Rudis.

My first two books (published in 1994 and 1995) were written on legal pads and produced by my wife using the word processor. Since that time, I have entered the world of computers, which makes book writing easier and certainly more enjoyable. I couldn't have done it back then without her help. Thank you, Emma, for being a major part of my life.

INTRODUCTION

IN THE EARLY YEARS, VARIOUS tribes of Indians inhabited the area. It was in the late sixteenth century that the Chesapeian tribe occupied the region. According to documents in the City of Chesapeake's Circuit Court, the area that became South Norfolk had its beginning in 1661 when the Southern Branch Chapel of the Church of England was built. The opening of the chapel marked the beginning of formal record keeping of births, deaths and marriages. In 1701, the chapel had moved to Great Bridge and was located at the southwest corner of what is now Battlefield Boulevard and Cedar Road. In 1728, it was still called the Southern Branch Chapel, but by October 1749, according to records, it was known as the Great Bridge Chapel. In 1750, it was enlarged. During the Revolutionary War, the chapel was used as a fort and sustained considerable damage from cannon fire. Apparently, the church was not abandoned and dismantled until 1845.

The earliest family records are those of the Portlocks. Although records show that John Portlock first visited the area in 1685, it is believed that the earliest representative of the family came from England in 1634 and located near what became known as Portlock Estates in the vicinity of Norfolk. John soon returned to England. In 1687, he once again visited the colony of Virginia and this time brought several families with him. Those families were his responsibility until they were well settled in the colony. For this, John was rewarded with fifty acres of land for each person he transported to Virginia. This became known as the headright system, which was the basis for the distribution of land in the colony. John's property eventually extended from what would become known as Ferry Point (later Berkley) along the Southern Branch of the Elizabeth River all the way to Great Bridge. John built his home on part of the land he received from King James II of England. This home, referred to as The Homestead, is believed to have been built in the vicinity of Freeman Avenue where the old Belt Line Railroad tracks crossed and the mergence of Mill Dam Creek with the Elizabeth River took place. This would be near where Money Point is today. There weren't any roads at the time, and since most travel was by boat, early settlers tried to build their homes near the water.

There were many other individuals and families who figured in the early years of South Norfolk. Most of their names will appear elsewhere in this history. (For short biographies of many of those influential in the city's development, see volume 2, chapter 11, "Founding

Fathers.") Certainly one of the earliest was the Poindexter family, which settled in the area before the War Between the States.

Throughout the colonial period and most of the nineteenth century, the area that later became South Norfolk consisted mostly of individual farms and plantations. There was a large amount of marshland and many drainage ditches, some of which still exist today. At that time, the entire south side was considered Berkley, and in earlier years, South Norfolk was regarded as its suburb. By the time Berkley became a town in 1890, several homes had already been built in South Norfolk and developers began to make plans for its growth as early as 1889.

Before September 1919, South Norfolk was a flourishing community in the Washington Magisterial District of Norfolk County. On September 19, 1919, the village of South Norfolk was incorporated as a town and on January 5, 1921, it became a second-class city. The Virginia Constitution required that a city's population reach ten thousand before it could become a city of the first class status.

In the meantime, the small village of Portlock was chartered as a town on March 11, 1948, and in 1951 was annexed by the City of South Norfolk. Before the annexation, South Norfolk's boundaries covered approximately five miles by seven miles. As a result of the annexation, South Norfolk's population more than doubled, bringing it to 20,896 and the area of the city increased by 224 percent. Soon after the annexation, South Norfolk became a city of the first class. With these new citizens, there was much talk of changing the city's name. Originally old-timers say it was known as McCloudtown, after some of the first settlers, or as Scuffletown, after a series of old-time square dances or "hoedowns" held regularly in one part of the village. A referendum was held June 12, 1951, and the voters decided 851–558 to keep the name South Norfolk.

Before 1930, local addresses of businesses and homes consisted of one, two or possibly three digits. For example, the building located at 1 Chesapeake Avenue before 1930 became 1000 Chesapeake Avenue in 1930. Before 1930, G.W. Forehand's grocery store was located at 2 Ohio Avenue; in 1930, the address became 1409 Ohio Street. J.R. William's Funeral Home was located at 13 Chesapeake Avenue (an appropriate number for his business). In 1930, it became a part of the 1000 block of Chesapeake Avenue.

Some time before 1895, the public road through South Norfolk and Portlock was known as the Berkley and Currituck Turnpike, it later became Bainbridge Street, then Bainbridge Avenue and finally Bainbridge Boulevard. What was Holly Street is now Holly Avenue, Jackson Street has become Jackson Avenue and Hawthorne Avenue has been renamed Hoover Avenue. Many of the once well-known streets have through time disappeared entirely. Completely vanished are the old County Road, the public road generally known as the old Jones Road and Whitier's Bridal Path or Scuffletown Road, which once ran through South Norfolk. Barron, Lawrence and McDonough Streets were west of Bainbridge Boulevard in that part of town that was known as Scuffletown (the locals called it Scufflintown). Kentucky, Indiana and Michigan Avenues were parallel to and east of Atlantic Avenue. West Munden was also in that part of town. Catalina Heights was at the end of Rodgers Street in the Portlock area. Another area along Bainbridge Boulevard near its intersection with what is now Chesapeake Drive was known as Jones's Switch. There was a streetcar switch in front of Mr. William Jones's store on Bainbridge Boulevard. That area at the corner of Holly Street and Bainbridge Boulevard was known as Knitting Mill Curve. It was there that employees of the Elizabeth Knitting Mill disembarked and boarded the streetcar each workday. When the overpass on Bainbridge Boulevard was constructed in 1937, the streetcar no longer ran to Portlock. The end of the line was on Holly Street. Passengers going to Portlock had to transfer to a bus.

South Norfolk was a close-knit, very friendly community and a wonderful place to grow up. There were many activities to enjoy. There was the annual church picnic in summer, athletics of all kinds, trips to the Grand Theatre, visits to Jus Maid ice cream store or Gornto's Bakery after the movie, and the beauty of Lakeside Park. When winter came and snow blanketed the small city, an afternoon of ice-skating could sometimes be enjoyed at Lakeside Park or Johnson's Pond. Most of the local businesses used a horse and wagon to make their deliveries. Many of the homes relied on kerosene lamps for light, hand pumps for water and coal or wood stoves for heat. The "johnny" in the back yard served as the necessary house. The wooden icebox in the kitchen was dependent on the daily delivery of ice. A square sign was placed in one of the front windows to let the iceman know how many pounds of ice to deliver. The choices were twenty-five, fifty, seventy-five or one hundred pounds. At Mr. Tucker's meat market, a roast for Sunday's dinner could be purchased for 20 cents per pound, while five pounds of croakers (leave the heads on) could be bought for a dollar at Mr. Spivey's fish market. Today, a pound of croakers sells for $3.19. As a young lad, my family often had fried fish and corn bread for Friday evening's meal.

Many years would pass before the streets of South Norfolk were paved. In the 1920s, strips of concrete were laid in the middle of a few main roads, and until that time, the streets were dusty in summer and mostly muddy in the winter. When my family moved to Seaboard Avenue in April 1932, grass was growing in the middle of the street. Curbing was added around 1937.

In the 1930s, there were several business ventures that a young person could undertake to earn money or prizes. One was the sale of Cloverine salve (it was supposed to cure everything). Many prizes were available for those who were able to sell enough of the salve. Each can sold for 25 cents. The same amount (one ounce) now sells for $6.99 per can (when you can find it). Another business was the delivery of newspapers. The afternoon paper sold for 3 cents per copy or 15 cents a week for six papers. The morning paper, which included the Sunday edition, sold for 20 cents a week. A note of interest: Haircuts were 15 cents, and when I ran short of money, which was most of the time, I would swap the cost of the afternoon paper with David Smith, a local barber. Mrs. Hand who lived on Chesapeake Avenue near Poindexter Street had a green house in her back yard where she raised and potted plants. She owned a large wagon that she filled with plants and hired the local children to pull it through the streets of South Norfolk. The young people were to receive a percentage of their sales. When the country was in the middle of the Great Depression, people spent what little money they had on necessities instead of on plants. As a result, no one, including Mrs. Hand, made any money for his or her efforts.

In the spring of each year, the boys looked forward to the marble championship. The Norfolk Ledger-Dispatch newspaper sponsored this event. The winner was always treated to an all-expenses-paid trip to some special place. In 1939, Gibson Harrell from South Norfolk won the championship, and he and his mother were treated to a trip to the New York World's Fair. Also in the spring, the annual yo-yo contest was held on the school grounds by a group of Filipinos. Sweatshirts with "yo-yo champion" on the front were awarded to the winners.

Two popular organizations that were well supported by the local boys were the Boy Scouts of America and the South Norfolk Boys Club. One of the early meeting places for the Boy Scouts was the Chesapeake Avenue Methodist Church. Two members of the church, D.T. Allen and V.L. Sykes, served as Scoutmasters. Another meeting place was the house in the corner of the schoolyard at the corner of Twenty-second and A Streets. This was the home of Troop 54 until it moved to St. James Street. James O. Lowe was the Scoutmaster. Eventually another troop of Scouts was formed, and Henry Gallup served as its Scoutmaster.

Josh Campen and Joe Lassiter organized the South Norfolk Boys Club. The club met at the Woodmen of the World (WOW) Hall on Twenty-second Street. The club's drum and bugle corps was well known throughout Tidewater and participated in functions such as the dedication of Foreman Field in Norfolk on October 3, 1936, and the dedication of the South Norfolk overpass on June 18, 1938. The membership dues were a whopping 10 cents per month.

Campen was also involved in organizing the South Norfolk Grammar School Safety Patrol. The safety patrol later came under the sponsorship of the American Automobile Association (AAA).

Several days each week during the hot summer months, the block of Twenty-second Street between A and B Streets was closed to traffic and a large sprinkler was connected to the fire hydrant. Children from all areas of South Norfolk came in shorts or bathing suits and enjoyed the coolness of the water.

On more than one occasion, many citizens of South Norfolk answered our country's call. Most of the old-timers remember the draft board on A Street. Some may have earlier memories of the St. Helena Naval Training Station and how the sailors marched from Berkley to the corner of Jefferson and Jackson Streets in South Norfolk. The men would then stack their rifles, rest for a while and then march back to Berkley.

With the onset of World War II and the many shortages that accompanied it, rationing became a way of life. In May 1942, the Office of Price Administration (OPA) opened local board no. 65-4 at 701 St. James Street where war-rationing books were issued to all the families of South Norfolk. Before the war ended in 1945, gasoline, tires, fuel oil, shoes and most food items were rationed. Ruth Tucker, Vivian Dail, Lillian Rice, Effie Ferbee and possibly others served as issuing officers.

A few years ago when interviewing older residents of South Norfolk, some of them spoke of having seen a race track from Phillips Street along Seaboard Avenue to Holly Street. It seems that the track, which existed in the 1890s before houses were built, was known as the half-mile track. More recently the City of Chesapeake repaired the streets in the 1400 block of Ohio Street between Seaboard and Chesapeake Avenues. A resident of Seaboard Avenue reported having seen trolley tracks beneath the road surface in that block of Ohio

Street. This is quite possible because the early trolley barn and stables were located on the property behind the South Norfolk Baptist Church (wish I could have seen them).

South Norfolk was a busy community both day and night. Most places were within walking distance and those that were not could be easily reached by riding a local streetcar. Some of the stores were open until 11 p.m. or later. The downtown area was well lighted; lights from the Grand Theatre, Preston's Pharmacy, Rosedale Dairy Store and other businesses could be seen from several blocks away. It was always possible to walk up to Preston's corner and find some friends to talk to. South Norfolk offered its residents a friendly small-town identity in the midst of nice homes, local schools and churches.

In South Norfolk's history, we can watch the emergence of a town from farmland, and the evolution of a city of the second class and then to the first class. The 1952 Progress Edition of the *Norfolk Ledger-Dispatch* compared South Norfolk to a train that was well on its way and stated that the city was growing by proverbial leaps and bounds. At that time, it was impossible to imagine what would take place in a little more than ten years when the city merged with Norfolk County. The political scene changed, and the new city council felt that the merger would lead to bigger and better things. Today it is hard to find any former resident of the old city of South Norfolk who will admit he or she voted for the merger. Somebody is not telling the truth, or is it possible that the newly installed voting machines were manipulated to change the count? That story has been going around for years. The only person who knows for sure is deceased and he shall remain anonymous. It is now between he and his maker. Some employees of the former city supported the merger because they felt that, in a larger city, their income would increase several times over what they were then receiving. Some city politicians thought they could bargain with the leaders of Norfolk County. That did not work out because the good, old country boys were always one step ahead of the city slickers. As I have said before, most of those persons are now deceased, and I never did see a Brinks truck in any of the funeral processions. One thing for sure is that the pro-merger politicians rented Carl Parker's Restaurant on Poindexter Street for a victory party long before the election took place.

After the merger, the once prosperous city did not receive its fair share of tax dollars, and as a result, it started to decline. Some of the longtime residents sold out and moved to what they considered more fashionable areas of Chesapeake. When nearby cities began cleaning up the slums, some residents then moved to South Norfolk—as did drugs and crime. Also presenting a problem were absentee landlords, who accepted rent checks but did not give back to the community. Today it seems that things may be turning around. A few young people have begun to purchase and renovate the once-beautiful old homes. Part of the area has been declared an historical district and is on the national register. The City of Chesapeake has employed Urban Design Associates from Pittsburgh, Pennsylvania, to produce ideas on how to revitalize South Norfolk. The drawings they have generated are beautiful (more on this subject will be addressed later). It is the hope of many that these new citizens of South Norfolk will not become discouraged and leave.

It has been more than forty years since the city of South Norfolk merged with Norfolk County to form the new city of Chesapeake. A large number of Chesapeake citizens have no idea how the city was formed. It is my hope that the information in this book and others that I have had the privilege to write will shed light on the subject. As the saying goes, if you do not know where you came from, it is certain that you cannot know where you are going.

I invite you to join me and step back in time when life moved at a slower pace and the community blossomed with friendship, trust and goodwill. We will meet prominent families and travel dirt streets lined with horse-drawn wagons and a variety of vendors. It is a cold 1930s winter day and snow is beginning to fall. Here comes the streetcar. Let's catch a ride to Lakeside Park and see if the lake is safe for skating.

CHAPTER I

SOUTH NORFOLK—
VILLAGE, TOWN, CITY

O N NOVEMBER 18, 1618, IT WAS ORDERED by the Virginia Company's London Council that the colony be divided into four large corporations. For purposes of local administration, each was to be a parish of the Church of England. Each corporation was to have a chief executive and military officer and later either justices or a court of law. As each corporation was an ecclesiastical parish, each was required to have a minister, churchwardens and vestry.

The duties of churchwardens were to keep the church in repair, provide books and ornaments, collect the minister's dues, render an account of disbursements and present to the court blasphemous, wicked and dissolute persons. The law required that twelve of the most able men of each parish should be chosen by the majority of the parish to be a vestry, out of which the minister and vestry members were to select two churchwardens yearly.

The Church of England was the church of the colony of Virginia and Governor George Yeardley's instructions from July 24, 1621, required him to "keep up religion of the Church of England as near as may be."

Between the years of 1632 and 1634, the Virginia colony was divided into eight shires, or counties. The eight original shires were Accawmack (now Accomack), Charles City, Charles River (later York County), Elizabeth City, Henrico, James City, Warrosquyoake (later Isle of Wight) and Warwick River. Elizabeth City County extended on both sides of Hampton Roads. The area from which South Norfolk eventually emerged was part of Elizabeth City County in 1634, New Norfolk County in 1636, Lower Norfolk County in 1637 and Norfolk County in 1691. In 1639, the area was part of the Southern Shore Parish, and soon after 1643, it was included in the Elizabeth River Parish. South Norfolk had its beginning in 1661 when the Southern Branch Chapel of the Church of England was built near present-day Barnes Road in the vicinity of Lakeside Park.

The Elizabeth River Parish was divided in 1761 "on account of illegal practises [and] oppressing its inhabitants," according to an act of the assembly. The first election for new vestrymen was held June 6, 1761. The results and the number of votes received were as follows: John Portlock, 251; Robert Tucker, 250; James Webb, 249; Joshua Corprew, 249; William Smith, 240; Thomas Nash Jr., 239; Samuel Happer, 232; James Wilson, 228; Henry Herbert, 205; John Wilson, 186; Malachi Wilson Jr., 176; and William Happer, 155. John Portlock and William Smith were selected to serve as churchwardens. Candidate

Thomas Nash Jr. was the grandson of the man who had served as clerk of the Southern Branch Chapel in 1728.

As provided in the act of the Virginia General Assembly dividing the Elizabeth River Parish, vestrymen of Saint Bride's Parish sold the land at public auction to John Tucker for 6 pence per acre. With 172 acres, this amounted to 520 pounds and 6 shillings. The deed was dated October 20, 1761. Apparently the land was auctioned to acquire funds to pay parish debts, according to the last entry in the old parish's vestry book: "Here end every Transaction of the Vestry of Elizabeth River Parish till the said Vestry was dissolved and the said Parish was divided into three distinct Parishes."

On August 1, 1763, William Smith and his wife Ann, conveyed to Minister James Pasteur, John Portlock and the vestrymen of Saint Bride's Parish two hundred acres of land in the parish for 350 pounds.

The area that became South Norfolk experienced some settlement during the colonial period but remained rural until the late nineteenth century. The city of Norfolk, located across the Eastern Branch of the Elizabeth River, did not reach its full potential until after the post–Civil War depression, when railroads began to bring coal and produce from the west and south. The new railroads were a boon to Norfolk and also to the farms and villages of Norfolk County. Norfolk's location on the Elizabeth River gave it a prime position for shipping but prohibited a natural expansion across the river's Eastern Branch. When the railroads came through Norfolk County, development was encouraged all along the line. New industries grew up along the Eastern and Southern Branches of the Elizabeth River, and new businesses and housing appeared near the railroad lines.

Although several homes had already been built in the area, information indicates that developers began to make plans for development of South Norfolk as early as 1889. This land adjacent to Berkley began to be developed by the laying out of streets and building lots. The farm comprising the land between the town of Berkley and what is now Poindexter Street was known as the Green House Tract. Alvah H. Martin and others purchased this property for the sum of $3,500. The men divided the land into lots and put them upon the market under the name of Elmsley. Elmsley was that land bounded by Poindexter, Eighteenth, Liberty and B Streets.

W.S. Butt owned large amounts of land along the Southern Branch of the Elizabeth River in Berkley as well as in South Norfolk between B and D Streets. Around 1887, at the end of South Main Street there was a footbridge across the creek that connected Berkley to the Butt plantation in South Norfolk. Later the Greenleaf Johnson Lumber Company purchased a large part of Butt's land.

Development of adjoining land soon followed. Alvah Martin and his wife Mary donated two lots, each with thirty feet fronting Liberty Street and having a depth of one hundred feet, to be used for the construction of the Liberty Street Methodist Episcopal Church, South. The deed was dated October 13, 1890, and the church, which was the first in South Norfolk, was dedicated in May 1892.

Among the early settlers of the South Norfolk area were Admiral Carter W. Poindexter and his family. The admiral had served in the British navy, and when he came to the area, he built his home, called the Anchorage, on the waterfront across from the Gosport Navy

This drawing depicts the Poindexter home as it appeared in 1894 when it was on Ohio Street. It was later moved a short distance to what became the 1100 block of Stewart Street. In 1918, one of the neighborhood boys set fire to the house, destroying the kitchen and dinning areas at the back of the house. The house, minus those areas, was rebuilt and still stands in the 1100 block of Stewart Street.

Yard. The Poindexters had three children, Reginald, Parke and Bettie. Reginald has been credited with naming the community "South Norfolk" before 1890. Poindexter Street was named after the family, and the admiral was responsible for having named most of the other streets in South Norfolk. Among them are Jackson, Rodgers, Decatur, Stewart, Hull, Bainbridge, Perry, Porter, Lawrence, Barron and Truxton. A study of the War of 1812 reveals that the above names were those of sea captains who fought in the war. Guerriere Street was named for the HMS *Guerriere*, which was captured by Captain Isaac Hull and the crew of the USS *Constitution* during the War of 1812.

Later, the Poindexter family moved from the waterfront to a home on Ohio Street in what is now the 1000 block. The house was two stories with an A-line roof and painted red. The admiral owned two large sailboats, which he used in his import business. He made trips to the Orient and brought back spices, coffee, tea and other commodities. On one of his trips to China, he brought back a ginkgo tree, which he planted in the front yard of his home on Ohio Street. Although the house has since been moved, the tree is still there along with a magnolia that he planted. Of Chinese origin, the ginkgo has fan shaped leaves. In the fall, the tree bears yellow fruit that produces an unpleasant smell and the leaves turn a brilliant yellow in color. A small shoot from the Poindexter tree was planted in the front yard of the house located across the street at 1007 Ohio Street and has since grown to maturity.

Eventually the red house with an A-line roof was removed to 1148 Stewart Street. In 1918, a little "firebug" in the neighborhood set fire to it, completely destroying the kitchen

This photograph was taken in the 1100 block of Stewart Street on April 24, 1996. The house in the middle is the Poindexter house as it appears today. The house to its left was the home of the Tavenner family.

and dinning room, which were built off the back of the house. The same boy later set fire to a garage on the corner of Ohio and Stewart Streets. When the Poindexter house was repaired, a slanted roof was installed to replace the original roof. The kitchen and dinning room were removed at that time. This dwelling, which now serves as a duplex, may be the oldest remaining home in South Norfolk.

When the Poindexters moved from Ohio Street, they relocated to a house that J.P. Andre Mottu had built on his property in the vicinity of what is today the corner of Rodgers and Jefferson Streets. This very large house sat in a field, which included the present-day 1200 blocks of Rodgers, Decatur and Stewart Streets and all the land in between. A fence protected the area and the entrance was by way of a gate, which was operated by a man known as Solomon the gatekeeper.

Mottu had served as consul from Belgium. Upon leaving South Norfolk, he purchased the Colley Farm in Norfolk, which was located in the Atlantic City area on the west side of The Hague, near Christ and St. Luke's Church.

By this time, Carter Poindexter and his wife Mary were deceased and their son Reginald was living in California. As the story goes, Reginald was a very handsome young man and possibly became a silent film star. Parke and his sister, Bettie, were the only occupants of the home. Parke L. Poindexter had engaged in farming for several years but later turned his attention to the development of industries and land. The February 26, 1898 Berkley edition of *TIPS Weekly* (a local newspaper) reported the following information about Parke L. Poindexter: "He was instrumental in securing the first manufacturing enterprise of importance in what is now known as South Norfolk—the firm of Johnson & Waters, of Baltimore, which firm afterwards became Greenleaf Johnson Lumber Company. Later Mr. Poindexter was one of the largest stockholders in building the Chesapeake Cotton Mills and was the direct cause of the construction of the Elizabeth Cotton Mills by the donation of land, in addition to being a liberal subscriber of stock."

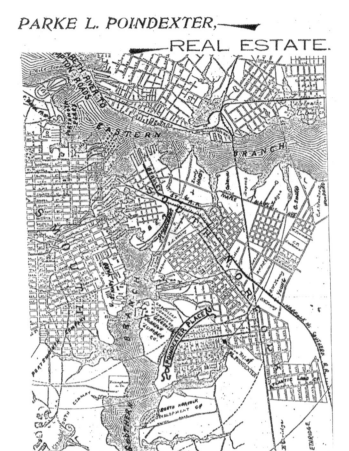

This map, which accompanied an article in the February 26, 1898 Berkley edition of the *TIPS Weekly* newspaper, served at least two purposes. It advertised the fact that Parke L. Poindexter was a real-estate salesman, and it also showed areas of South Norfolk, Berkley, parts of Portsmouth, the U.S. Navy yard and other properties of interest.

In addition to his large residence, Parke Poindexter owned a substantial amount of property, which was known as Poindexter Place. He also dealt in real estate, selling building lots, factory sites and waterfront property with railroad accessibility. Probably his last employment was as a justice of the peace for Norfolk County. His duties included trying minor civil and criminal cases, administering oaths and solemnizing marriages. His office and courtroom were in the Flatiron Building, which was also referred to by some as the Berlin Block. This building, which housed the municipal offices and a movie theater (where for six cents, one could see a silent film), was located on Liberty Street near the Belt Line Railroad crossing.

Parke Poindexter carried his pistol and daily newspaper in a market basket on his arm and rode the streetcar to and from work each day. It has been said that he would stop in the middle of a court session and send a policeman to the saloon, which was in the same building, to fetch him a pitcher of beer. This he would consume while continuing to perform his judicial duties.

It was reported that Parke was plagued with poor health in the latter part of the nineteenth century; however, it must have improved, for he fathered a son with Lucy Saunders Deans.

Parke Deans Jr. was born December 13, 1907, and died June 22, 1922, at the age of fourteen years, six months and nine days. He was buried in the Magnolia Cemetery in Berkley. Parke died shortly after the move from Ohio Street, and his sister Bettie followed shortly thereafter.

After the passing of the Poindexters, the property was acquired by Jesse Cuthrell, who used it to start a dairy. Each day, the cows were driven down Ohio Street almost to the Royster plant, where they would graze all day before being driven back to the barn in late afternoon for milking. At that time, none of the streets in South Norfolk were paved and much of the land was marshy. There was a large marsh bordering the dairy, which Cuthrell had dug out so that it would fill with water from nearby drainage ditches and the rain. This hole in the ground was filled with three-hundred-pound blocks of ice from John Cuthrell's ice plant and was used as cold storage for the milk. Jesse Cuthrell later relocated his dairy to Princess Anne Road in Norfolk.

Around 1916, Jerry G. Bray Sr., O.J. Parker, D.W. Lindsey (many of the men liked to be called by their initials) and one other person purchased this large piece of property. The men had Rodgers Street extended from Ohio Street, disassembled the large house, divided the property into lots and sold them. This became known as the Beechwood Tract. Bray was into contracting, and using the lumber salvaged from the old Mottu/Poindexter house, he was able to build several smaller houses, which are still standing.

By 1900, the area now designated as the historic district of South Norfolk had been divided into housing lots. Although the old County Road continued to run through the district, most of today's streets had been laid out. The section bounded by Park Avenue, the old County Road and Stewart Street was given the name Quincy Place. It covered a large part of the southern section of the district near where Lakeside Park is today. At one time this land had been the Quincy farm. In 1900, there were only two houses in Quincy Place.

The Elizabeth Land Improvement Company owned the area bounded by Bainbridge Boulevard and Stewart, Holly and Poindexter Streets on the western side. The company had laid out streets and lots, but there weren't any houses on the property, which continued for several blocks to the west. The land did include the Elizabeth Knitting Mill, which was south of Park Avenue and west of Bainbridge Boulevard.

A triangular-shaped section enclosed by Stewart Street, Park Avenue and the old County Road did not have street and lot divisions, but this section did include a house and outbuilding owned by J.P. Andre Mottu and three open lots carrying the names Whitehead, Tilley and Woodard.

The most developed section in 1900 was the addition built by real estate developers Thomas H. Synon and Daniel E. Frost. (Synon and Frost had offices at 17 Granby Street in downtown Norfolk. Synon was also president of the Berkley Street Railway.) The land contained a large triangular section bounded by the old County Road, Poindexter Street and Seaboard Avenue. The Baptist Church, which was a wooden building, stood at the corner of Guerriere Street and Chesapeake Avenue. Earlier, in August 1891, a two-room wooden school building had been erected on Jackson Street in the middle of what is now the 1100 block.

Some residential development in South Norfolk had gotten under way before 1890, but it did not really pick up speed until the 1890s and around 1900. By the turn of the century, the population was almost 1,500. In early 1900, Decatur Street was only one block in length, from Buchanan Street to Eighteenth Street. Johnson Park covered the rest of the area up to Poindexter Street. Later, Decatur Street was extended from Poindexter Street to Park Avenue. Chesapeake Avenue terminated at Holly Street; Rodgers Street stopped at Ohio Street. Hull Street began at Poindexter Street, as it does today, and came to an end at Park Avenue. It has since been extended to Holly Street. Stewart Street also came to an end at Park Avenue, and a footbridge was used to cross a creek to Hull Street. A baseball field covered much of the area that is now the 1400 and 1500 blocks of Chesapeake Avenue and a portion of Park Avenue.

Contributing largely to the growth and development of the community was the extension of the Berkley Street Railway from the limits of Berkley to the intersection of Chesapeake Avenue and Guerriere Street. At a later date, the streetcar line was extended to the limits of South Norfolk and on to Money Point, which became part of the village of Portlock.

It was thought that South Norfolk would become a streetcar suburb; however, for the most part, this did not take place. Most of its residents did not take advantage of the streetcar to ride to work in Berkley or Norfolk. The two railroads that passed through South Norfolk created employment, as did new industries that located along the Southern Branch of the Elizabeth River.

South Norfolk had been laid out into large lots and broad streets, giving it somewhat of an advantage over Berkley, whose lots were generally much more narrow. These advantages helped to build up South Norfolk and make it a place of handsome homes.

The home of E.M. Tilley at the corner of Chesapeake Avenue and Guerriere Street was among the first of many stately homes to be built in South Norfolk. Tilley settled in Berkley after the Civil War, went into the lumber business and helped in the founding of Berkley. Construction of his house, which has twenty-two rooms and seven fireplaces, was begun in 1890 and completed in 1893. Originally there was a breezeway on the back of the house that separated the main living quarters from the kitchen. There were two reasons for this design. One was to protect the main residence from a kitchen fire and the other was to contain food smells to the kitchen. The breezeway had steps leading to the servant quarters on the second floor. Tilley's stable was at the rear of the property and faced Guerriere Street. Its floor was made of wood, and passers-by could hear the horses stamping flies. This was especially bad during the hot summer months. The carriage house, which was on Jackson Street, backed up to the stable. In later years, the carriage house was renovated and converted to a dwelling that still stands at the corner of Jackson and Guerriere Streets. Tilley owned additional property on Jackson Street. It was on this land that the first school in South Norfolk was built.

A large drainage ditch ran beside the Tilley property and meandered through South Norfolk, eventually reaching the large hole in the ground at Cuthrell's dairy. Part of the ditch then branched across Park Avenue and emptied into a creek. This creek flowed into a spillway that was in the area where Lakeside Park is today. The water from the spillway flowed into Scuffletown Creek, which connects with the Elizabeth River.

Shortly after the Civil War, Edward Munro Tilley entered the lumber business along the waterfront in Berkley. In 1890, he began construction of this house on Chesapeake Avenue in South Norfolk. This large stately home was completed in 1893. It contains twenty-two rooms and seven fireplaces. The kitchen is separated from the main residence by a breezeway. Quarters for the servants were built over the kitchen, which is off the back of the house. The carriage house, which was originally at the back of the property and faced Guerriere Street, was later removed to Jackson Street and now serves as a residence. After Tilley's death on December 21, 1917, The family of Q.C. Davis Jr. moved into the house. *Photo courtesy of Quinton C. Davis III.*

All the land between Tilley's home and that of his son-in-law John Jones was vacant and would remain so for several years. Jones built his house around 1888. After 1930, this became 1130 Chesapeake Avenue.

E.M. Tilley had two other large homes built around this time. One was diagonally across from his home at what would later become 1049 Chesapeake Avenue. This was the home of his son George Thomas Tilley. E.M. also had a large and impressive home built at 17 Ohio Street for his son William Munro Tilley. After 1930, the address became 1007 Ohio Street. The Portlock family purchased this house in 1910.

William Tilley eventually took over management of Tilley Lumber Company. George worked in his father's business for a while but later entered the real estate and insurance business. All of the Tilley interests coincided to promote the development of South Norfolk.

In 1873, J. Alonzo McCloud operated the only store in a South Norfolk area that was then known as McCloudtown. By 1888, Sam W. Wilson's grocery store was located in a small frame house on Liberty Street near the Norfolk & Western Railroad. Wilson's capital stock in the business then amounted to $50.

In 1895, Dr. N.G. "Nick" Wilson began the practice of general medicine at the home of his Aunt Carrie Edwards on Liberty Street Extended. On November 28, 1895, he

The Tilley mansion has had many owners since the Davis family. One owner even had stalls, very much like public rest rooms, built on the second floor and rented rooms to local schoolteachers. As can be seen in this 2000 photograph, more recent owners have put forth an effort to restore the old home to its original elegance. *Photo courtesy of Kathy Keeney.*

married Beulah Halstead. They resided in a new white house with a white picket fence. Her father, Dr. G.N. Halstead, had the house built (most likely it was a wedding gift). This later became 1401 Poindexter Street and was known as Wilson's corner. In 1938, Preston's Pharmacy was built at that location. In 1904, Dr. Wilson built a large handsome house at 13 Chesapeake Avenue.

Around 1900 and 1901, there were a number of other businesses in South Norfolk. On Liberty Street were confectioners, dry goods merchants, a laundry, an eating house, a fish and oyster dealer, a furniture dealer and a saloon. John Jackson, a physician, lived in a large house on Chesapeake Avenue that later became 1041. The Berkley Street Railway Company had its offices at the corner of Avenue C and Thirteenth Street. Miss Rena B. Wright was the principal of the South Norfolk Public School on Jackson Street, the Reverend Paul Bradley was pastor of the Methodist Church and Samuel Robinson was minister of the South Norfolk Baptist Church. By 1902, a thriving community existed where farms and strawberry fields had been just a few years earlier, and the estimated population of South Norfolk was 2,000. At the turn of the century, some industry was already moving into South Norfolk.

In 1887, Foster Black came from New York, bringing with him his young nephew, William Sloane. Sloane's mother was Black's sister. William, who was just nineteen at the time, worked for his uncle, became superintendent of his knitting mills and eventually became a junior partner in Foster Black & Co. Young William Sloane assisted his uncle when he decided to lease the Chesapeake Knitting Mill in Berkley. Foster Black died in 1903 and is

Many images of early South Norfolk appeared on postcards that could be purchased at Preston's Pharmacy. This picture, which was reproduced from one of them, shows two early houses in what became the 1000 block of Chesapeake Avenue. The streets were dirt, and the sidewalks and curbing were made of wood. The house on the right was at the corner of Chesapeake Avenue and Guerriere Street. It was originally the home of George Tilley, then Robert B. Rowland Jr., the Williams family and the Dowdy family. The South Norfolk Baptist Church eventually purchased the house. It was then demolished to make room for a parking lot. The house near the center of the image was originally the home of Dr. Jackson. When this picture was made, Dr. T.B. Wood lived there. *Image courtesy of Stuart Smith.*

This March 1995 photograph shows a portion of the 1100 block of Chesapeake Avenue. The house on the corner of Chesapeake Avenue and Guerriere Street was the home of J.T. Lane, who ran a drugstore on Liberty Street in the latter 1800s and early 1900s. He sold the store to Dean Preston in 1913. His brother William Lane owned the house next to his.

Here we see the early homes of J.T. and William Lane as they appeared in the year 2000. *Photo courtesy of Kathy Keeney.*

This picture was taken from the middle of the 1200 block of Chesapeake Avenue in 1947. The church on the left was the old Chesapeake Avenue Methodist Church. This sanctuary was demolished in early 1970 and replaced by the present structure. The house across the street from the church was originally the home of Ed Reass, owner of the Grand Theatre. The streetcars that carried the local residents to and from Norfolk used the tracks in the middle of the street. At one time, beautiful trees lined both sides of the street and met in the center, forming an arch.

buried in the Magnolia Cemetery in Berkley. After his uncle's death, Sloane acquired the business and changed the name to William Sloane & Co.

The Chesapeake Knitting Mill was located at the corner of Twelfth and B Streets. It covered that area from B Street past where Bainbridge Boulevard is today. This was the dividing line between Berkley and South Norfolk. In 1935, Sloane retired and the new owner soon thereafter moved the operation to Martinsville, Virginia (my grandfather, Jesse Lee Harper, moved with the company). Eventually the main building was torn down; however, the building that was used for boxing and shipping remained and was used by other companies. The S.L. Williams candy factory, which had its beginning on Chestnut Street in Berkley, relocated to this site and remained there until the construction of Interstate 464 forced the removal of the building. The candy company is now located at 1230 Perry Street in South Norfolk.

The success of the Chesapeake Knitting Mill was the direct cause of the construction of the Elizabeth Knitting Mill. The Elizabeth Knitting Mill was located on land donated by Parke Poindexter west of Bainbridge Boulevard at Park Avenue, where the Rena B. Wright School is now located. Parke Poindexter, E.M. Tilley and William Sloane held large amounts of stock in the mills.

Many local residents worked in the knitting mills, which manufactured union suits (one-piece long Johns with a flap in the back) and sweat shirts. A common sight was the delivery wagon drawn by two white horses carrying crates of union suits to the Norfolk & Western Railway station at Seaboard Avenue and Guerriere Street. These crates were shipped north for protection against the cold winters. In the summer, on the way back to the mill, the driver would stop in the shade of the elm trees on Ohio Street to let the horses cool down and dry.

The Tilley and Black families as well as Sloane came to the area from the North after the Civil War, settled in Berkley and then moved to South Norfolk. William Sloane and Florence Knapp were married in 1895 and had their home built on the corner of Chesapeake Avenue and Ohio Street. Sloane lived at what is now 1203 Chesapeake Avenue with his wife, two sons (William Jr. was born in 1904 and Edwin Knapp was born in 1906) and a white chauffeur. In 1907–1908, the Sloanes had a summer home built on property that had been a part of the Swann farm. The description in the original deed describes the tract of land known as The Hermitage as situated at the mouth of Tanners Creek and containing 175 acres. This is now known as the Loch Haven section and is located in Norfolk. Today, this beautiful home at 7637 North Shore Road houses the Hermitage Foundation Arts Museum.

The front of the Elizabeth Knitting Mill faced Perry Street, the back was near the 1400 block of Porter Street and one end was near Park Avenue. The structure was torn down about 1933, and in 1934, the bricks were salvaged and cleaned by a group of citizens who were paid according to the number of bricks cleaned. The bricks were used in the construction of individual homes. The following summer, this land was used by a circus; it has been said that flies plagued the entire neighborhood.

One of the most important developments was the processing of seabird droppings, or guano. Farmers learned in the mid-nineteenth century that those droppings made a particularly effective fertilizer. In a busy horse-and-buggy era in Tarboro, North Carolina, a former country boy by the name of Frank Sheppard Royster opened his first fertilizer

William and Florence Sloane were married in 1895 and had their home built on the corner of Chesapeake Avenue and Ohio Street (what is now 1203 Chesapeake Avenue). Sloane lived there with his family and employed a full-time chauffeur. In 1907–1908, the Sloanes built a summer home in the Lochhaven section of Norfolk. Today it is the Hermitage Foundation Arts Museum. This snowy photograph of the South Norfolk home was taken January 7, 1904, and a look at the left side of the picture shows Ohio Street to be a mass of weeds. The homes in the background are on Seaboard Avenue. *Photo courtesy of Bill and Debbie Rountree.*

This is the Sloane house as it appeared *circa* 1920s. By that time, the Forehand family owned the house, some of the original land had been sold and other houses had been built nearby. Eventually the Sloane house was cut up into apartments and began to deteriorate. In recent years, Bill and Debbie Rountree acquired this once-beautiful old home and are investing in its restoration. *Photo courtesy of Bill and Debbie Rountree.*

factory in 1885. In 1891, Royster sent his young protégé Charles F. Burroughs Sr. to the Norfolk area to start up production in a Berkley warehouse.

Soon thereafter, the company built a large fertilizer plant in South Norfolk and operated under the name Columbia Guano Company. In 1898, Royster made Norfolk his permanent headquarters, and on August 12, 1900, changed the firm's name to F.S. Royster Guano Company.

By 1910, the Pocomont Guano Company and A.S. Lee and Sons, lime manufacturers, were also operating on the waterfront. Arthur S. Lee of Richmond, Virginia, established the firm of A.S. Lee and Sons.

The number of houses continued to increase in South Norfolk. More appeared on Chesapeake Avenue and on scattered lots throughout the southern section of the community. An inlet from the Southern Branch of the Elizabeth River reached as far as the area where Lakeside Park would eventually be located. This inlet was a part of Scuffletown Creek. There were a large number of houses in the blocks bounded by B, D, Eighteenth and Twenty-second Streets. Seaboard Avenue was probably the most populated of all the streets at the time.

The residents of Seaboard Avenue included carpenters, grocery merchants and employees of the local guano, lumber, knitting, creosote and dredging businesses. Most were native born with one exception, Emanuel Price, a house carpenter who had been born in Sweden.

As a note of interest, the two-story house at 1119 Seaboard Avenue was built around 1910. There were two lots numbered and designated as lots 58 and 59 on the plat of D.E. Frost's property. This house and lots sold for $1,025 in October 1931.

Among other early residents of South Norfolk were the Funks. A tugboat captain, Captain George Funk, built his home at 1416 Poindexter Street in 1894. The front of his house was built to resemble the bow of a tugboat. Across the street was the home of George L. Grimes. Grimes married Anna Eliza Hockaday on June 21, 1888, in the village of Berkley and moved to South Norfolk soon after the wedding. On one corner of Twenty-second Street at A Street was the Madrin home; this house was later occupied by the Sawyer family, which converted a part of the first floor into a confectionery store. The two-story house directly across the street on the other corner was in the early 1900s, the home of the White family. Their son Bill ran a confectionery store in the Preston building and later moved the business to Poindexter Street. Around 1909, the fire department used the house as its headquarters; by that time, the property was at the corner of the South Norfolk schoolyard. The fire department stored the fire hose and reel in a building next to the Madrin house. When the fire department no longer used the building for storage, Jack Brown acquired the property. It was there that Brown stored his horse and cart, which he used to pick up trash. This was the beginning of trash collection in the village of South Norfolk.

In 1915, the firemen built a new two-story fire station next to Brown's building on Twenty-second Street, and the house they vacated became a classroom for the domestic science, or home economic, classes of the South Norfolk school. The sewing classroom consisted of cutting tables, foot-pedal Singer sewing machines and a potbellied stove in the middle of the room. Mrs. Julia Parker was the teacher.

In the meantime, the construction note for the new fire station became due and the department could not raise the necessary funds. The building was put up for sale and was

Captain George Funk built this house on Poindexter Street in 1894. The Funk family sold it to Doc Monroe. The structure has served as the South Norfolk Welfare Department, Dr. Woodley's office and now the office of E.C. Beacham and Associates Accounting and Tax Service. *Photo courtesy of Linwood L. Briggs Jr.*

This old home in the corner of the schoolyard at Twenty-second and A Streets was originally the home of Bill White's parents. In 1892, it became the first fire department headquarters. The building was later used by the South Norfolk School as the domestic science classroom, and it also served as the welfare department during the Depression. The Boy Scouts met there at one time, and the boy's club used it for a woodworking shop. This photograph was taken August 13, 1937 by an unknown photographer. *Courtesy of Linwood L. Briggs Jr.*

This 1932 garbage cart is a far cry from the trash trucks of today. In the early years the driver had to empty the trashcans into the small horse-driven wagon and men using push brooms and shovels cleaned the streets.

In 1915, members of the South Norfolk Volunteer Fire Department constructed this building on Twenty-second Street. It was to serve as the second fire station, but when the note came due, the department was unable to raise the necessary funds and had to sell the building. It was purchased by the Woodmen of the World (WOW) lodge. On March 10, 1920, the WOW Hall, as it became known, burned. When it was repaired, the bell tower was removed. During its existence, the hall housed the police station, court, town hall, election headquarters, boys club, Junior Chamber of Commerce and possibly others. *Photo courtesy of Hardy Forbes.*

purchased by the Woodmen of the World lodge. It then became known as the WOW Hall. Around the same time, Brown's building was removed and a house was built between the Madrin home and the WOW Hall. This became the residence of Johnny Brinn, who worked for Dean Preston, owner of Preston's Pharmacy. Preston built his own large home on D Street at the corner of Twenty-second Street. In later years, Preston moved to Kemp Lane off Indian River Road, and the house in South Norfolk was owned by the Briggs family and then the Overtons.

Sam Wilson, owner of the South Norfolk Market, lived on Poindexter Street. When he purchased a triangular piece of land that was bounded by D, Decatur and Buchanan Streets, he sold the house on Poindexter Street to the Consolvo family and made plans to build a large home on the newly acquired land. The year was 1907, and construction was under way on the various state houses and buildings that would be featured at the Jamestown Exposition. All the construction workers in the area were employed on that project, meaning construction of the house was put on hold and the Wilson family could not move when promised. Eventually some kind of agreement was reached between the Wilson and Consolvo families.

After work on the exposition buildings was nearly complete, Wilson was able to hire a contractor to build his home. Buchanan Street, which ran behind the new home,

Sam Wilson's home at 64 D Street was built in 1907. Luton is standing behind his mother, Mrs. Sam Wilson Sr. (Jennie) and Bill Darden is standing behind Christine Wilson. The little girl with roller skates sitting at the top of the steps is Eloise Wilson. Sometime later, Christine married Bill Darden and they lived in the 1200 block of Chesapeake Avenue next to the Sloane/Forehand house. *Photo courtesy of Richard Womack.*

This image was made from a postcard, but the original picture was taken at the intersection of D and Decatur Streets and shows how the area looked shortly after 1907. Trees hid the home of Sam Wilson. The streetcar traveled D Street on its way to and from Norfolk. Two ladies can be seen on the sidewalk to the left of the streetcar tracks. The whitewash used on the trees added to the neat appearance of both streets. *Image courtesy of Kathleen Wilson.*

was the location of the garage, and Wilson's horse and delivery wagon were housed there when the store was not open. The area also included a rose garden, fig trees and a playhouse. The playhouse was an ideal place for one of the Wilson boys and his friends to congregate and play poker. When his father discovered this, the building was demolished. The address of the home was 64 D Street; it still stands but the address has changed to 604 D Street.

In 1910, members of one of the oldest families in Norfolk County, the Portlocks, moved into South Norfolk. The Portlocks were descended from early settlers and gave their name to the community of Portlock. Frank Livingston Portlock Sr. and his wife Marion Hunter (West) Portlock acquired the home that had belonged to William M. Tilley at 17 Ohio Street. The Portlocks had three children: Marion, who was born in 1900; Eugenia, in 1906; and Frank L. Portlock Jr., in 1908. Frank Jr. died May 10, 2003, at the age of ninety-four.

The Norton family lived on Chesapeake Avenue at the corner of Poindexter Street and owned several adjacent lots facing Chesapeake Avenue. In 1910, when the Christ Disciple Church wanted to build on Chesapeake Avenue, Joseph Herbert Norton moved his house to one of the other lots and donated the corner to the church.

Dr. Frank Wilson and his wife, Ruth, lived on Chesapeake Avenue across the street from his half-brother Dr. Nick Wilson (the doctors were not part of Sam Wilson's family). Sometime after 1914, Frank bought his brother's house at 13 Chesapeake Avenue, where Frank practiced general medicine until January 1919. He then sold the house to J.R. Williams, who moved his funeral business from Chestnut Street in Berkley to the large home on Chesapeake Avenue in South Norfolk.

In 1904, Dr. Nicholas Wilson had this handsome home built at what was then 13 Chesapeake Avenue. Rooms at the ground level served as space for his medical practice. When he moved his practice to Norfolk in 1914, his half-brother Dr. Frank Wilson moved into the house. In January 1919, Frank moved to Boston to study pediatrics and sold the house to J.R. Williams, who had an undertaking establishment on Chestnut Street in Berkley. Williams then moved his business to 13 Chesapeake Avenue. In later years after the funeral home closed, the South Norfolk Baptist Church rented the rooms for a Sunday school annex. This beautiful old home, shown in a *circa* 1945 image, has been demolished and all that remains are the front steps leading to the sidewalk. The building to the left is the Grand Theatre.

Josey C. Brothers, superintendent of a knitting mill, lived on Seaboard Avenue before moving to 1035 Chesapeake Avenue. After Dr. John Jackson moved, Dr. T.B. Wood acquired the large home at 1041 Chesapeake Avenue. In later years, the home was divided into apartments and given the name Carver Hall. William "Uncle Nukes" Lane lived across the street at 1044 Chesapeake Avenue and his brother James Thomas Lane, owner of J.T. Lane's Drug Store on Liberty Street, lived next door at 1050 Chesapeake Avenue. These homes were built around 1895.

After the George Tilley family left the home at 1049 Chesapeake Avenue, Robert B. Rowland Jr. lived there with his wife, two sons and two servants. At that time, the carriage house—behind the home and facing Guerriere Street—became outfitted with two new Cadillacs. Rowland was in the fertilizer business and was among the rich and famous of South Norfolk. In later years, he built a home off Indian River Road on Kemp Lane. (An early picture postcard identified 1049 Chesapeake Avenue as the home of Mayor B.H. Gibson of South Norfolk. I did not find any evidence to suggest that Gibson ever lived there. Gibson did, however, live on Decatur Street between Poindexter and Guerriere Streets.)

In 1893, the South Norfolk Baptist Church was constructed on the corner of Chesapeake Avenue and Guerriere Street in what became the 1100 block. It was a small wooden building, which burned on June 13, 1914. Thomas Black, brother of Foster Black, lived next to the church, and his home sustained fire damage in the amount of $250.

Some of the other residents of the 1100 block included the Ambrose family, who lived next to the Blacks. The Reverend Richard B. Scott, pastor of the Methodist Church, lived at 1129 Chesapeake Avenue. Eventually Joe Forbes, a streetcar motorman, moved next to the McHorney family. After E.M. Tilley died on December 21, 1917, Q.C. Davis Jr. and his family occupied the large house across the street from the Baptist Church at what would later become 1106 Chesapeake Avenue. The Abbots lived next door at 1114. Waverly T. Lane lived at 1118, and the VanVleeks' home was at 1126, which later became the office of Dr. G.W. Simpson.

John W. Jones, son-in-law of E.M. Tilley, built his home at 1130 Chesapeake Avenue around 1888. Glenn R. Leroy, a retail grocery merchant, resided at 1138. He and Mrs. Leroy converted the front of their house into a store, which the local residents referred to as the "Little Store." The store burned and was not rebuilt when repairs were made. Thomas Miningder, who lived at 1137 Chesapeake Avenue, was also a retail grocery merchant. William B. Ashburn, a physician, had his office in the small house at 1140; he lived next door at 1144 with his wife and children. Dr. Ashburn had graduated from medical school in Virginia and practiced in South Norfolk until his death in 1923. His son Horace Godwin Ashburn, who established his clinic at 1301 Ohio Street in 1927, succeeded him. T.B. Wood, another physician, and Dr. John O. Belcher, a dentist, had offices in the same building.

In 1919, the large vacant lot at the northeast corner of Chesapeake Avenue and Ohio Street became the location of the Chesapeake Pharmacy and apartments. Foster Black lived in the large three-story house in the 1200 block at the corner of Chesapeake Avenue and Ohio Street. A heart-shaped driveway, which was superimposed over a very large green lawn, flowed gently down to the dirt road. It would be several years before Chesapeake Avenue became a paved street. After Black died in 1903, Louis Furman occupied the house. Around 1920, this property was made available to the Liberty Street Methodist Episcopal Church, South and today the Chesapeake Avenue United Methodist Church stands on this corner.

Across the street from Black was the residence of William Sloane, owner of the local knitting mills. Sloane had this house built in 1895 and lived there with his family and a full-time chauffeur. After Sloane moved to Norfolk, the Forehand family occupied the home. Dr. L.C. Ferbee's office was at 1222 Chesapeake Avenue. A house contractor, Fred Sherman, lived at 1238, the large house on the corner of Chesapeake Avenue and Jefferson Street. William Sykes, a real estate agent, lived at 1416 Chesapeake Avenue. Dr. Irvin Lee Chapman lived at 1446, which is the corner of Chesapeake Avenue and Holly Street, and his office was in the basement. Steve Hollowell was Dr. Chapman's full-time driver. After Dr. Chapman, Drs. Bocock, Myers and Jennings used the office. Dr. Stanley Jennings retired in 2004. James A. Stephenson, who ran an insurance business, owned the house at 1500.

When my family moved to 1119 Seaboard Avenue in April 1932, our neighbors were the Doziers, Boyers, Berrys, Roberts, Miss Indiana Young and her sister Mary, the Dunning

This was the home of George Lafayette Grimes at the corner of Chesapeake and Park Avenues.

The house at the corner of Chesapeake Avenue and Holly Street was the office of Dr. I.L. Chapman. After his death, his medical practice was taken over by Dr. Bocock. Dr. Bocock passed away at an early age, and the practice was passed on to Dr. Jennings. Dr. Jennings recently retired. *Photo courtesy of Linwood L. Briggs.*

One of the most impressive homes in South Norfolk is this large Queen Anne-style house at 1146 Rodgers Street. Built in 1903 in a combination of cement block, brick and wood, this was the home of the John Cuthrell family. Francis A. Gay bought the home from the family in 1939 and turned it into a funeral home. In this early photograph, the carriage house can be seen off the back of the main structure. This is now the location of the Francis A. Gay chapel of the Oman Funeral Home.

This is the Francis A. Gay Funeral Home as it appeared in the early 1940s.

family, a family of Rountrees, the Meacoms and the Altman family. Dennis Curling, his family and his mother-in-law, Mrs. Ferrell, were our next-door neighbors. The other families in the block were the Lindseys and Taylors. Sam Taylor ran the grocery store at the corner of Seaboard Avenue and Ohio Street.

Some of the families in the 1200 block were the Winslows, two families of Womacks, the Harpers, the Weavers, the Blounts, the Dowdys and the Hatches. Nat Dowdy lived at the corner of Seaboard Avenue and Ohio Street, and ran the fish market behind his house. Also living on the 1200 block were Dutch Kriss and family; a Mrs. Bunch who had a jungle of flowers and bushes in her front yard; two families of Forehands; the Starboards; the Culpeppers; Rosses; and the Hargroves.

In the 1300 block were the Swains, Sprouts, Sawyers and Davises. The elderly Davis lady was an American Indian who enjoyed sitting on the front porch smoking her pipe. Other families in the 1300 block included the Lucases, the Whites, the Ashleyes, the Gibbs, Joe Harper (and family), the Doziers, Captain Jack Duncan and family, the Panels and the Snyders.

Some of the families I knew in the 1400 block were the Jordans, Bells and Jenningses; others included the Bunches, the Rountrees and the Hodges family.

In 1919, a three-story building, which still stands, was constructed at 1 Chesapeake Avenue at the corner of Phillips Street. Dean Preston, proprietor of Preston's Pharmacy, had it built. On the front of the building, near the top there is a large cement rectangle with Preston's name and the year 1919. Also in 1919, the Grand Theatre opened in what later became 1019 Chesapeake Avenue.

One of the most impressive houses in South Norfolk is the large Queen Anne–style house at 1146 Rodgers Street. Built in 1903 in a combination of cement block, brick and wood, this was the home of the John Cuthrell family. It has been said that John mixed the cement himself and built the house to the second floor before enlisting the help of an architect and contractor to finish the job. He lived in the house with his wife, Sarah; his children; a boarder; and one female servant, Mary Elizabeth Addington. When Mary Elizabeth died, she was buried in one of the Cuthrell family plots in Magnolia Cemetery. Cuthrell owned an ice plant at the end of B Street across the Belt Line Railroad—this location later became the Grower's exchange. In 1910, John owned a feed store, and by 1926, he was president of the Bank of South Norfolk. Directly across the street at 1145 Rodgers Street was the Mercer home. Mrs. Mercer and Sarah Cuthrell were sisters. In 1939, Francis and Mildred Gay bought the house from the family and turned it into a funeral home. In May 2003, Sid Oman and his son Robert bought the funeral home.

South Norfolk's Incorporation

By the second decade of the twentieth century, South Norfolk had churches, a school and stores, and a large number of residents owned their homes and either had businesses or were employed by nearby companies. South Norfolk was a flourishing unincorporated community in Washington Magisterial District, Norfolk County. Although South Norfolk was a city in size and importance, it was without public improvements. There weren't any smooth surface streets, a sanitary sewerage and storm-disposal system or any health facilities. Just before the close of World War I, some citizens decided that county government was not advantageous to a large and growing community such as South Norfolk. By August 1919, it was obvious that Norfolk had intentions to annex South Norfolk. Most South Norfolk citizens thought that annexation by Norfolk would result in lower taxes and better services. On August 19, 1919, South Norfolk citizens were called to discuss annexation and the issue of applying for a town charter. As a result of this meeting, strong opposition to annexation arose. Q.C. Davis Jr., a member of the Virginia General Assembly and an attorney, was most instrumental in the change of position. Davis, with the assistance of state Senator Corbitt and the backing of the community leaders Thomas Black and E.E. Meginley, prepared a bill for the Virginia legislature. In a rapid succession of events, the bill to incorporate the Town of South Norfolk became law on September 11, 1919, and South Norfolk began to function as a town on September 19. Davis was the first mayor and E.L. Harper was appointed president of the nine-member council. The town had assets of more than $4 million.

The August 19, 1919, meeting was one of the most important ever held in this area. In 1872, Norfolk was squeezed between Smith's Creek on the north and Newton's Creek to the east. On July 1, 1887, the City of Norfolk started a series of annexations from Norfolk County that would not end until 1955. Between 1887 and 1955, Norfolk annexed a total of twenty-three areas from the county. If South Norfolk had become a victim of annexation, Norfolk would have eventually gobbled up the rest of Norfolk County and the cities of South Norfolk and Chesapeake would never have become a reality.

Ordinances approved by the South Norfolk Town Council in 1919 included a $5 fine for shouting in streets or alleys; a $15 fine for fast and dangerous driving (fifteen miles per hour on streets, ten miles per hour on corners) of gasoline-driven or horse-drawn vehicles; a fine of between $1 and $25 for drunkenness or disorder; and a $1 fine or sixty days in jail for gambling or betting.

By December 22, 1920, the population of South Norfolk was 7,691, and Mayor Davis prepared a petition for the town to become a city of the second class. This occurred on January 5, 1921, with F.L. Rowland as mayor; Q.C. Davis Jr., first city attorney; W.T. Madrin, clerk; P.M. Warden, city sergeant; S.H. Dennis, treasurer; and E.H. Brown, commissioner of revenue.

At that time, South Norfolk comprised the territory bounded on the north by Berkley Avenue, on the east and south by the Virginian Railroad, and on the west by the Southern Branch of the Elizabeth River and Berkley.

The growth of South Norfolk was rapid. Numerous ornamental and attractive homes had been built on Chesapeake Avenue, which was to become the elite section of the community. Eventually, beautiful tall trees lined both sides of the street. Their branches formed an archway, producing shade from spring until early fall.

By 1928, many new stores were beginning to appear on Poindexter and Liberty Streets. The early streets were of dirt, rocks or oyster shells, and sometimes a combination of these. When it rained, the streets were mostly mud. The sidewalks were boards fastened together. On one side of Liberty Street, boardwalks extended from the Norfolk & Western Railway to the Belt Line Railroad near the Berkley line. A bond issue was floated in 1922 enabling the city to run sewer lines down the center of the principal streets, and twelve miles of lines were laid. Some of those are still buried beneath Poindexter Street. A two-lane concrete strip was paved down most of the streets. Curbs and gutters were added in 1937 under a federal Works Progress Administration project (WPA). The construction of the South Norfolk City garage was another WPA project. The building was completed in June 1937 at a cost of $6,117.96.

The new South Norfolk High School was built in 1929 at a cost of $140,430. In 1934, the city, at a cost of $5,000, built Cascade Park, one of the largest athletic fields in the vicinity of Norfolk.

Lakeside Park and Other Recreation Sites

Before the turn of the twentieth century, the area that became Lakeside Park was marshy and an inlet from the Southern Branch of the Elizabeth River reached that far. In the early 1900s, part of it was cleared and a large roof-covered dance pavilion was built (probably in the area where Byrd Avenue is today). The pavilion was approximately two hundred feet by one hundred feet. There were bleachers on both sides and a center bandstand, where dances were held several nights a week. The Berkley Street Railway and Light Company promoted this spot, and the company ran trolley cars from Chestnut Street in Berkley to Holly Street in South Norfolk. To encourage use of the trolley, the company donated funds for installation of electric lights around the area. Most of the activities took place at night. A favorite activity was the cakewalk, which was a musical promenade where a cake was awarded to the couple who demonstrated the most imaginative or intricate dance steps. A narrow footbridge crossed the marsh to the pavilion. In the next few years, a merry-go-round and several concessions were added. There were also slides and barbecue pits. The local residents, visitors from Berkley and workers from the nearby Elizabeth Knitting Mill used the facility.

For the next thirty years, the dance pavilion, merry-go-round and other structures were not maintained and fell into disuse and decay. But, in the spring of 1933, city attorney Q.C. Davis Jr. went to Washington, D.C., as chairman of a committee formed to acquire funds for construction of Lakeside Park. He was successful— receiving nearly $140,000—and work started in the summer, with J.H. Massey as the consulting engineer. The work was done by hand, and many previously unemployed men were put to work. The lake was dug with shovels, and the dirt was carried away in wheelbarrows. Because the community had used the area for drainage, pumps were required to keep the water out. Gravel walks were laid, and a rustic bridge was built with lumber donated by Carl Jordan of Jordan Lumber Company. Greenbrier Farms planted trees and shrubs. Most of the trees were pines, which have since been replaced with oaks and magnolias. Plaques were placed in the ground at the base of each tree to commemorate those from South Norfolk who had died in World War I. Sadly, all of the plaques disappeared over the years. Some were thrown into the lake, and others just walked off into the sunset.

Federal funds were acquired in the spring of 1933 and construction of Lakeside Park was begun that summer. The Depression had gripped the nation, and many men were unemployed. This was one of several projects that afforded local people the opportunity to work and support their families. The park was completed in the spring of 1934. This photograph, taken shortly afterward, shows the lake and the original rustic bridge. *Photo courtesy of Anne Howell Mahew.*

This photograph, taken by A.B. Howell in 1934, shows the bridge and part of the gravel walks that were laid in the original park. *Photo courtesy of Anne Howell Mahew.*

Here we see some of the trees and shrubs planted by Greenbrier Farms. Reflection of the tall pines in the lake and the early homes in the background add to the already existing beauty of the park. *Photo courtesy of Anne Howell Mahew.*

A spillway on the edge of the lake near Bainbridge Boulevard was constructed to keep the water level of the lake constant. A circular structure was built in the center of the lake. The plan was to install a water fountain, but the pipes were not connected. The lake was stocked with fish. The project was completed in the spring of 1934, and on June 16, 1934, Governor George Campbell Peery dedicated the park. A shovel that was used to plant the first dogwood tree in the park was inscribed by the governor, "To my friend, Q.C. Davis."

Over the years, many notable events have taken place in the park. One in particular is the sport of ice-skating. Even when the marsh was there, the water would freeze solid and people would come from miles around to skate, especially during the severe winter of 1918. During my youth, the lake froze almost every winter.

In March 1995, the City of Chesapeake spent approximately $1 million on a major renovation of Lakeside Park. It is still a place of beauty where band concerts and other events take place. One of the most popular gatherings is the family day in the park, which is held every July 4. Another event that has become an annual affair is the Art and Craft Festival, held each September.

Another place that provided recreation in the early years of the twentieth century was Johnson's Pond. Early residents of South Norfolk indicated there were two ponds; one was referred to as the big pond and the other, small pond. The big pond ran from Stewart Street across the section where Bainbridge Boulevard is today, near the Belt Line Railroad, and continued to where the city dump was located in later years. The structure that served as

Overton's grocery warehouse was built on land that had been the edge of the pond. Part of the pond was filled and served as the location for construction of Hutchinson's Market. A small section of the pond still remains in the 200 block of D Street. There was a large drainage ditch, which began approximately one hundred yards from Poindexter Street between what is now the 1000 block of Stewart Street and Bainbridge Boulevard. This ditch, the edges of which were covered with willow trees, emptied into the big pond. This body of fresh water would freeze in winter and many residents gathered there to ice-skate or to watch others skate.

The small pond was on the opposite side of the Belt Line Railroad tracks near Berkley and ran down to the Elizabeth River. There was a dam, which prevented the pond from emptying. This was a saltwater pond, which was used by the Greenleaf Johnson Lumber Company. Logs that had been floated down the river were pulled through a gorge to the pond, where they were stored until the company was ready to process them.

The area south of the big pond was known as Johnson's woods and was at one time a part of the Tunis-Johnson farm. Before World War II, Bainbridge Boulevard came to an end at Poindexter Street and the area between Poindexter and Grady Streets was woodland. There were approximately four houses on the other side of the woods on what was known as Bainbridge extended. In the early 1940s, four hundred apartments were built off Bainbridge extended, the woods were removed and Bainbridge Boulevard was continued on to Berkley. The apartments backed up to the Elizabeth River in the vicinity across from the Navy yard, where Admiral Carter Poindexter built his first home. It was determined that an appropriate name for the apartment complex would be Admiral Roads. The original Admiral's Road began at the Poindexter home (the Anchorage) on the waterfront, meandered through the

Prior to World War II, Bainbridge Boulevard came to an end at Poindexter Street on the edge of Johnson's woods. During the war, the woods were removed, Bainbridge Boulevard was cut through and four hundred apartments were built. The apartments were constructed on land that, many years before, had been the beginning of Admiral's Road. In light of this fact, a decision was made to name the community the Admiral Roads apartments. This photograph of the main entrance was taken on Sunday, November 12, 1944. *Photo courtesy of Linwood L. Briggs Jr.*

areas that became South Norfolk and Portlock, and came to an end at the old Providence Church at the corner of Great and Chair Roads. Today, Great Road is Campostella Road, and Chair Road is Providence Road.

A familiar sight along the Southern Branch of the Elizabeth River was that of the steamboat *Emma Kay*. The *Emma Kay*, whose skipper was Captain Snow, brought produce from the farms of North Carolina and Norfolk County to the Roanoke Docks in Norfolk. The steamboat made several stops along the way and picked up passengers. One regular passenger was Margaret West, a student at Deep Creek School. She rode the boat to and from school each day. After completing her education, Miss West taught English and history at South Norfolk and Oscar F. Smith High Schools for almost fifty years. Margaret's sister Marion Lee taught seventh grade at the South Norfolk School and another sister, Frances, taught at the Portlock School.

The schedule of the *Emma Kay* was well known to the boys of South Norfolk and Berkley. In the summer months, most of them swam nude in the Elizabeth River. When the boat appeared around the bend, they ran for cover until it passed.

Landowners

Before the end of the nineteenth century and up until the South Norfolk High School was built on Holly Street, the section was mostly woods and marshland. Eventually, part of the land was cleared and became a ball field for the local boys and another part was used by the neighbors for gardens. This tract of land was part of the Portlock estate and stretched from Holly Street to the Virginian Railroad. In 1927, Irvin Truitt of Truitt-Smith Realty Corporation purchased this land from the heirs of William Nathaniel Portlock and began development of a new residential section that became known as Avalon. It was advertised as the ideal location for a home and only minutes from any action of the city. There weren't any utility poles on the streets; instead, they were installed in the alley behind the houses. There was a building restriction that the construction of each house had to cost at least $5,000.

The part of Jackson Street that became the 1600 block was low and marshy. There was one house in the area, and the only way to reach it was by way of a footbridge. This house, which later became 1611, was built and occupied by a Mr. Adams. Sam Wilson and his wife Kathleen were its next owners. Avalon had been built on part of John Etheridge's wheat field. Etheridge cultivated his land and the land belonging to others. For this privilege, he agreed to pay the landowner's taxes.

Etheridge lived on Hardy Avenue in Berkley and operated a livery stable and blacksmith shop on Chestnut Street. A part of his business came from South Norfolk and Berkley residents who parked their horse and buggies on his property and boarded the ferry to Commercial Place in Norfolk. Etheridge was a large man with a black bushy mustache and appeared, at times, quite debonair in his three-piece suit and gray bowler.

Also in the area were Rosa Etheridge, who owned land from Chesapeake Avenue over to Jackson Street, and Mrs. Indy Seymore, sister of John Etheridge, who owned the property from Rodgers Street to Decatur Street. Mrs. Indy lived in Colonial Place in Norfolk. The

John S. Etheridge, a landowner in South Norfolk, lived on Hardy Avenue in Berkley and operated a livery stable and blacksmith shop on Chestnut Street. A part of his business came from the residents of South Norfolk who parked their horse and buggies on his property and boarded the ferry to Commercial Place in Norfolk. The large man standing at the entrance to the livery stable is Etheridge. As can be seen by the sign in the window of the place of business second to the left, this picture was taken before prohibition. This large brick building was old and in need of repairs. The stars mounted in the mortar were placed there to add strength, *circa* 1914.

In 1937, this overpass was built on Bainbridge Boulevard over what was then the Virginian Railroad. In recent years, the overpass received extensive repairs and the pictured plaque has vanished. *Photo courtesy of Linwood L. Briggs Jr.*

estate of William Nathaniel Portlock included the land from Jackson Street to Rodgers Street. The Portlocks owned two strips of land in this area plus a third strip, which was dug out and the dirt was sold for the construction of the overpass over the Virginian Railroad on Bainbridge Boulevard. Some of the dirt was also used in the construction of the overpass on Campostella Road near the George Washington Carver School. Henry Clay Hofheimer was awarded the contract to build the Bainbridge Boulevard overpass, which was built at a cost of $197,000 and was dedicated in 1937. (Hofheimer died February 6, 2005, at the age of ninety-eight.) Frank L. Portlock Jr. served as timekeeper on the project. This was one of the few jobs he held in his lifetime.

John Massenburg owned the tract of land across the Virginian Railroad and down by the creek, which is now next to the Southgate Plaza Shopping Center, that is a part of Jones Creek. All the low land along Rodgers Street across from the Oscar Smith stadium was part of Big Hill and the Massenburg property. The Massenburg Cemetery was located in front of what is now the main entrance to the stadium. The land between the stadium and the Oscar F. Smith High School was at one time the city of South Norfolk dump. The area at the end of Chesapeake Avenue along the Virginian Railroad was also used as a dump.

There were many stories associated with Big Hill and the Massenburg Cemetery. My friends and I, without parental knowledge, would mount our bicycles and head for the cemetery on Sunday afternoons. Once over the railroad crossing on Jackson Street, we would ride about the equivalent of one city block, turn right and pedal through the woods to the cemetery. The imagination of our young minds often worked overtime. Many of the graves dated back to the 1700s and were sunken because there was nothing left in them. There was supposed to be a giant in one of the graves, but I don't recall ever seeing one that large.

In the 1930s, there was a popular story about the town drunk. It seems that every Saturday night, he would tie one on. One Saturday night after he passed out, his fellow drunks reportedly picked him up and carried him to the Massenburg Cemetery where they carefully placed him in one of the sunken graves. As the story goes, he spent the night there, and when the sun appeared Sunday morning, he woke up, looked around and upon seeing all the surrounding tombstones, he knew he had died the night before. It has been said that he never took another drink and acquired some new friends.

When Frank L. Portlock Sr. surveyed the property in the vicinity of the Norfolk & Western and Virginian Railroads, he laid out Chesapeake Avenue and Jackson, Rodgers and Decatur Streets to run straight through to Portlock Road. In later years, the Richardson family acquired that land in the vicinity of Virginia Avenue, the Norfolk & Western Railway and the spur line between the Norfolk & Western and Virginian Railroads. The Richardsons also purchased the Briquette Plant at the end of Virginia Avenue. An English company had originally owned the plant. There was a tall, steel tower that was used to unload coal dust from the train. This dust was mixed with oil and compressed into briquettes. When they were used in a stove or furnace, they produced a very hot fire. Eventually the plant closed and the surrounding land was developed with total disregard for the original survey. Today there are many streets winding in and out, and quite a few cul-de-sacs. The rationale behind all of this was that more houses could be built by changing from the previous survey.

Before Rodgers Street was extended over the Virginian Railroad, there was a crossing at Jackson Street. In the 1950s, the City of South Norfolk acquired land on Rodgers Street from the Commonwealth of Virginia. The purpose was to build a new high school to replace the one on Holly Street. It was about this time that people began buying land and building new homes along that part of Rodgers Street. The early residents had to contend with the smoke and smell from the old city dump. They gambled, and it paid off because the city soon closed the dump and filled the land.

With all of this, it was felt that a railroad crossing was needed at Rodgers Street. A meeting was held with representatives from the Virginian Railroad, and a decision was reached to close the crossing at Jackson Street and make a new one at Rodgers Street. The original survey was for the crossing to remain at Jackson Street, but a greater need prevailed. Around this time, the Portlocks sold their strip of land in the vicinity of the Massenburg property to Scotch Hall, Ralph Haywood and Sidney McPherson.

Until recent years, the spur line ran between the Norfolk & Western and Virginian Railroads. In the early 1960s, the area between the spur line and Freeman Avenue became Varsity Manor. This property had been part of the Tapley Portlock farm. The old farmhouse, which still stands, was built *circa* 1789. After the Portlocks, the Gibsons owned the property and the surrounding area was known as Gibson Hill. Gibson Acres is the land between Freeman Avenue and Portlock Road. Elmer Gordon developed most of this area.

This is the back of the Portlock homestead as it appeared in 1902. The people on the porch are Frank Livingston Portlock Sr. and his wife Marion West Portlock standing near the steps. Bet Towns, the maid, is standing at the left end of the porch. Emmie Argyle Portlock and Marion Hunter Portlock (age two years) are in the buggy. *Photo courtesy of Frank L. Portlock Jr.*

In 1854, Nathaniel Portlock (1814–1863) built the farmhouse that he referred to as the Oaks. It stood near what is now the corner of Portlock Road and Franklin Street, near Bainbridge Boulevard. Portlock Road ran straight to the front gate. In order to reach Bainbridge Boulevard, one had to detour down Freeman Avenue. The Portlock family used a lane that ran from the farm to Freeman Avenue. Portlock Station was on the corner of Freeman Avenue and Bainbridge Boulevard. This is where the streetcar stopped to pick up passengers. The entire tract of land covered fifty-two acres and was originally granted to the Portlock family by the king of England. The boundaries were Freeman Avenue, Franklin Street and Mill Dam Creek. Judge William Nathaniel Portlock, the next owner, named it the Home Place. He was the son of Franklin and Eugenia Herbert (Tatem) Portlock. William's brother Franklin Livingston Portlock Sr. and his family lived there and tended the farm until moving to South Norfolk in 1910.

A man known as "Uncle Virgil" came from North Carolina and went to work as a hired hand for Franklin L. Portlock Sr. He did various jobs around the Portlock farm, and when the family moved to South Norfolk, he went with them. The Portlock house on Ohio Street had a large basement with seven-foot ceilings. It was there that Virgil made his home. Uncle Virgil milked the cows, kept the lawn and did other chores as needed at the new house.

This beautiful old home was the Portlock homestead, which was built in Norfolk County in 1854. It stood at what is now the corner of Portlock Road and Franklin Street until 1939. At that time, Robert B. Rowland Jr. purchased the house and surrounding farm. Rowland's mother, Mary Rowland, paid $7,000 to have the old homestead and a small brick annex moved to Mill Dam Creek. The house now faces Hamilton Street in the Portlock section of South Norfolk. *Photo courtesy of Frank L. Portlock Jr.*

On April 13, 1922, more than a third of Berkley was destroyed by fire. The funeral establishment of Elis Pendleton was burned down. The fire required the undertaker to move one body to at least three locations. It has been said that the body was that of Uncle Virgil.

After the family moved to South Norfolk, Franklin Portlock rented the farm to A.S. Jones. Ownership of the farm remained in the family until 1939. On September 2, 1939, Robert B. Rowland Jr. purchased the property. His intention was to have the farmhouse torn down and develop the farm into single-family homes. His mother, Mary Rowland, saved the house by having it moved. She paid $7,000 to have the old homestead and a small brick annex moved to the edge of Mill Dam Creek. The house now faces Hamilton Street in the Portlock section of South Norfolk. Rowland, along with Simeon Leary, developed the area and gave it the name of Portlock Terrace. There were two oak trees in the back yard of the farmhouse, and when the house was moved, the oak trees were left standing. Today one remains on what became an extension of Portlock Road across from Dyanax Street and the other is at the corner of what is now Bernard Street near Portlock Road.

On December 8, 1948, a deed of gift was made between Robert B. Rowland Jr. and his wife Ella C. Rowland and the Town of Portlock. This deed conveyed Corden Avenue, Maryview Avenue, Mary Ellen Avenue, Gallop Avenue, Lyndall Avenue and Bernard Street to the Town of Portlock. These properties are shown on the plat or map titled "Map of Portlock Terrace" made by R.R. Savage, Norfolk County surveyor, in October 1947. The plat was recorded in the Office of the Clerk of the Norfolk County Court in map book 31, page 8. It is part of the property conveyed to Rowland by deed from Eugenia Tatem Butt on September 2, 1939, and recorded in deed book 654, page 496 in the Norfolk County clerk's office.

Chapter II

Early Industries

After the post–Civil War depression, the industrial potential of South Norfolk began to be realized through two railroad lines, the Norfolk & Western and the Virginian. With its proximity to Norfolk, South Norfolk was a natural for suburban development. The railroad lines and the Elizabeth River also made it a natural for industry.

Early South Norfolk was like the hub of a wheel. The bulk of the industries were either in South Norfolk or the territory immediately surrounding it on both sides of the Southern Branch of the Elizabeth River. It was there that large amounts of manufactured goods were shipped out and raw materials shipped in. A large number of the fertilizer, chemical, guano and oil companies were located in the Money Point section of Portlock.

It was about 1870, when Carter W. Poindexter and his son Parke brought the first manufacturing plant of importance to this area by encouraging Johnson & Waters of Baltimore, Maryland, to locate here. This plant later became the Greenleaf Johnson Lumber Company. Other manufacturing mills soon located in the vicinity and drew a large number of people for employment.

One of the earliest industries was the processing of lumber. Logs were chained together and floated to the area by way of the Intracoastal Waterway from the Carolinas and southern parts of Virginia. Among the early waterfront lumber mills were Lekies and Collins, E.M. Tilley (located at Montalant), Tunis and Serpell, Arbuckle, and Greenleaf Johnson. Tunis and Serpell later became the Tunis Lumber Company. Its president, Theophilus Tunis, also served as a Virginia state senator.

Another major industry was the creosoting of piles, lumber, ties, post and other wood products. Creosote is made by the distillation of coal and wood tar, and is used as a coating to preserve wood. Wood treated with creosote can spend many years in the ground without rotting. There were several creosoting works at Money Point on the Southern Branch of the Elizabeth River. Among them were the Old Dominion Creosoting Plant and the Norfolk, Republic, Eppington-Russell, Wycoff and Atlantic creosoting companies. Over the years, these plants contributed heavily to the pollution of the Elizabeth River. Currently, there is a movement to clean up the river. The U.S. Army Corps of Engineers is using the area between Scuffletown Creek and the Jordan Bridge as a test site. If this is successful, other parts of the river will follow.

This photograph shows the plant of the Nichols Fertilizer Corporation at Buell. The large water tank, which was used by the railroad, can be seen beside the plant *circa* 1942. *Photo courtesy of Willard Hill.*

Another predominant industry of the time was the manufacture of fertilizer and guano. The first guano plant was built by Frank S. Royster and operated as the Columbia Guano Company, later changing its name to F.S. Royster Guano Company. Royster built his home on the corner of Warren Crescent and Colonial Avenue in the Ghent section of Norfolk in 1901.

Industries continued to expand, as did the shipments of coal over the Norfolk & Western and Virginian Railroads. By 1910, in addition to F.S. Royster Company, there was the Pocomont Guano Company and the Swift and Company Fertilizer Plant. Two major oil companies, the Mexican Petroleum Company and the Texas Oil Company, operated large distribution plants. There were also six mills that manufactured lumber, boxes, laths, shingles, hardwood, mahogany and other millwork.

The James G. Wilson Corporation made steel blinds as well as rolling and sliding doors of all kinds, many of which were exported. The company employed approximately five hundred men and worked an average of eight and three-quarter hours per day and five and a half-days per week. The company also produced partitions, which were used in the largest buildings in the world.

The firm of A.S. Lee and Sons Company Inc., manufacturers of agricultural lime and fertilizer, had its factory on Barnes Road. Arthur S. Lee of Richmond had established the company. In December 1933, Walter B. Mann and his associates acquired the business, which then became the Reliance Fertilizer and Lime Corporation. After Mann's death in March 1947, James Justin Joyce became president and Mrs. Marguerite Joyce Mann of South Norfolk became vice president.

The F.S. Royster Guano Company occupied a large portion of the Southern Branch of the Elizabeth River near the Jordan Bridge. This photograph was taken on February 5, 1957. *Photo courtesy of Richard Spratley.*

Looking east we see completed pier 7 with piers 8 and 9 in the background. Also in the background is the F.S. Royster Guano Company's plant as it appeared on June 3, 1957. *Photo courtesy of Richard Spratley.*

Joyce was working in Shulman and Company Inc., a man's furnishings store, when he met his future wife, Eugenia Herbert Portlock. They were married October 21, 1931, in South Norfolk. Before her marriage, Mrs. Joyce taught in the South Norfolk High School.

By 1926, there were three factories manufacturing lime and fertilizer, and they supplied the farms in the vicinity of South Norfolk and Norfolk County. The Virginia Portland Cement Corporation completed the area's first cement plant with a capacity of 3,600 barrels per day. The plant employed 180-day laborers in addition to the salaried men for a weekly payroll of $1,250. This figure did not include the monthly salaried employees—a laboratory and clerical force of about ten. This plant later became the Lone Star Cement Plant. The Norfolk & Southern Railroad shops and other railroad facilities also helped to provide an economic base for the community.

In 1902, Joseph Herbert Norton, who lived on Chesapeake Avenue, opened the Shirtwaist Factory on Poindexter Street. The factory was charted by the county court in July. On July 30, 1902, the *Virginian-Pilot* newspaper announced that the factory was ready to start operation in ten days and would employ about one hundred people. Sometime later, Norton moved the factory to Thirteenth and Liberty Streets, and later still a Mr. Hoffner, who owned the building, turned the former factory into apartments. Many young newlyweds of South Norfolk began their married life in one of the Hoffner apartments. The apartments were demolished in November 1951.

The first cement plant was completed in 1926 by the Portland Company and had a capacity of 3,600 barrels per day. The plant employed 180-day workers and a force of about ten laboratory and clerical people. A large expansion was accomplished in 1957, and the plant became Lone Star Cement Plant. It was located at the end of Ohio Street in South Norfolk. *Photo courtesy of Linwood L. Briggs Jr.*

This aerial view shows the Lone Star Cement Plant on the far right. Oil tanks can be seen on the left and center of the picture.

The E.H. Barnes Company opened and produced box shooks and lumber. The company also purchased logs for processing. Consumer's Box Company, at the corner of Seaboard Avenue and Guerriere Street, manufactured barrels, wooden strawberry crates and other types of wooden containers; John Loeffeet was the proprietor. One of the office employees, John Gaydell, who was also known as "Uncle John," painted the large murals on the walls of the Grand Theatre.

Other plants of importance included N. Block and Sons-Salvage, Interstate Sand Company, Riley Tar Company and Eastern Tar Products. These plants represented an investment of millions of dollars and paid thousands of dollars in taxes to the community. They also furnished employment for a large number of citizens of South Norfolk and the surrounding areas.

South Norfolk advertised the availability of industrial sites, three trunk line railroads and the Norfolk and Portsmouth Belt Line Railroad, which handled trade to and from all points without additional cost to the shipper and consignee. The city publicized an ample water supply, cheap electric power and deep water on the Southern Branch. South Norfolk cooperated with prospective industries to see that their requirements were supplied. For example, the city spent $3,400 to reinforce a concrete road that led to the Virginia Portland Cement Corporation plant.

In a special twentieth-century edition of the *Virginian-Pilot* newspaper, South Norfolk boasted of a population of 1,500 that was served by three railroad lines, two box factories, four sawmills, one chemical works, three guano plants, two churches, two public schools, a post office and its own waterworks. The article ended with a promotional blurb stating, "With our good schools, smooth streets, nice sidewalks, plenty of churches, pure water, employment for all and money to let, we can say those desiring a good investment could do no better than to cast their lot here. We are looking for good citizens and no others need apply." Sounds like a Marine Corps recruiting ad.

CHAPTER III

THE KNITTING MILLS

IN THE 1890s NORFOLK HAD A lot to gain by investing $600,000 to build her five knitting mills, which employed large numbers of operators and, in ways too numerous to mention, added much to the welfare of the community. Many kinds of factories were lacking in the Norfolk area at that time. That was a great drawback throughout the entire South because there was not a local market for much of the mill's materials and they had to be exported.

In the fall of 1880, a number of enterprising businessmen formed the Norfolk Knitting and Cotton Manufacturing Company to establish a mill where knit underwear could be manufactured. Money was raised, an expert was sent North to purchase the required machinery and, within a few months, the first mill in the area was in operation. Located in Norfolk's Atlantic City at the corner of Colley Avenue and Avenue B, the first knitting mill south of the Mason-Dixon Line cost $100,000. For some time, it was a source of little profit and was a disappointment to stockholders. After a few years, a large block of stock was sold to Dickson and Johnston, who persevered and obtained the most current equipment, and things started to improve. It was said that the factory contained everything needed to transform a bale of cotton into knit cloth of the finest quality. At that time, the factory was operating six sets of cards, six spinning mules, twenty-eight cylinders and with automatic take-ups. The finishing department was supplied with the latest improved machinery. Employment was at two hundred, of which 49 percent were women. The finished negligee shirts and underwear were sold through New York's William Iselin & Co. The main building was brick with thirty-five thousand feet of floor space, and the plant had five hundred square feet of land.

The officers of the company were D. Lowenberg, president; C. Hardy, treasurer; and C. Brooks Johnston, secretary and manager. Other company directors were Dr. Alex Tunstall, W.A.S. Taylor and V.D. Groper. Lowenberg was involved in the construction of the Chesapeake Knitting Mill in Berkley and the Lowenberg Mill in South Norfolk. The mill in South Norfolk became the Elizabeth Knitting Mill.

Lowenberg built the Chesapeake Knitting Mill in 1890, but Foster Black was the lessee of the mill and a large stockholder. In 1897 when being interviewed by a reporter from the *New Daily Pilot*, Black said that for some time the entire capacity of the mill was needed in order to meet the underwear demand, and that all the goods manufactured were sent North. He also

Above: This is the Chesapeake Knitting Mill as it appeared April 20, 1920. It is not certain if the fenced-in recreational area was a part of the mill. *Photo courtesy of Hardy Forbes.*

The view below of the Chesapeake Knitting Mill shows more of its size and a part of the building facing the road, possibly old Thirteenth Street. The fenced-in recreational area shown in the previous photograph does not appear in this July 5, 1920 snapshot. *Photo courtesy of Hardy Forbes.*

stated that the northern trade had fallen off somewhat and that the knitting-mill business seemed to be going from bad to worse. He further stated that the goods manufactured could only be sold at ruinous prices. The mill's specialty was a cheap line of underwear; however, the company was gradually being forced into producing a better quality of goods. This was a new industry and, as with most new undertakings in the manufacturing business, the mill owners struggled with problems incident to a new enterprise. As for the future, Black

Left: Here is the wash room of the Chesapeake Knitting Mill on July 3, 1920. The many rolls of cotton cloth have been washed or are waiting to be washed. *Photo courtesy of Hardy Forbes.*

Right: Two young ladies grace the entrance of the Chesapeake Knitting Mill office on April 20, 1920. Do you realize that the baby being held by its mother, if living today, would be eighty-five years old? *Photo courtesy of Hardy Forbes.*

This photograph was taken from the roof of the Chesapeake Knitting Mill on April 20, 1920. There is a lot of activity in this picture. Several of the cottages built for employee use can be seen, numerous trucks being loaded or unloaded, and in the right center background, there seems to be a large tent. This could be part of a carnival, an event that was popular around that time. *Photo courtesy of Hardy Forbes.*

indicated that the volume of manufacture would be limited not by demands of the market but by overproduction, which was already threatening manufacturers.

Mr. Bailey was the superintendent of the Chesapeake Knitting Mill. A tour of the mill would begin with the lapping, or opening, department before moving to the card room, where there were six lots of cards, six spinning mules and twenty-eight knitting cylinders with automatic take-ups. The cloth passed from the card room to the washroom where it was cleaned and dried. The better the wool and the more care taken in the carding, drawing and roving processes, the more excellent the spinning would become. Also warmth, dryness, cold and moisture had a great influence on the ductility of the cotton.

The building had an office as well as carpenter and machine shops. The mill employed 150 people. E.M. Tilley, a retired lumber manufacturer, was president of the company. Foster Black was the secretary, part owner and lessee of the mill.

South Norfolk's Lowenberg Mill—which was later named the Elizabeth Knitting Mill and was known in the trade as the Elizabeth Cotton Mill—was built in 1892. The largest of all the mills, it was equipped with the latest machinery and appliances for opening, break-in, carding, spinning, knitting and dressing the material and for measuring and cutting the cloth. A low-pressure engine with steel boilers supplied the motive power. The engine was rated at 150 horsepower. The mill employed 175 hands and occupied four acres, where the company built several handsome cottages for employees. Cottages were also available at the Chesapeake mill.

Black was a mysterious, many-sided man who was engaged in the importing business in New York before coming to Norfolk. The officers of the Lowenberg Knitting Mills Company were W.H. Taylor, president, and Alvah H. Martin, secretary and treasurer. The directors also included W.W. Old, S.L. Foster, J.W. Perry and Foster Black. Taylor was also president of the Marine Bank and had served as adjutant to General Robert E. Lee during the War Between the States—the late unpleasantness.

The knitting mills in the Norfolk area were located at Atlantic City's Colley Avenue (founded in 1890), while Lambert's Point Knitting Mills were organized in Newark, New Jersey in 1882. Other Norfolk mills were: Chesapeake Knitting Mills (founded in 1890), Lowenberg or Elizabeth Knitting Mills (founded in 1892) and the Portsmouth Knitting Mills (founded in 1896).

The Elizabeth Knitting Mill was on Perry Street in South Norfolk, where the Rena B. Wright School is located today. The Chesapeake Knitting Mill was near the Berkley–South Norfolk line and employed a large number of South Norfolk residents. Most of the employees were paid by the piece (piecework).

CHAPTER IV

SCHOOLS OF SOUTH NORFOLK
AND PORTLOCK

IT WAS IN 1796 THAT THOMAS Jefferson introduced his plan for the "General Diffusion of Knowledge" for Virginia. Through his influence and suggestion, on December 22, 1796, the Virginia General Assembly enacted the school law, An Act to Establish Schools. Two years later, Norfolk County adopted Jefferson's plan and put into operation a system of public education.

The future president described the type of educational program that he thought was needed by the commonwealth when he wrote, "A system of education which shall reach every description of citizens from the richest to the poorest, as it was the earliest, so will it be the latest of all public concerns in which I shall permit myself to take interest." The county's leaders accepted this point of view, and it has served as a guide during ensuing years for citizens of Norfolk County and in the area that became the town of South Norfolk.

For a number of years, the children from McCloudtown (as South Norfolk was then known) and nearby farms attended the schools of Berkley. After the Civil War, during the Reconstruction, the people who could afford to do so employed tutors for their children. Around 1872, the Providence School was established at the intersection of what is today Campostella and Providence Roads. The next public school was at Money Point.

Classes were held in a church until a one-room, frame-building school was completed in the village of Portlock around 1895. The history of Rosemont Christian Church relates to using the school for prayer meetings in 1902. When the school was completed, Miss Rena B. Wright, the teacher at Money Point, moved with her students to Portlock. Miss Wright taught at this school for two or three years. For a while, the school at Portlock continued to be known as the Money Point School.

On August 31, 1895, School District Number Five of Norfolk County acquired a parcel of land in Washington Magisterial District from the Shea family (all eight members of them). The land was situated on the east side of the public road, which had been formerly known as the Berkley and Currituck Turnpike. The road was forty feet wide. It is interesting to note the descriptive location of the stakes placed by the surveyors—one in the branch near a spring on the road side, another in the center of a cove—and the reference made to the lines of the lands of B.F. Gibson and A.A. Spain. The deed stated that the piece of land "contained an acre, less a fraction of an acre" and that the school district would have the right to use the spring on the roadside located near the northwest

[Form B—No. 2.]

Commonwealth of Virginia.

PUBLIC FREE SCHOOLS.

Teacher's First Grade Certificate.

It is hereby Certified, That *Miss Sue Tatem*

having passed the required examination on Orthography, Reading, Writing, Arithmetic, Grammar, Geography, History, Physiology and Hygiene,

_____ *and on* The Theory *and Practice of Teaching, and having furnished satisfactory evidence of Professional Ability, Zeal, and Experience, and also of Good Morals and General Fitness, is hereby* Authorized to Teach *in the* Public Free Schools *of*

Norfolk County, *during the term of three years, ending July 31st, eighteen hundred and ninety- One, unless this certificate be annulled.*

Given under my hand, *this* 23 *day* Sept

A. D., eighteen hundred and ninety- eight.

John T. West, *Supt. of Schools.*

Norfolk *County.*

NOTE.—This certificate may be renewed for any period not exceeding two years, and may be made valid in any other county of the State by endorsement of the Superintendent of Schools of such county.

The Regulations provide that "no first grade certificate shall be issued to any person who is under twenty years of age, and who has not taught successfully ten school months."

This certificate from the Commonwealth of Virginia, which was signed by Superintendent of Schools John T. West on September 23, 1898, certified that Miss Sue Tatem was qualified to teach the first grade. John West was the first superintendent of Norfolk County schools after the Civil War.

Miss Rena B. Wright taught and served as assistant principal and principal of the local schools for more than forty-five years—probably more like fifty years. She retired from the South Norfolk school system in 1942.

corner of the land. This property, on which a new four-room, brick school was eventually built, was purchased for $150.

The first school to be established in the village of South Norfolk was a private school. Around 1892, the Elizabeth Knitting Mill was operating on Park Avenue between Perry and Porter Streets. At that time, there were not any labor laws and a number of children worked six days a week at the mill. When an economic depression occurred in 1893, the mill cut back its operations to three days a week—Thursday, Friday and Saturday. This meant that there were three days that the children could not work. The parents collectively asked Mrs. Edward Williams if she would teach the children. Since Mrs. Williams was teaching her own children, she consented to teach the others as well. For two years, she used the second floor of her home for this purpose. During this time, she had about fifteen students and received $1 per month for each student. The Williams homestead was located near Scuffletown Creek at what later became known as 1710 Porter Street.

A public school was organized in South Norfolk as early as August 1891. A group of men formed the South Norfolk School Society and erected a two-room, wooden school on property acquired from E.M. Tilley. The South Norfolk Public School was built on Jackson Street in what is now the 1100 block between Guerriere and Ohio Streets. The cost of the school, including the furniture and outbuildings, was approximately $2,200. The teachers were Miss Annie Gammon and Miss Lucy Scott (who later became Mrs. H.W. Keeling). Captain John T. West was superintendent of Norfolk County schools at that time.

This picture of the South Norfolk Public School on Jackson Street was taken in 1903. *Photo courtesy of Linwood L. Briggs Jr.*

The enrollment continued to increase, and a third room was added. The faculty then consisted of Miss Grace Coggin (principal), Miss Blanche Hines Barrie and Miss Frances Wray. When Miss Coggin married, Miss Rena B. Wright took her place. There was a rule that married teachers, except under extenuating circumstances, would not be employed by the school. This rule was followed until there was a severe shortage of teachers during World War II. In 1946, after the war ended, married teachers were no longer placed under contract, and each received a letter from the superintendent of schools thanking them for their service during the emergency. It also stated that they would not be rehired.

In 1899, Rena B. Wright was teacher of the Senior Department of the school, Blanch Hines Barrie was teacher of the Intermediate Department and Nancy Shafer was teacher of the Primary Department.

Commencement exercises for the South Norfolk graded school was held Thursday June 22, 1899, in the Odd Fellows Hall on Poindexter Street (this building still stands today). The roll of honor included the following: Senior Department: Bertha Adams, Geneva Daughtery, Mattie Jones, Alma Jones, Eve Haskett, Mamie Mercer, Mamie McLeroy, Bessie McLeroy, Eva McMaster, Arthur Nash and Willie McMaster; Intermediate Department: Paul Bradley, Othie Sherman, Wesley Jones, Edwin Jones, Oscar Parker, Waverly Parker, Richard Vellines, Vernie McCloud, Bertha Geraud, Lillie Eason, May Gallope, Jessie Harrell, Mary Dean and Edna Vellines; Primary Department: Wilbur Howard, Noel Howell, George Hand, Elvie White, Pansy Dean, Maude Marr, Lucy Andrews and Annie Leroy.

Just before 1900, enrollment at the Jackson Street school had increased to the point where some classes were held in the Odd Fellows Hall. At that time, the school had 140 pupils and three teachers. Because the small wooden building was inadequate for the growing community, the Washington District School Board (D.G. Williams, M.C. Keeling and F.L. Portlock) purchased a block of land in Elmsley. The block was bounded by A, B, Twentieth and Twenty-second Streets. The first brick building of eight rooms was built around 1902 at a cost of $35,000. The five teachers in the new building were Miss Rena B. Wright, principal; Miss Mildred Wilson; Miss Sally Morrison; Miss Evelyn Walke; and Miss Donaho. Other early teachers were: Miss Sadie Sandridge, Miss Lottie Snead, Miss Emma Montague, Miss Margaret Borden, and Miss Fannie May Pierce.

In 1906, plans were made to form a high school, even though Miss Wright, Miss Wilson and Miss Annie Creekmur were the only teachers certified to teach the higher grades. This high school was among the first—if not the first—in Norfolk County. In the beginning, there were only four students taking high-school subjects. They were Georgia Monell, Hattie Schuerman, Oris Roache and Percy Sabine. Miss Wright taught these students for only one year. After the first year, each student left to either work or go to another school. During this period, pupils who wanted course work in the sixth grade or higher came to South Norfolk from Portlock, Campostella and from as far away as Oak Grove. Students from Portlock and Money Point rode the streetcar, and their fare was paid by the school board. Pupils from Campostella walked, and those from Oak Grove came on a mule drawn wagon driven by Lewis Curling Sr.

On July 16, 1908, a preconstruction notice appeared in a building journal called the *Manufacturer's Record*. The notice stated that bids for the erection of a four-room school building in Portlock would be opened July 22 and went on to explain how to submit a bid. It is not surprising that John W. Jones was awarded the contract. Jones was the son-in-law of E.M. Tilley, chairman of the school board. Thus the Portlock Public School was built at a cost of $7,000.

It is not certain if the school was wired for electricity or if it was equipped with a furnace. Most likely it was heated by burning coal or wood in several potbellied stoves. One thing for certain is that it did not have indoor plumbing. There was a wooden ramp from the back of the school to a frame outbuilding. The outhouse had two sides—one was designated for girls and the other for boys. In those days, natural lighting was relied on and it was typical for schools to have large windows on at least two walls of each classroom. Sometime in the early to mid 1900s, the ceilings were lowered.

At that time, Portlock was a village in the Washington Magisterial District of Norfolk County. When the Portlock School opened, Miss Sallie Wilson was its first principal and grades one through five were taught. Some of the early teachers were Catherine Bray, Mrs. Craver, Myra Odell, Mrs. Gibson, Christine Stokes, Lorraine Halstead, Mrs. Bondurant, Mrs. Bowen, Mrs. Foster, Mrs. Coleman and Mrs. Faulkner. Students in grades six through high school attended the school on B Street in South Norfolk. Students from Dozier's Corner and other distant surrounding areas came to school in a horse-drawn wagon with benches. As the story goes, children from Edmonds Corner came to school in a wagon pulled by a blind mule. In the morning, the children climbed in the wagon and gave the mule a slap on the rump to start him on his way to the Portlock School. Upon arrival, the children got out of the wagon and the mule went back home. In the afternoon, without a driver, the mule went back to school, the children climbed in the wagon and he took them back home.

After renovations in the early 1990s, the Portlock School reopened in May 1997 as Chesapeake's Museum and Information Center. Information about that project indicated that the lowered ceilings were removed.

Two other schools were constructed in 1908. One of them, the South Hill Elementary School, was built at the corner of Hill Street and Hanna Avenue and served about three hundred students. The other, named for George Washington Carver, was built off Campostella Road.

In 1908, A.H. Foreman became superintendent of Norfolk County schools. The following year, construction of a second building began in Elmsley on B Street. While the new building was under construction, the old school structure on Jackson Street was moved to B Street. This building didn't have any running water, so the larger boys were detailed to carry buckets of water to the classes in the morning and again in the afternoon. Outhouses were erected behind this temporary building. The new building was ready to accept students in September 1910 and was used as the high school.

Between 1906 and 1908, more students were advancing toward the high school level. In September 1909, a dozen pupils entered the first year of high school. Those students included Margaret Wilson, John Lawrence, Harry Blanchard, Clyde Rogers, Margaret Blanchard and Waverly Cherry. Three completed the four years: Margaret Blanchard, Clyde Rogers and Waverly Cherry formed the first South Norfolk High School graduating

When the wooden building on Jackson Street became inadequate, the members of the school board of Washington District purchased a block of land in Elmsley between A and B Streets and built the building on the left at a cost of $35,000. This took place around 1902. By 1906, plans were made for a high school and more room was needed. This photograph shows the second building when it was still under construction, *circa* 1909, but it was completed in time for the school year, which began in September 1910.

This structure was located on B Street near the first school building. It appears in pictures dated as early as 1909 and was possibly moved there from Jackson Street. The building didn't have any running water, so the larger boys in the school were detailed to carry buckets of water to the classes in the morning and again in the afternoon. One of the outhouses can be seen in the right background.

class in 1913. Margaret Wilson and John Lawrence transferred to Maury High School after three years, and Harry Blanchard became ill and died before graduation.

A large hall connected the two eight-room structures on B Street. This combination became known as the double building. Although both buildings contained a bell tower, only the first structure built was equipped with a bell. A rope with a loop in one end hung down from the bell. A long pole with a hook was connected to the rope and, through the use of one unit of manpower (that of the janitor), the bell was rung several times a day. The E.W. Vanduzen Company's Buckeye Foundry in Cincinnati, Ohio, manufactured this large bell in 1902. When the school buildings on B Street were razed in 1972, the bell was removed to the stadium of the new Oscar F. Smith High School on Rodgers Street. On May 22, 1995, the bell was relocated to the stadium of the new Oscar F. Smith High School at Great Bridge Boulevard and Tiger Drive. The bell, which was labeled the victory bell, was rung once too often and cracked during the 2004 football season. The school held a fundraiser in 2005 to help acquire funds towards the purchase of a new bell. Replacement will cost about $9,000.

The high-school teachers for the school year 1912–1913 were Miss Annie Creekmur, Miss Mary R. Daniel, Miss Sadie Sandridge and Miss Rena B. Wright. Miss Creekmur left during the school year and was replaced by Miss Indiana Young. When Miss Young came, she expected to stay only two months but remained until she retired in June

The Waterford Elementary School was built on Liberty Street in 1914 and received an addition in 1959. The school and grounds covered 1.3 acres and had a capacity of 510 students. *Photo courtesy of Acme Photo Co. Inc. of Norfolk.*

This was the third of three school buildings constructed on B Street. This large building was located at the corner of B and Twentieth Streets and was put into use in September 1916.

1935. Miss Young and her sister Miss Mary Young were my neighbors, residing at 1126 Seaboard Avenue.

In 1914, the Waterford Elementary School on Liberty Street was built. It received an addition in 1959. The school and grounds covered 1.3 acres and had a capacity of 510 students. The name was later changed to the Edward Wilson School.

Enrollment at the schools on B Street continued to increase and a third building was added at the corner of B and Twentieth Streets in 1916. An unconfirmed rumor stated that this large building was initially designed to serve as a hospital. The structure consisted of three floors and sixteen classrooms. The rest rooms, furnace room and cafeteria were located on the ground floor. In 1924, the high-school chemistry laboratory was also in that part of the building; in 1940, the wood and machine shops were also there. Classrooms occupied the second and third floors. This stand-alone structure with its high ceilings and large rooms was larger than the other two buildings and was referred to as the "big building." Many former students have stories relating to the steep stone steps (which were actually made of concrete) and the difficulties experienced when trying to climb them, especially when they were covered with snow.

Longtime School Figures

Three long-employed custodians of the school on B Street were Mr. Hanbury who lived across the street from the school at the corner of B and Twenty-first Streets, Victor Branch and James Wynn. Hanbury died in the 1930s when I was attending the school. The school flag was flown at half-mast.

Rena B. Wright, born in Bowling Green, came to South Norfolk expecting to stay for only two months but spent most of her life in the Norfolk, Norfolk County and South Norfolk areas. At the age of sixteen she became governess to the Hyslop children at their home in Brambleton. At one time, Wright was the tutor to the daughters of Dr. G.N. Halstead. Wright taught and served as assistant principal and principal at the local schools for more than forty-five years, retiring from the South Norfolk school system in 1942. After retiring, she went to live with a sister in Colonial Place in Norfolk. Rena B. Wright died on March 16, 1946.

Community Involvement

On December 22, 1912, the South Norfolk graded school prepared a "pounding" for the poor. This was under the direction of W.C. Giraud. Deputy Sheriff W.J. Rawls furnished the horse and wagon used in the distribution of groceries. The young people who assisted included Annie Maude Cuthrell, Farcie Smith, Eve Vellines, Sybel Deans, William White, Grady Nichols and Julian Gregory.

The South Norfolk Civic League—later called the South Norfolk Home and School League, and which still later became the Parent Teacher Association (PTA)—was organized October 29, 1915, in the auditorium of the South Norfolk High School on B Street. The first officers were the Reverend W.M. Black, president; R.A. Woods, first vice president; Rena B. Wright, second vice president; Mary F. Barner, secretary; and Bascomb Etheridge, treasurer. In 1916, Portlock's first PTA was organized; Patty Bartlett was its president. In 1917, James Hurst became the seventh superintendent of schools for Norfolk County. Hurst would serve until 1942.

South Norfolk organized its first school board on April 21, 1921. The organizing meeting was held in the office of Q.C. Davis Jr. Davis, who was elected board chairman; George L. Grimes, clerk; W.C. Adams, member; and Rena B. Wright, principal of the schools. At that meeting, the members voted to contact the Virginia State Board of Education to request a division superintendent be appointed to serve the schools of South Norfolk. At that time, the superintendent of Norfolk County schools was also the superintendent of South Norfolk schools.

When the school board met on June 20, 1921, the most important order of business was the appointment of a principal. There were two delegations of citizens present: One delegation wanted to retain Rena B. Wright as principal, and the other felt that a man should hold the position. Even though Wright had more hands-on experience, at that time it was strictly a man's world and the board hired Grover Cleveland Outland, both as principal of South Norfolk High School and as supervising principal of the entire school system. Wright, after having guided the school through its formative years, was appointed to the position of assistant principal. This injustice had followed Rena B. Wright throughout her career until she retired in 1942. Outland's salary was set at $225 per month. At the same meeting, a janitor was hired at a monthly salary of $220.

The second school board took office in September 1921 and included the Reverend O.D. Poythress, R.B. Rowland Jr. and A.M. Nichols.

A home-economics department was added in 1922. The classes, which were designated as domestic science, were held in the house that stood in the corner of the schoolyard at Twenty-second and A Streets. Julia Parker was the teacher. The room was filled with several cutting tables, chairs and two foot-pedal-operated Singer sewing machines. A small stove in the center of the room provided heat on cold days.

Also in 1922, work was begun on the first high school yearbook, *The Tiger*. This was volume one and when completed it covered the years 1922 and 1923. On October 2, 1924, the premier issue of "The Tiger's Cub," the school newspaper, was presented to the student body. The paper was advertised as having a two-fold purpose; first was to bring the student body into closer contact with each other and to further literary attainments; secondly, to place in the hands of the citizens of South Norfolk an accurate report of the various phases of school activities. The paper was published bi-monthly by the officers of the Washington and Jefferson Literary Societies. The subscription rate was 50 cents per school year.

Portlock High School

In 1922, the Portlock High School was built behind the small Portlock School that had been constructed in 1908. J.H. Lassiter was the principal. The first senior class graduated in 1924

In 1924, the domestic science class of South Norfolk High School met in a house in the corner of the schoolyard. The classroom was equipped with foot-pedal Singer sewing machines and cutting tables. As can be seen, a single stove in the center of the room served as the source of heat on cold days.

The Portlock High School was one of several three-story schools built in Norfolk County in 1922. Located behind and to the left of the four-room school that was constructed on Bainbridge Boulevard in 1908, this building was demolished in August 1965.

with only three pupils: Nannie Elizabeth Roane, Rosser L. Gwyn and Mary Halstead. This was probably the only time in history that every member of the class was an officer.

Eventually there was a Y-shaped concrete walk that ran from Bainbridge Boulevard to the two front entrances of the high school. The left entrance was designated for girls and the right entrance for boys. The gymnasium was built behind the school and faced Godwin Avenue. The gymnasium still stands and is used for many functions, such as bingo games. Across the street—where the South Norfolk Community Center is located (1217 Godwin Avenue)—was another school building that housed the cafeteria and later additional classrooms and storage space for textbooks. In addition to Lassiter, the other faculty members were Miss M.T. Winder, science; Miss Anna Rydingsvard, French and English; and Miss G.M. Davis, mathematics and Latin. The small school had an athletic department. The football team played only three games in the 1924 season; Doc Koontz, who ran the local drugstore, was the coach.

Portlock High School served the community of Portlock; students from surrounding sections of Norfolk County between South Norfolk and Oak Grove; and high-school pupils from Norfolk Highlands and Indian River until 1951. At that time, high-school students

The Portlock High School, which was built in 1922, was demolished in August 1965. *Photo courtesy of Vincent Curtis.*

began attending South Norfolk High School. From 1951 to 1964, the former high-school building served as an elementary school. The building was demolished in August 1965.

South Norfolk Schools

A meeting of each South Norfolk class was held for the purpose of reorganizing and electing officers for the school year 1924–1925. The officers from each class were:

Senior Class		Junior Class	
President	Sarah Mercer	President	Carrie Grimstead
Vice President	Herbert Stallings	Vice President	Sudie Page
Secretary	Sarah Marshall	Secretary	Catherine Wallace
Treasurer	Ethel Baker	Treasurer	Edward Meginley
Sophomore Class		Freshman Class	
President	Herman Askew	President	Marjorie Poole
Vice President	Sadie Harrell	Vice President	Birchman White
Secretary	Nicholas Brinn	Secretary	Paul Forehand
Treasurer	Margaret Johnson	Treasurer	William Lynch

In September 1924, there were eleven new faculty members. The new high-school teachers were Margaret Keister (science) and Elizabeth Pulleyn (commercial subjects). The new elementary-school teachers were L.M. Spain, first grade; M.L. Ives, fourth grade;

H.M. Beale, fifth grade; E.C. Branche, fifth grade; L. Zion, fifth grade; M.B. Clayton, fifth grade; L.B. Sinclair, sixth grade; and G.J. Lankford and M.C. Bland, seventh grade.

When the school year began in 1925 the South Norfolk High School faculty consisted of ten teachers: Margaret West taught both English and history; Mary Thompson taught English; Lucille Scaff and Sara Lee Hutchins were the mathematics teachers; Indiana Young taught history; Margaret Keister and Louise Baker taught science; Louise Baker also taught Latin along with Rena B. Wright; Sara Lee Hutchins taught French; Elizabeth Pulleyn was the tearcher of commercial subjects; and Judith Parker taught classes of domestic science.

The South Norfolk Grammar School faculty and grades taught were:

First Grade	Second Grade
Shanna Pulliam	Evelyn Walke
Ruth Wright	Nonie Bonnie*
Lilly Spain	Edith Parker
Louise Stephenson	Ruth Pollard
Third Grade	**Fourth Grade**
Charlotte Omohundro	Edith Pulliam
Lula Briggs	Marie Jones
Vivian Lane	Elsie Grey
Elizabeth Brothers	Myrtle Ives
Virginia Plonk	
Fifth Grade	**Sixth Grade**
Nonie Price	Annie Hudgins
Helen Beale	Mary Young
Ethel Branche	Eva Powers
Lucille Zion	Felix Williams
Mary Clayton	
Seventh Grade	**Special Teachers**
Florence Rountrey	Coach and Physical Director
Laura Harding	Ted Myers
Gladys Lankford	Public Health Nurse
Mary Bland	Miss. Elizabeth Davis**
	Manager of Lunchroom
	Mrs. Edwin Carr

* Married teachers could not be employed unless there were extenuating circumstances. Nonie Bonnie was secretly married for many years and continued to teach.

** Elizabeth Davis, public health nurse, eventually married the Reverend Clyde Sawyer, pastor of the South Norfolk Baptist Church. They had three children and all of them graduated from South Norfolk High School.

In 1925, the South Norfolk School Board included the Reverend O.D. Poythress, chairman; and members A.M. Nichols and O.J. Parker.

In September 1926, the class that would graduate from a new high school on Holly Street in four years began its freshman year at the school on B Street. R.H. Pride became supervising principal of South Norfolk schools in September 1927 and remained until the end of the school year in 1940. Rena B. Wright was assistant principal.

The following is a typical South Norfolk school lunchroom menu from the 1927 school year.

Soup		Milk	
Vegetable	5 cents	Plain	5 cents
Bean	5 cents	Chocolate	6 cents
Roast beef & potatoes	5 cents		
Sandwiches		Deserts	
Veal	5 cents	Pineapple & raisin pie	5 cents
Plain ham	5 cents	Applesauce	5 cents
Ham, lettuce & tomato	10 cents		

How about those prices?

On July 31, 1928, the Virginia State Board of Education officially created a new school division in the city of South Norfolk. J. James Davis was chairman of the school board; other members were Robert B. Rowland Jr. and W.E. Taylor. When the board met on August 6, 1928, R.H. Pride was elected division superintendent. The grammar school enrollment in September 1928 was 1,060 and the high school enrollment was 345.

When the school on B Street became crowded, a six-acre site was acquired on Holly Street between Rodgers and Decatur Streets, and the new South Norfolk High School was built in 1929 at a cost of $140,430. The first students entered the school on February 3, 1930. Around 1997, the school was renovated and received a coat of gray paint. The reason given for painting the brick building was that the particular paint used would strengthen the mortar holding the bricks in place.

The members of the freshman class of 1926 were now seniors. The class, which started with ninety-eight members, had dwindled to forty-five. Mrs. Martha Lindsey was the senior-class homeroom teacher. The class officers were Vernon "Big Jim" Burton, president; Herman Dennis, vice president; Evelyn Hollowell, secretary; and Thelma Harrell, treasurer. The class graduated on June 9, 1930, becoming the first class to graduate from the new school.

In 1931, a young lady by the name of Aurelia Leigh arrived from Mary Washington College and began teaching commercial courses at South Norfolk High School. In 1954, Leigh would report to another new high school in the City of South Norfolk. That school received its name from Oscar Frommel Smith, a local industrialist. Miss Leigh served the school system for more than thirty years.

In September 1934, I entered the first grade at South Norfolk Grammar School on B Street. I was placed in the capable hands of Miss Shanah Pulliam, who had been teaching

When the school on B Street became crowded, a six-acre site was acquired on Holly Street between Rodgers and Decatur Streets. In 1929, the new high school was built at a cost of $140,430. The first students entered the school on February 3, 1930.

Aurelia Leigh, having just graduated from Mary Washington College, arrived at South Norfolk High School in 1931. During her tenure, she served as teacher of commercial courses, clerk of the school board, assistant principal and principal. Leigh served both South Norfolk and Oscar Smith High Schools.

since Shep was a pup and my life has never been the same since. Pulliam had taught my older brother, my father and maybe even my grandfather.

The school board in 1937 consisted of Chairman R.B. Rowland Jr. and members A.N. Nichols and C.L. Williams. R.H. Pride was superintendent of South Norfolk schools, and W.E. Warren was assistant principal of the high school. During the summer of 1937, a new industrial arts department was installed.

In July 1940, Pride resigned as superintendent of South Norfolk schools. On August 1, 1940, T.C. Anderson filled the position of superintendent and Harry C. Paxson Jr., who had served as coach and physical education teacher, was appointed to the position of assistant principal. Anderson had been principal of the Portlock schools for about fifteen years and coached the boy's athletic teams.

C.L. Williams was chairman of the school board, and the other members were R.B. Rowland Jr. and J.S. Rogers. Aurelia Leigh was clerk of the board. In 1944, Leigh became assistant principal of South Norfolk High School. By 1948, Rowland was no longer on the school board and W.R. Britton had filled his position.

Anderson served as superintendent until 1949. In July 1949, William J. Story Jr. replaced Anderson. The first position held by Story when coming to the area was that of coach at Cradock High School. When Granby High School in Norfolk opened in 1939, he became the coach there and later accepted a coaching position at Davidson College before coming to South Norfolk.

A Growing District

On January 1, 1951, the City of South Norfolk annexed a portion of Norfolk County. This increase in population enabled the second-class city to qualify as a city of the first class. With the annexation, the South Norfolk school division inherited the schools of Portlock, Riverdale, Providence and South Hill. This was an increase of 2,450 students.

The first school in Riverdale Manor was built in 1943 and was known as the Riverdale Elementary School. This later became Park Elementary and then Thurgood Marshal Elementary School. The school is located at 2706 Border Road. Charles T. Evanosky became principal in 1951 and was succeeded by R. Turnbull Gillete who served from 1952 through 1953. Then Aurelia I. Leigh, longtime faculty member and administrator, became the principal.

The George Washington Carver School, which was originally built in 1908 and received an addition in 1938, was replaced in 1952 with the George Washington Carver High and Elementary School. The school was constructed on a twenty-eight-acre site at a cost of $460,000. Desks and other school furniture cost about $10,000.

The increasing school enrollment called for other schools to be built. In early 1950, the City of South Norfolk acquired twenty-six acres at the foot of Rodgers Street from the Commonwealth of Virginia. In earlier years, the land had belonged to the Massenburg family. Apparently there were no heirs and the property reverted to the state. Linwood L. Briggs Jr. and others made the trip to Wall Street in New York City to arrange for a loan to build a new high school. It was on this property on Rodgers Street that the first Oscar

The original George Washington Carver School was built in 1908 and received an addition in 1938. Construction of the school began in 1952 on a twenty-eight-acre site and completed in 1953 at a cost of $460,000. Desks and other school furniture cost about $10,000.

F. Smith High School was built at a cost of about $1 million. John W. Daniels of Danville built the school that is now the Oscar F. Smith Middle School. When the new high school opened in September 1954, the high school on Holly Street became the Dorothy H. Truitt Junior High School. It is now called the Truitt Intermediate School. Truitt had been the elementary supervisor at the school on B Street. At that time, the grammar school was named for Rena B. Wright.

It wasn't until 1955 that the old Massenburg Cemetery was moved and construction of the Oscar F. Smith stadium was begun. Mrs. Ruth Elizabeth Smith had donated $50,000 to be used toward construction of the stadium and requested that it be named for her late husband. The South Norfolk School Board voted to name the school and stadium in memory of Oscar Smith. What most citizens of South Norfolk did not know at that time was that Carl M. Jordan, executive vice president and general manager of the Jordan Bridge, contributed $150,000 to start construction of the new high school. So then why wasn't the school named the Carl M. Jordan High School? In addition, $900,000 in proceeds from the Jordan Bridge were contributed to the social, educational and recreational facilities of South Norfolk.

Dorothy Truitt served as assistant principal and later principal of South Norfolk Grammar School. It was said that she drew a line on the floor in front of her desk and that students and teachers were not allowed to cross that line. Truitt lived on Cedar Street in Suffolk and drove to South Norfolk each day. The school building had a bell tower, which was accessible from the third floor. Truitt used this area for curing hams. When the building was demolished, it was reported that there was a very large area of grease beneath the tower. The building on Holly Street that once served as South Norfolk High School was named for Dorothy Truitt.

Edward Ernest Brickell Jr.—a graduate of South Norfolk High School Class of 1944 and the College of William & Mary—joined the faculty of his high school alma mater in 1950. He taught English and coached the baseball team. When Leigh was promoted to principal, Brickell became assistant principal. In 1959, Leigh was again promoted, this time to the position of director of instruction. Brickell then became the principal of Oscar F. Smith High School.

When Brickell was promoted to principal, John William Etheridge—South Norfolk High School Class of 1938 and a graduate of the University of Richmond—became assistant principal. There were at least two members of the Oscar F. Smith High School faculty that had been in the South Norfolk school system when the high school was on B Street. They were Margaret West and Lucille Scaff. West's sister Marion Lee later taught the seventh grade and another sister Frances taught in the Portlock School. The West sisters grew up in Deep Creek and attended the Deep Creek Schools. Another exceptional member of the

Portlock Elementary School was constructed in 1964 on a twenty-three-acre site at 1857 Varsity Drive. A new wing was added and the entire school was renovated in 1995. The new wing featured a media center, computer lab, kindergarten classrooms, special education classrooms and a guidance wing.

high school administrative staff was Cora J. McDowell. McDowell taught in the schools of Isle of Wight County and came to South Norfolk from Windsor High School. She taught English and served in the positions of guidance director and dean of girls.

In 1964, the Portlock Elementary School opened on Varsity Drive. It was situated on twenty-three acres and contained thirty classrooms. The building, which was valued at $560,000, was designed by John Waller and Ben Britt, architects, and built by Tugwell Construction Company. In 1967, its enrollment was just shy of one thousand students and was the largest elementary school in the city of Chesapeake.

Schools in the Late Twentieth Century

In the 1960s, a new elementary school was needed, and on October 24, 1971, the new Rena B. Wright Elementary School on Park Avenue was dedicated. Later the old buildings on B Street were torn down and a McDonald's was built near the corner of B and Twenty-second Streets. About half of the land is still vacant.

In September 1994, just forty years after the first Oscar F. Smith High School received its first students, a new Oscar F. Smith High School opened on Great Bridge Boulevard and Tiger Drive. This marked the first time in more than eighty years that there wasn't a high school in South Norfolk.

It is now the twenty-first century, and plans have been made to demolish the Oscar F. Smith middle school and stadium on Rodgers Street and build a much larger complex on the same property. The plan is to remove the stadium first, build the new school on that land, move the students into the new school, tear the old school down and build the new stadium where the original school was. The reasoning for the plan is to prevent interruption of classes. Sound confusing? It will just be a flip-flop.

CHAPTER V

CHURCHES—EARLY RELIGION

N OT ONLY DID EARLY CHURCHES serve as places of worship, but they also hosted events such as school graduations, picnics and other happenings of the day. The first church in South Norfolk was the Liberty Street Methodist Episcopal Church, South, which was dedicated in May 1892. The Methodist church was soon followed by the South Norfolk Baptist Church, which opened as a chapel on January 5, 1893, and became a fully constituted church on November 5, 1893.

In 1761 when the Elizabeth River Parish was divided, the areas that would become South Norfolk and Portlock were included in the Saint Bride's Parish. The nearest Episcopal Church in 1900 was Saint Bride's, which was located in Berkley. The same was true of the nearest Catholic Church, Saint Matthews. Saint Bride's Episcopal Church is now located at 521 Sparrow Road in Chesapeake and Saint Matthews Catholic Church is at 3314 Sandra Lane in Virginia Beach.

Liberty Street Methodist Episcopal Church, South/ Chesapeake Avenue United Methodist Church

It was in early 1890 that the members of the Board of Stewards of the Chestnut Street Methodist Episcopal Church, South in Berkley became concerned about the need for a church in the rapidly developing South Norfolk area. In a short amount of time, church members raised $4,000 for construction of a church in South Norfolk. Alvah H. Martin Sr. and his wife Mary E. (Tilley) Martin donated two lots on Liberty Street at the corner of Twenty-second Street. The deed for the lots was dated October 13, 1890, and described the property as follows: "lots numbered 15 and 16, each thirty feet fronting Liberty Street and having a depth of 100 feet and being in square Q, according to the plan of Elmsley." Thus, the one-room church built on this corner became the Liberty Street Methodist Episcopal Church, South. Dedication took place in May 1892 by the Reverend A. Coke Smith. The Reverend Robert Tankard Waterfield became its first pastor.

At that time, the young village of South Norfolk consisted of dirt streets and wooden boardwalks. The area where the church was located contained a short section of boardwalk in front of the building and the remaining sidewalk was a dirt path bordered by young, tall trees. The main mode of transportation was the streetcar, which ran down the middle of

The Liberty Street Methodist Episcopal Church, South, was the first church in South Norfolk. It was built in 1892 at the corner of Liberty and Twenty-second Streets. At that time, Liberty Street was a dirt road with wooden boardwalks and young, tall trees. The streetcar ran down its middle, taking people to and from Berkley and Norfolk. Many members of the congregation rode the trolley to church services.

Liberty Street. As would be expected, the streets were muddy during most of the winter months and dusty in the summer. Many of the men of the church were members of the local volunteer fire department and, when the fire bell rang during services, the majority of the men left to go fight the fire.

In those days, everyone either walked or rode the streetcar to church. Pearl Grimes often spoke of walking the length of Chesapeake Avenue each Sunday to Liberty and Twenty-second Streets to attend Sunday school and church. The year was 1910, and she was seven years old. Grimes became a church member in the fall of 1917, during a revival conducted by Reverend J.O. Babcock. A young divinity student by the name of Walter C. Gum assisted Pastor Babcock (when Chesapeake Avenue Church held its dedicatory service June 20, 1943, Dr. Walter C. Gum was district superintendent and later became bishop).

The church was one large room. Sunday school began with a short devotional period after which the classes divided into separate groups, and each moved to its own little corner for the lesson. Following the lesson, everyone assembled together for the closing exercise. The worship service would begin with the preacher requesting a member of the congregation to lead them in a word of prayer. During the worship service, when the preacher made a point of special emphasis, the older, more respected members of the congregation would reply with a reverent "Amen;" however, the younger members were expected to keep quiet. On communion Sunday, everyone drank from one cup passed among the congregation.

The interior of the Liberty Street Church consisted of one large room with wooden pews and light bulbs mounted on fixtures hanging from the ceiling. On Sunday morning, the congregation met together before dividing into classes, and each class had a designated corner for Sunday school. After Sunday school, everyone came back together for a church service.

It is most unfortunate that the church records before 1911 are missing. It is possible that they were lost in the move from Liberty Street or were in the possession of one of the early members who has since died. Another possibility is that some overly ambitious person thought the papers were junk and just tossed them. One saving grace that helped identify some of the early members is a Sunday-school record book I acquired some years ago. This book contains the records of attendance, money received and money expended from January 5, 1896, through December 25, 1898. There are 158 names listed in the book. The records show that on at least one occasion, the Sunday school borrowed money from Dr. George N. Halstead to cover expenses for the Christmas celebration. The classes were not given names but were numbered instead. There were thirteen classes.

Four quarterly conferences were held each church year. They were usually conducted at the church or parsonage. The first quarterly conference for the year 1910–1911 was held at the Liberty Street Church on January 25, 1911. At that time, the value of the house of worship was $5,000 and that of the parsonage was $4,500. The indebtedness on the parsonage was $1,600. The amount allocated for the preacher in charge was $1,000. The Liberty Street Church was in the Portsmouth District. The members present at the conference were the Reverend Richard B. Scott, John W. Jones, C.C. Sykes, W.J. Miller, J.E. Grimes, C.H. Lambeth, O.L. Hanbury, M.B. Upton, W.C. Lindsey and Dr. Nicholas G. Wilson.

An adult Wesley Bible class was established before the September 11, 1912 conference. The Reverend Scott reported that the general state of the church was fairly good and that the Rose Bud Society (the youth of the church) was doing well. He also commented about winning the heathens for Christ. A social was held on Tuesday night, January 14, 1913, to welcome the new pastor, the Reverend Cameron E. Pleasants.

When the first quarterly conference for the church year 1912–1913 met February 12, 1913, there was a church membership of 372 and a shortage of Sunday school space was reported. The church leader (now referred to as lay leader) was Dr. N.G. Wilson.

The second quarterly conference met May 14, 1913; it was reported that the debt of $1,448.09 on the parsonage had been paid off. John Jones, C.C. Sykes and Jerry G. Bray Sr. were elected delegates to the district conference. A cradle roll department had been organized with Beulah Wilson serving as teacher of the twenty-three members.

On August 18, 1913, John W. Jones, C.E. Pleasants and N.G. Wilson were appointed to inquire into the advisability of beginning a mission Sunday school at Campostella Heights and one at Rosemont.

The first quarterly conference for 1913–1914 was held at the parsonage on April 20, 1914. The Reverend George William Martin Taylor had been assigned as preacher in charge. The Liberty Street membership had grown to the point that it was too large for the existing church building. A committee was elected to recommend a building site. The property at the southwest corner of Ohio and Jackson Streets was available for $1,250 and the committee recommended purchasing it. A called meeting of the conference was held at the parsonage on July 14, 1914 with the Reverend Taylor presiding. Church members moved and seconded that John Jones try to purchase the property for $1,200. The church acquired the property, but the records do not indicate how much was paid for it.

The next preacher at the Liberty Street Church was the Reverend Robert N. Hartness. When he met with the other members at the first quarterly conference of 1914–1915 on February 2, 1915, plans were made to erect the Sunday school on the property acquired at the corner of Ohio and Jackson Streets. The Reverend Hartness must have been an old-fashioned fire and brimstone preacher. According to him, everything about the church and the community was wrong. He commented that "there is no Sunday school plant and an influence is making itself felt in the community for the pulling down of the school." According to him, the Sunday school material was inadequate. He continued, "In order for

Liberty Street Church to do the work needed, she must provide adequate facilities for taking care of the Sunday school in an up-to-date plant."

The fourth quarterly conference met on October 5, 1915. When the meeting adjourned and the business had not been completed, they agreed to meet in November at the home of Edward M. Tilley. At that time, it was reported that the value of the church and parsonage was $8,500 and the lots at the corner of Jackson and Ohio Streets were valued at $1,500.

Because of a lack of funds, construction of a new building was not begun. During this time, however, the congregation was instrumental in organizing and building a new Campostella Heights church, which was completed in 1916. That church is now Saint Paul United Methodist Church and is located on Providence Road.

The Reverend Thomas James Chandler (T.J.C.) Heath came to Liberty Street Church late in 1916. The church was in need of funds to build a new building and the members were constantly seeking ways to alleviate financial problems. Mrs. Winnie Heath, the pastor's wife, suggested a lilliputian wedding as a means of raising funds. The mock wedding, which consisted of some seventy children, was held on the front lawn of the Forehand house at the corner of Chesapeake Avenue and Ohio Street. Mildred Simpkin (later to become the wife of Francis Gay) was the bride, and Melvin Young was the groom. This became a popular form of entertainment in the community. (The Winnie Heath Circle was formed during the ministry of the Reverend Heath and still meets the third Thursday of each month at the Chesapeake Avenue United Methodist Church.)

The first quarterly conference for the church year 1917–1918 was held January 22, 1918. At that time, the Reverend James C. Babock was the pastor. His salary for the year was set at $1,100 and use of the parsonage. It was reported that E.M. Tilley had died December 21, 1917. The minutes read, "Bro. E.M. Tilley after a long and useful life has fallen asleep."

Babcock was very pessimistic. On one hand, he complained of the lack of attendance; on the other hand, he stated that the church in all of its various departments was greatly hindered by the lack of a new building. A committee of three was appointed to consider and recommend ways to raise funds for a new building. The trustees were also authorized and requested to sell the existing church sanctuary at a suitable price.

When the second quarterly conference was held at the Liberty Street Church on April 9, 1918, it was learned that E.M. Tilley had left $5,000 to be used toward the construction of a new building. The condition being that the church must raise an equal amount in order to receive the money. The ways and means committee had received a bid of $2,750 from the Knights of Pythias to buy the church property. The church and its land were valued at approximately $5,000. Because of the unsettled times—World War I would not end until November 11, 1918—the committee felt it could not make a decision regarding the knights' bid and recommended a full vote of the conference. On motion, the committee was asked to continue with its investigation and give a more definite report at the next meeting.

The third quarterly conference was held at the church June 24, 1918. At that meeting, the ways and means committee reported that the offer made by the Knights of Pythias Berkley Company Number Six, Uniform Rank, had been adopted by the conference. On motion, presiding elder J.O. Babcock, O.L. Hanbury, R.M. Rich and C.H. Lambeth were authorized to enter into a legal contract with the Knights of Pythias Berkley Company. In hindsight this was a bad decision for, during time of war, prices were up and then following World War I, the entire country experienced a time of prosperity.

Selling of the property posed another problem. Where would the congregation meet while a new building was under construction? A letter was written to the Knights of Pythias, asking if they purchased the property would they agree to rent the property to the church until the congregation could move into a new home? A response was received from George E. Vogler of the Knights of Pythias agreeing to rent the property for $15 per month, beginning six months from the date of acceptance of their original offer. This meant church members did not have a place to meet for at least six months. Information in the church records does not state that the church ever rented from the Knights of Pythias; however, it is known that the congregation met at the Odd Fellows Hall on Poindexter Street while the new building was under construction on Chesapeake Avenue.

In preparation for a service of dedication in 1978, a history of the church was written. At that time, a few of the older members stated that the church property on Liberty Street was not sold to the Knights of Pythias but to another congregation that had the building moved to Atlantic Avenue in South Norfolk.

However, that version was not supported by my research, as evidenced in the following information from the Chancery Order book 13, page 389.

> *January 22, 1919:*
>
> *In the matter of the petition of the trustees of Liberty Street M.E. Church, South, to sell church property.*
>
> *This day came W.C. Lindsey, F.L. Rowland, A. Guy Hall, V.L. Sykes, O.L. Hanbury, C.H. Lambeth, and C.C. Sykes, trustees of Liberty Street Methodist Episcopal Church, South of South Norfolk, Norfolk County, Virginia, and presented their petition in writing asking permission to sell to Berkley Company No. 6 United Rank of Knights of Pythias, for the sum of twenty seven hundred and fifty dollars, the following property, which they hold in trust for said church, to-wit:*
>
> *All those two certain lots, pieces or parcels of land with the buildings and improvements thereon, fronting thirty feet each on Liberty Street, and having a depth of one hundred feet, situated, lying and being in South Norfolk, in the county of Norfolk, in the state of Virginia, and being lots numbered 15 and 16, in square Q according to the plan of Elmsley, which plan is recorded in the Clerk's Office of the Circuit Court of Norfolk County, Virginia and the same property conveyed to the trustees of the Methodist Episcopal Church, South, now Liberty Street Methodist Episcopal Church, South, by Alva H. Martin and his wife by deed dated the 13th day of October, 1890, and duly recorded.*
>
> *On consideration whereof, it appearing to the court from the evidence produced that it is the wish of the said church to sell the said property above described, for the sum of twenty seven hundred and fifty dollars to Berkley Company Number 6 United Rank of Knights of Pythias, the court doth hereby authorize the said trustees to make a deed conveying the property to the said Berkley Company No. 6 United Rank of Knights of Pythias, upon the payment to them of the sum of twenty seven hundred and fifty dollars,*

which amount is to be used by said trustees to build another church building on other property of said church.

Ordered that court be adjourned until tomorrow morning at ten o'clock.

C. W. Coleman

The above was required in order for the trustee to sell the church property. A deed was made January 24, 1919, (deed book 458, page 270) between the trustees of the church and the trustees of Berkley Company Number Six, Uniform Rank, Knights of Pythias. F. L. Portlock was the notary public, and the deed was admitted to record in the clerk's office of the Circuit Court of Norfolk County on February 7, 1919. G. Tayloe Gwathmey was the clerk.

It is possible that the Knights of Pythias in later years sold the property to the other congregation, who then moved the building to Atlantic Avenue.

Not long after the Liberty Street property was sold, the large three-story home at the corner of Chesapeake Avenue and Ohio Street was offered to the church. As this property was larger than what the church owned on Jackson Street, the members felt it would be beneficial to sell that property and build the new church on Chesapeake Avenue. Owned by Foster Black and considered one of the finest in South Norfolk, the home was set back from the road in the middle of a well-kept lawn and was accessible by a heart-shaped driveway.

It was reported in the *Norfolk Ledger-Dispatch* on August 9, 1919, that a contract had been let for $50,000 to construct a new church in the English-parish style at the corner of Chesapeake Avenue and Ohio Street in South Norfolk. John W. Jones was the general contractor, and A. J. Makinson was the brick and stone contractor. The year 1919 is inscribed on the cornerstone, but it was not laid until January 31, 1920. Throughout the years, it has been said that the ceremony was carried out during a snowstorm. This has not been verified, but it would certainly have added excitement to the occasion.

The regular meeting of the board of stewards met at the home of D. T. Allen on January 6, 1920, and the Reverend Wallace R. Evans, pastor was asked to secure a speaker for the laying of the cornerstone. When the board met again on January 20, 1920, Evans announced that Dr. Booker and Dr. Simpson (not the physician) would be able to come on January 31, 1920. Brother Parker was asked by the Reverend Evans to arrange with the Masons for laying of the cornerstone. At the January 20 meeting, Parker reported having received a letter from a Mr. Old, attorney for the Tilley estate. Old advised that he expected to soon be in a position to pay the $5,000 willed to the church. This was more than two years after Tilley's death. Church records indicate that the church did receive part of the estate money, but it is not certain if it ever received the entire amount.

The cornerstone of the Chesapeake Avenue Methodist Church was laid January 31, 1920, by Berkley Lodge Number 167, A.F. & A.M., and Doric Lodge Number 44, A.F. & A.M. Right worshipful Ivor A. Page Sr., D.D.G.M., presided. According to records, a box containing certain period mementos was placed in the cavity within the foundation stone. This box should have been recovered when the building was torn down in 1970; however, no one seems to know if there was a box and, if so, what became of it. Most likely it is in possession of a church member and may be lost when that person dies. One of the original programs from that day is in possession of the church.

After laying the cornerstone, the building committee undertook the task of raising money to complete construction of the church. Attempts were made to acquire loans and donations. William Sloane, owner of the local knitting mills, sent a check for $500. Hugh Rountrey was asked to contact Captain Frederick Matt Halstead and ask if he would lend the church some money. D.W. Lindsay approached John Cuthrell for a loan from the Merchants and Planters Bank. Lindsay was able to get a loan of $5,000. L.D. Rawls had plans for soliciting funds to buy an organ. The firm of George Hardy Payne made the church's leaded, stained-glass windows. The cost was $1,770, and the windows were donated by individuals as memorials. The church extension board donated $1,000 toward construction of the building. In order to save a few dollars, members of the board accomplished most of the cleanup.

After many hardships, it appears the congregation moved into the new building in January 1921. The Reverend Evans was still pastor of the church and would remain so until the end of the year. The summers were hot, and there wasn't any air conditioning (anywhere). The Merchant and Planters Bank; White and Deshields, a coal and wood dealer in Berkley; Tabbs Department Store; S.W. Wilson's Market; and local funeral homes donated hand fans.

The cornerstone of the church shown here was laid on Saturday January 31, 1920. After completion, the name was changed to the Chesapeake Avenue Methodist Episcopal Church, South.

Financial problems continued. Various members of the board were appointed to contact local businessmen to ask for contributions. The ladies of the church worked diligently to help raise funds. They made and sold soup, held oyster suppers and gave lawn parties with homemade ice cream. The stewards performed tasks such as repairing broken chairs, wrapping steam pipes in the Sunday school rooms, landscaping and preparing the lawn, laying cement sidewalks around the church, wallpapering the parsonage and any other job that they could possibly do themselves to save money.

In 1923, the church and parsonage roofs began to leak, and the church gutters and downspouts were in urgent need of repair. Rainwater was standing on the church grounds and a committee was appointed to determine the best way to drain the water away from the building. For a structure that was about two years old, a lot of problems were showing up. When the building was demolished in 1970, it was confirmed that many shortcuts had been taken in its construction.

The Reverend Charles E. Green, who became minister of the church in 1921, reported that the church extension board would grant Chesapeake Avenue Church a loan of $15,000. A wire was sent to the extension board requesting that the necessary application papers be forwarded as soon as possible. The records do not state whether the church received the loan or not. We can only assume that they did.

Although the Chesapeake Avenue Church continued to have financial problems, on July 7, 1924, a $1,000 donation from the church poor fund was donated to the Reverend Wallace of the Campostella charge.

Fund-raising efforts continued, and in February 1925, it became obvious that the parsonage porch was in need of a new slate roof. A committee was appointed to sell brooms. It was decided to hold a revival, beginning the last Sunday in March and continuing through April 12, 1925. Usually large sums of money were collected during a revival that lasted for a period of two weeks. On October 5, 1925, the Williamsburg Methodist Church donated $50 toward the building fund. Other donations received from the church organizations included the Men's Bible Class, $25; Young People's Class, $18.50; and the board of stewards, $6.50. The total internal contributions amounted to $50. The church ended the year with a deficit of $40.50.

The year 1926 brought more problems. Plumbing was swapped around to fix leaks, as there wasn't enough money for repairs. A motion was approved to turn over to the general fund $4,000, which had been raised by the music committee for a motorized organ. Additional chicken and oyster dinners were held, each added about $100 to the church fund. The ladies held an ice cream supper and used the profits to paint the parsonage. As one of the many efforts to save money, it was agreed to turn off the water in the church during the week.

The general report from the third quarterly conference of 1926 made reference to holding revivals at Mount Pleasant Church during the first part of August and at Chesapeake Avenue Church the first Sunday in September. The report further stated that the Reverend Annie Agnes Smith would assist in the meetings.

By March 16, 1927, $1,140 had been raised toward the church debt. Another revival was planned to begin the first Sunday in May. It was reported on June 18, 1927, that

H.E. Hodgson & Sons had completed building the new pipe organ and installing it in the Chesapeake Avenue Church. The Reverend Linton D. Stables reported that the church had raised about $2,000 since the last conference, to be used toward the debt and organ. Stables had replaced the Reverend Green and would serve the church for a period of five years.

There are several entries in the records, which refer to activities involving the Mount Pleasant Church. At this point it is not known if it is the same church that exists today. The history of Mount Pleasant Church as printed in the *United Methodist Church History, Norfolk District, 1984* indicates that the church was one of nineteen on the Princess Anne Circuit in 1846. Is it possible that the original church became inactive and in 1926 became a mission of Chesapeake Avenue Church? On March 10, 1926, Mount Pleasant had a Sunday school but no other organizations. When new members were received at Mount Pleasant, their names were recorded in the records of Chesapeake Avenue Church.

At the regular meeting of the fourth quarterly conference on October 21, 1927, the following resolution was adopted:

> *Where as the parsonage property of the Mount Vernon Circuit has ceased to be used for a parsonage and the same has been directed to be sold and some question has arisen as to who are the proper trustees of said parsonage property, as the records in the clerk's office of the circuit court of Princess Anne County, Va. do not show that George S. Fentress, T.C. Munden, D.S. White, and C.M. Williamson have been removed as said trustees, yet the minutes of the quarterly conference shows that these parties have been removed.*
>
> *Therefore be it resolved that it is the wish of the quarterly conference that the said George S. Fentress, T.C. Munden, D.S. White, and C.M. Williamson be removed as trustees of the parsonage property of the Mount Vernon Circuit and that the said L.F. Cason, Y.B. Miller, and John Wesley Hackworth be and are to remain trustees of the said parsonage property for the purpose of holding legal title to the same.*
>
> *A. Guy Hall, Sec. Geo. W. Jones, P.E.*

A called quarterly conference of the Chesapeake Avenue charge was held at Mount Pleasant Church on May 1, 1928, at 3:00 p.m. Y.B. Miller Sr. reported that the parsonage and furniture of the Mount Vernon Circuit had been sold. The parsonage was sold for $2,120 and the sale of the furniture brought $120.35. The expenses recorded against the property were deed release, $2; insurance, $7.25; notary fee, $6; auctioneer, etc., $100; and church extension, $200. Total expenses were $315.25. The amount realized after expenses was $1,925.10.

It was ordered that a committee of three be appointed to serve as trustees of this fund and invest it in a safe and secure manner. The interest acquired was to be apportioned in such a way that two-thirds would go to the support of the ministry of Mount Pleasant Church and one-third for the support of Cana Church on the South Norfolk Circuit. The presiding elder of the conference appointed F.E. Kellam of Princess Anne County and Y.B. Miller Sr. and V.L. Sykes of South Norfolk as trustees of the fund.

The second quarterly conference of 1928–1929 was held at the church April 12, 1929. The Reverend Stables wrote, "[W]e are planning an evangelistic campaign beginning next

Sunday; Walter C. Gum of South Boston will do the preaching and L.E. Vining of Berkley will lead the singing."

The annual conference began October 15, 1930, at Epworth Methodist Church. The Reverend L.D. Stables closed his ministry at Chesapeake Avenue Church on Sunday evening, October 26, 1930. The auditorium was packed to overflowing to hear his farewell address, "A Message from God to You." During his pastorate, part of the church debt had been paid off, a new organ was installed and paid for, additions to the Sunday school plant had been made and the church auditorium was redecorated at a cost of about $1,000.

The Reverend Stables was assigned to Memorial Methodist Church in Richmond and began his duties there November 2, 1930. The Reverend Lee G. Crutchfield, former pastor of Fairmount Avenue Methodist Church in Richmond, preached his first sermon at Chesapeake Avenue Church on Sunday, November 2, 1930.

A called session of the South Norfolk Circuit was held at Hickory Methodist Church on December 18, 1930. Representatives from all five churches, South Norfolk, Cana, Hickory, Oak Grove and Good Hope were present. The Reverend Dr. R.H. Potts, presiding elder, was in the chair. The trustees of the special fund from the sale of the parsonage and furniture of the Mount Vernon Circuit were ordered to pay to its parsonage trustees one-third of the sum invested and that it be used for the improvement of the South Norfolk Circuit parsonage. This special committee—consisting of F.E. Kellam, Y.B. Miller Sr. and V.L. Sykes—was asked to make certain that the interest from the remaining two-thirds be used to supplement the salary of the preacher serving Mount Pleasant Church.

A called meeting of the quarterly conference of the Chesapeake Avenue charge was convened at the church on December 23, 1930. At that time, the trustees of the special fund were commended for their faithful discharge of the trust. The committee was then instructed to turn over to C.M. Williamson, E.H. West and W.W. Sawyer, trustees of the South Norfolk Circuit parsonage, one-third of the $1,925.10 or $ 641.70, as had been ordered at the meeting on December 18, 1930.

In 1930, our nation was experiencing the beginning of the Great Depression and the clutches of poverty grasped a large part of the country. Many people in desperation would hide in railroad cars and jump off when they reached cities where they might find work. Seaboard and Chesapeake Avenues, being near the Norfolk & Western line, received quite a few of these people who were cold, hungry and out of work. It was not unusual to hear a knock on the door, open it and find a person in need of food and other necessities. During one severe cold spell, a man arrived at the door of the parsonage asking for a cup of coffee. Pastor Crutchfield invited him in to join his family at the dinner table. This man was clothed in a shirt and sweater, which were not enough to protect him from the elements. Pastor Crutchfield had recently bought a new topcoat and still had his old one. The good pastor, seeing this man in need, went upstairs, returned with the newer coat and gave it to him.

Although the Reverend Crutchfield left Chesapeake Avenue Church in 1932, a part of him remained for years to come. His daughter Ruth became the wife of Jerry Bray Jr. Ruth, Jerry and their children served the church in a variety of ways. Their son Steve became a minister in the Methodist church and served as a district superintendent in northern

Virginia. At the annual conference in October 1932, the Reverend Leonard R. Black was assigned to the Chesapeake Avenue Methodist Episcopal Church.

When the quarterly conference was held on September 21, 1933, it was announced that the men's classroom, which had been built that year and was valued at $800 had been paid for and would be dedicated the following Sunday. This was probably the small building that housed the Beacon Bible Class. R.H. Pride, chairman of the church board of trustees, reported that the two churches (Chesapeake Avenue and Mount Pleasant) were valued at $60,000 and the parsonage behind the Chesapeake Avenue Church was valued at $8,000.

Pastor Black asked that a bulletin board be placed in front of the church. Mr. R.M. Rich agreed to build the frame; Mr. Miller contacted the local Board of Christian Education and asked if it would buy the inside parts and sign letters. The board of stewards voted to purchase the glass and necessary lumber.

On January 9, 1934, Pride, who also served as chairman of the music committee, recommended that A. Guy Hall Sr. serve as director of the choir, A. Guy Hall Jr. serve as organist and Willie Edwards serve as assistant organist. The members of the choir asked that a light be installed over the back steps leading to the choir door. A. Guy Hall Sr. agreed to give the matter his attention.

On Tuesday March 27, 1934, when the board of stewards met, Brother Sykes reported that R.C. Gilliam, owner of the pharmacy across the street, had sent a notice to the newspaper stating his intention to apply for a license to sell beer and light wines (Prohibition had been repealed in 1933). The board voted to have the secretary write a letter to Gilliam informing him that the board had gone on record to oppose his application and asking him to withdraw it. Gilliam requested that the board meet with him on April 1, 1934, and graciously and kindly agreed to withdraw his application. Pride moved that the board give Gilliam a vote of thanks and promise its cooperation toward his business undertaking.

The parsonage and church were in constant need of repairs. After inspecting the parsonage in May 1934, the board voted to tear away the front porch to the corner of the house and build a small front entrance. Mitchell, the architect, commented that the change proposed to the front of the parsonage was very appropriate.

Among the topics discussed at the November 13, 1934 board meeting was the accumulation of old church records. J.C.Green felt that they were of no further use and in his opinion should be destroyed. The board left the matter in his hands. Those records could very well have been the ones missing from 1892 to 1911. People without a strong interest in history may consider past records to be junk and tend to toss them. Recently, I was able to publish a pictorial using old photographs that had been thrown in a Dumpster.

It is ironic that at a meeting of the board on March 26, 1935, Brother Ansell made a motion that a church history be written and recorded by Pastor Black. It was decided to appoint a committee at a later date. When the board of stewards met on April 16, 1935, Chairman, Brother Nichols appointed Mrs. Dickinson, Mrs. J.G. Bray Sr., Mrs. Carrie Abbott and Mrs. Miller to compile the church history. Mrs. Dickinson was appointed chairwoman. On May 28, she reported that her plans to have a tea and invite all of the older church members to record their memories and knowledge of the early church. It is not certain if this history was ever written; no copies have yet been found.

In late summer of 1935, church school attendance decreased dramatically because of an epidemic of infantile paralysis. Without a cure, children either died or were left crippled for the rest of their lives. An iron lung was used but was not very effective.

Although the board drafted a resolution asking for the return of the Reverend Black for a fifth year, when the conference met in October 1936, the Reverend Francis B. McSparran was assigned to the Chesapeake Avenue Church. His first meeting of the new church year was held November 10, 1936.

On December 12, 1936, devoted church member O.L. Hanbury died, leaving property to the church. From his estate, the church received the dwelling at 1321 Twenty-first Street. The total value of the house and lot was $2,000. Hanbury was a maintenance man at the grammar school across the street from his home on B Street.

The Reverend Black left his mark on South Norfolk and the Chesapeake Avenue Methodist Church, for his son Billy married Eleanor Rawls. (I had the pleasure of knowing Billy Black when he, James Benton, Jim Burton, David Pierce and Mike Smith organized the first community football league in the early 1940s. Billy Black and his wife Eleanor were the parents of Cole Black.)

Unfortunately, the Reverend McSparran did not serve the church very long. He died June 29, 1937, while visiting his adopted daughter, Mrs. J.W. Greyard. McSparran had celebrated his sixty-first birthday. Dr. William Archer Wright conducted the funeral at the Chesapeake Avenue Church and burial was in Oakwood Cemetery in Richmond.

A special meeting of the board of stewards was called for July 7, 1937, at that time R.H. Pride read the resolution expressing sympathy to the family of the Reverend McSparran. Dr. William Archer Wright was petitioned to appoint the Reverend R. Alfred White (McSparran's son-in-law) to fill the vacancy, and a third resolution was read extending to Mrs. McSparran the use of the parsonage for the remainder of the church year. At the same time the pastor's salary was set at $2,100.

Another special session of the board of stewards was called August 10, 1937. It had been learned that the Reverend Louis Oakey Wilburn and not the Reverend White had been appointed as pastor of the Chesapeake Avenue Church.

J.C. Green suggested that a letter be written to the Virginia Electric and Power Company (VEPCO) in reference to the noise created by the trolley as it ran past the church during services. Eventually churches along the streetcar line posted signs out front that read, "Run Slow Do Not Ring Bell." At the August 1937 meeting, Pastor Wilburn suggested that a chain be installed to prevent the lawn from being used as a shortcut between Ohio Street and Chesapeake Avenue. Also about that time, the church had problems with pigeons on the roof, and T.E. Gregory had asked the city council for permission to kill them. Most likely Gregory was given permission. Those were wild times, and it was not against the law to fire a gun inside the city limits.

On December 13, 1938, the Reverend Wilburn announced that Christmas services would begin the following Sunday evening with the choir presenting the "Christmas Cantata," followed by the Christmas pageant on Wednesday. Wilburn would deliver a Christmas message on Christmas morning. He planned to close the day with a candlelight Christmas carol service. This was a very ambitious schedule for the Christmas season.

There was nothing definite reported in the church records, but it appears that the property on Twenty-first Street was sold sometime around May 1939. That probably accounted for the financial report presented at the quarterly conference in October.

The report given by the Reverend Wilburn at the fourth quarterly conference that met October 6, 1939, was the most optimistic in the history of the church up to that time. The church year was coming to a close, and preparations were being made to attend the annual conference. Shortly after the 1938 conference, the church acquired a mimeograph machine, which enabled church members to produce a church bulletin; the choir loft was carpeted; and 150 new hymnals were purchased and paid for. Vacation Bible School, which was held in June, had approximately 150 children registered and several of the workers assisted at the St. James Colored Church. The interior of the parsonage had been improved as a result of new wallpaper, paint, screens, floors and water heater. Finances for the year were in excellent condition; for the first time, there was not a deficit, all current bills had been paid, all assessments were met in full, the church debt was reduced by $1,110 and the parsonage debt had been removed.

When the annual conference met, the Reverend George T. Forrester was assigned as pastor of the Chesapeake Avenue Church. He would serve from 1939 to 1944. One of the highlights of his ministry was the dedicatory service, which took place June 20, 1943. The membership at that time was 735 and the Sunday school enrollment was 447. Bishop W.W. Peele; Dr. Walter Gum, district superintendent; and the Reverend Forrester led the morning service. The board of trustees comprised C.H. Lambeth, chairman; A. Guy Hall Sr.; T.E. Gregory; A.M. Nichols; F.L. Rowland; J. Paul Smith; and V.L. Sykes.

The dedication service took place at 11:00 a.m. and burning of the note was carried out at the evening service. To quote Flora Bray Howell:

> *I remember the dedication and hard work of those folks involved with the financial campaign to pay off the debt of the original church (Chesapeake Avenue Church) which stood on this corner. Mr. O.J. Parker and my father, Jerry G. Bray, Sr. and others served on the committee. My mother, Mamie Shaw Pegram Bray, kept the books for the campaign and the ladies of the church worked diligently in their own areas of expertise to raise funds. Mr. Robert Rowland contributed $5,000 to complete the payment of the note as the end appeared in sight. On the appointed day, Mr. Rowland and Mamie Bray were asked to come to the chancel rail and, as one held the note, the other lit the fire.*

Robert Rowland, who lived at 1049 Chesapeake Avenue, was half owner of Smith and Rowland Fertilizer Company. This later became Smith and Douglas Fertilizer Company.

At the quarterly conference, which was held September 29, 1944, the announcement was made that the Reverend Forrester had decided not only to conclude his pastorate of Chesapeake Avenue Church but also retire from the active ministry.

When the appointments were made at the annual conference, the Reverend Clay Williams Hillman was assigned to serve Chesapeake Avenue Methodist Church. His first Sunday was October 29, 1944. In a letter to the district superintendent and members of the church, he expressed his feeling that the church was well organized and thanked the ladies for the delicious supper that was waiting for his family upon their arrival.

In 1945, the financial condition of the church continued to be excellent. All bills were paid and on time. By February, the church had received fifteen new members by certificate or transfer. The members had supported the Crusade for Christ program and raised $8,000. To quote the Reverend Hillman, "The only debt we owe is our debt to the world in this time of chaos and we are ready to begin payment of that debt. The Consecration Service this morning testified to that fact. We are looking forward to a great year."

By April 15, 1947, the church building fund had almost reached the $5,000 mark and a new piano had been purchased for the main auditorium. The final cost of the piano, after a deduction by the company, was $875.

The pastor's report on March 8, 1948, announced that the adjoining lot to the church had been purchased, giving plenty of room for future expansion. Hillman also reported that a young people's choir had been organized and, thanks to S.W. Wilson and W.H. Darden, the members were properly robed. During the quarter, C.L. Lambeth and J.H. Tatem, both longtime workers in the church, died.

The Reverend Hillman had served the church well, and when the annual conference met in October the Reverend Millard Fillmore Draper replaced him. In the pastor's report to the quarterly conference on January 26, 1949, the Reverend Draper said he and Mrs. Draper had been graciously received by the good people of the Chesapeake Avenue Church and that, shortly after their arrival, they were the recipients of a splendid reception given at the parsonage. The treasurer's report at this conference showed disbursements from October 1, 1948 to January 26, 1949 amounting to $4,473.74, of which $1,855 had been spent for a new furnace. The balance on hand was $223.50.

On Saturday evening, May 28, 1949, the marriage of Raymond Lee Harper to Emma Lee Rock took place in front of the fireplace in the parsonage. It was cold outside, and the good pastor had a roaring fire in the fireplace. About halfway through the service, all hands had to move away from the fire as they were well done on the backside.

On September 18, 1950, the pastor reported that the Reverend George W. Potts Sr. had held two weeks of evangelistic services. Vacation Bible School, which had been held in June, had an enrollment of 126 and 23 workers. The pipe organ had been rebuilt, and extensive work had been done to the church, including a new roof, copper guttering and downspouts, as well as the replacement of bad timbers and painting. The parsonage had two coats of paint as well as roof and gutter repairs.

By early 1951, the members began working toward some badly needed building projects. The nominating committee met April 17, 1951, at the parsonage to nominate a committee to build a parsonage and then an educational building. In the pastor's report to the quarterly conference on September 7, 1951, Pastor Draper announced that the congregation would vote on the building project September 23, 1951. A special church conference was held that morning with the Reverend Draper being assisted by district superintendent, the Reverend Edgar A. Potts. Church members moved to proceed on a building program of two units. The first project was to either build or buy a parsonage and use the existing parsonage as temporary quarters for the Sunday school. Web Townsend felt that the educational building should be started as soon as the church had $50,000 in the building fund. The building program was put to a vote, seventy members voted in favor of and six voted in opposition, with some members not voting. It seems that there was considerable discussion among several members. This was finally settled by adjourning the meeting.

When the annual conference met in 1952, the Reverend Dewey B. Mullins was assigned to the Chesapeake Avenue Methodist Church. Pastor and Mrs. Mullins were especially interested in youth work; Mrs. Mullins became superintendent of the youth department. Arthur Ostrander was lay leader in 1952 and Mrs. L.W. (Maisie) Mann was chairwoman of the commission on education.

The Reverend Mullins didn't stay but two years, and the Reverend Paul R. Best assumed pastorate of the church in 1954. Best had just completed a two-year ministry at Hickory Methodist Church and previously served six years at LaCrosse in Mecklenburg County.

A settlement sheet dated July 9, 1954 listed the sellers of the property at 1209 Chesapeake Avenue, South Norfolk, as E.F. Reass Jr. and Elizabeth M. Reass, and Bettie J. Reass Hamilton and Albert M. Hamilton. The buyer was Jerry G. Bray Jr. The purchase price of $8,500 was paid by a certified check. Bray took title to the property in order to hold it until the church could decide whether to buy the property for use as a parsonage.

A special meeting of the quarterly conference was held July 21, 1954, to discuss the purchase of the house at 1209 Chesapeake Avenue for use as the church parsonage. A motion was made by William Nicholas that the property be purchased for $8,500; George Banks seconded the motion. Another motion was made by Nicholas authorizing the trustees to borrow $6,000 from the Merchants and Planters Bank or some other lending institution to be used with $2,500 from the building fund to purchase the property at 1209 Chesapeake Avenue. Banks again seconded the motion. The motions passed.

The Chesapeake Avenue Methodist Church congregation met at the South Norfolk church on August 4, 1954. Dr. Kenneth Haddock, superintendent of the Norfolk district, chaired the meeting and opened the proceedings with prayer. J.C. Green was elected recording secretary for the meeting. Haddock announced that the meeting was called to act upon recommendations of the quarterly conference. Arthur Ostrander spoke about the need for expansion of the educational facilities. Jerry G. Bray Jr. then outlined an expansion program, which included purchase of the property at 1209 Chesapeake Avenue for use as a parsonage and using the existing parsonage at 1206 Chesapeake Avenue as a temporary educational annex. C.A. Harrell, Sunday school superintendent, then moved that the property at 1209 Chesapeake Avenue be purchased for $8,500. Hubert H. Rountrey Jr. seconded the motion. Rountrey, N. Duval Flora, Harrell, George Banks and Mrs. J.C. Etheridge each spoke in favor of the motion. T.E. Gregory and W.M. Townsend spoke against it. A motion was then made by Gregory and seconded by Townsend to vote on the issue by a secret ballot. This motion did not pass. The question regarding the purchase of 1209 Chesapeake Avenue was put to a vote, and the motion passed by a vote of 69–4.

Apparently Haddock wrote the letter of approval that same night, for it was dated August 4, 1954. It stated in part that the Norfolk District Board of Church Location and Building had visited the Chesapeake Avenue Church and reviewed the plans for purchasing the property at 1209 Chesapeake Avenue at a cost of $8,500. It was further understood that the minister and his family would move into the house at 1209 Chesapeake Avenue and that the existing parsonage at 1206 Chesapeake Avenue would be used for church school classes.

On October 8, 1954, E.H. (Mike) Smith, treasurer of the building fund, received a letter from Bray, listing the expenses incurred in purchasing the property at 1209 Chesapeake Avenue. The total—which included the purchase price, recording the deed (Reass to Bray), third-quarter taxes, insurance, repairs to the chimney, new roof and exterior repairs (paid to Caleb Briggs)—came to $9,217.80. Bray executed a deed conveying the property to the trustees of the church. In connection with recording this deed, the following expenses were incurred: documentary stamps, $9.35, and recording the deed (Bray to trustees), $15.75.

Dr. Harry W. Backhus, district superintendent, presided over the quarterly conference that met January 20, 1956. The purpose of the meeting was to discuss building the first unit of the educational building. The first motion was made by B.W. Lockhart and seconded by Hubert Rountrey. The motion was "that this quarterly conference authorize the construction of the first unit of an educational building on the property adjacent to the present sanctuary and that it request the proper officers of the church to call a meeting of the members to pass upon the project."

The second motion was made by W.J. Breedlove and seconded by L.W. Mann. Additionally, it was decided that "the Commission on Education consisting of C.S. Mizzel, G.W. Pegram, Jr., Mrs. Lillie M. Holloman, Berle Jolliffe, C.C. Jacocks, Mrs. Marie Etheridge, Mrs. Malrie Lane, Miss Evelyn Walke, Mrs. Virginia Cahoon, Jim Burton, Duval Flora, Jerry G. Bray, Jr., and C.A. Harrell be appointed as a committee to estimate the cost of constructing the first unit of an educational building." Also, in case the members of the church approved the project, the committee should cause the necessary plans and specifications to be prepared and submitted to the official board for the letting of the contract. Both of the motions were unanimously carried. The district superintendent adjourned the meeting with prayer.

A congregational meeting was held February 8, 1956. The purpose of the meeting was to get permission from the congregation to build the first unit of a new educational building. Claude Mizzel and Duval Flora presented plans for construction of the building to the members. A motion was made by George W. Pegram Sr. and seconded by Authur F. Ostrander to approve the project as presented for construction of the first unit of the new educational building. The motion passed. Ostrander stated that a September 23, 1951, motion required there to be at least $50,000 in the building fund before construction of a new educational building was begun. Ostrander then moved to rescind the September 1951 motion. His motion was seconded by Joe Miles and passed unanimously.

The estimated cost of this unit was $65,000. E.H. Smith, treasurer of the building fund, reported having approximately $27,000 on hand. There were sixty-five members present at that meeting. Ostrander issued the dismissal.

Excerpts from the pastor's report at the quarterly conference held on May 17, 1956, stated that 165 new Methodist hymnals had been purchased and that there was approximately $50,000 in the building fund. He also reported that plans were almost complete for the new educational building, that trees had been removed and that the Beacon Bible Class building had been moved to clear the site for the new building. The building that was used by the

Beacon Bible Class was moved to Hawthorne Avenue across from Cascade Park and was converted into a residence.

A church congregational meeting was held on November 4, 1956, to gain approval to enter into a contract with L.J. Hoy to construct the first unit of the educational building at a cost of $71,845. A second motion was made and seconded that the existing properties serve as collateral for a loan of $40,000 from the Merchants and Planters Bank. The congregation approved both motions. The first unit was completed and occupied in 1957.

Pastor Best completed four years at Chesapeake Avenue Church in 1958, and when the annual conference met in June, the Reverend Edward A. Plunkett was assigned to serve as pastor .

Dedication of the first unit of the new educational building took place November 23, 1958. Special guests that Sunday were Bishop Paul Garber, Dr. Harry W. Backhus III, the Reverend Paul Best and the Reverend Dewey B. Mullins.

The pastor's quarterly conference report on March 27, 1960, stated that the next major church project would be to complete planning for a subsequent unit of the educational building. The next unit was to be an extension of the existing educational building. Pastor Plunkett also addressed an evangelistic survey made of the two newly developing sections of South Norfolk: Catalina Heights and Ardmore. He further commented that "we have been pleased this year with the great improvement of our choirs under our new choir director, Mrs. Elizabeth Lindsey."

A church conference was held on May 29, 1960, after the Sunday morning worship service. At that time, the preliminary plans for the next unit of the education building were presented to the congregation. The plans, dated April 27, 1960, were drawn by A. Ray Pentecost and put the estimated cost of the construction at $90,000. The commission on education recommended approval of the preliminary plans, as did the approximately 75 congregation members at the May 29 meeting.

A special quarterly conference met November 30, 1960, to authorize the church to enter into a contract for the construction of an addition to the educational building and to obtain a loan of $50,000 from the National Bank of Commerce. It was moved by J.C. Green and seconded by L.B. Rogers that officers of the church be authorized to enter into a contract with L.J. Hoy in the amount of $78,682 for construction of the addition. The motion was carried unanimously.

A church conference was called December 6, 1960, after the morning worship to approve the above resolutions. Both were approved by a unanimous vote of the congregation. A letter of approval dated December 12, 1960, was received from Joseph S. Johnson, district superintendent.

The new children's wing of the educational building was formally opened in a special service held October 1, 1961. It was reported October 5, 1961, that work was well under way on the renovation of the educational portion of the sanctuary building. It was further reported that emergency repairs had been made to the parsonage and that a decision should be made either to undertake extensive repairs or purchase a new home.

In a report to the fourth quarterly conference April 5, 1962, it was stated that renovation to the educational wing of the sanctuary building had been completed. This renovation provided offices for the pastor and secretary, robing and rehearsal rooms for the choirs, a library and committee room as well as additional adult classrooms.

The Women's Society of Christian Service report of June 1, 1962, through September 30, 1962, stated that a reception was given to welcome the new minister and his wife, Pastor and Mrs. Lyle H. Youell.

At the first quarterly conference on September 10, 1963, it was reported that beginning in June 1963 and continuing through the first Sunday in September, two identical services were held each Sunday. One was conducted at 8:30 a.m., and the other at 11:00 a.m.

Pastor Youell's report to the fourth quarterly conference on April 8, 1965, praised the counseling of young adult couples by Mr. and Mrs. Max Jennell as well as the work accomplished by Mr. and Mrs. Gerald Wood in working with the Junior High Methodist Youth Fellowship (MYF). Pastor Youell also said, "[W]e consider our ministry of music, directed by Mrs. Elizabeth Lindsey to be the finest in the area." His report included the expectation of retirement of the existing debt by midsummer and the engagement of the services of a structural engineer as the initial step in the renovation of the sanctuary.

In July 1967, the parsonage at 1201 Orville Avenue was purchased from Alton Overton. In June 1968, the Methodist Church joined with the Evangelical United Brethren and Chesapeake Avenue Methodist Church became the Chesapeake Avenue United Methodist Church

During the 1968–1972 ministry of the Reverend Robert H. Eason, inspection of the sanctuary revealed termites had done irreparable damage and the building would have to come down. The congregation voted to demolish the sanctuary and build another on the same land. Worship services would be held in the fellowship hall during the demolition and construction period. After the vote, Dr. J.W. Creef stood to remind the congregation that they had just voted to put themselves in debt for approximately $250,000 and that it was possible they would not be able to raise that much money. Where there is a will, there is a way, especially if it is the will of God. The complete church debt—which included the sanctuary, education building and parsonage on Orville Avenue—was satisfied in only eight years.

The congregation held a special service in the fellowship hall on May 10, 1970, at 3:00 p.m. for the ground breaking of the new building at the corner of Chesapeake Avenue and Ohio Street. This was the same site on which the previous church had stood. Dr. Carl J. Sanders, Norfolk District superintendent, threw the first shovel of dirt. The Reverend Robert H. Eason led the service. The architectural firm of Pentecost, Wade and McLellan designed the new sanctuary. H.L. Temple was the contractor.

During construction of the new sanctuary, services were conducted in the fellowship hall. A new Moller pipe organ was installed in December 1970 and a service of consecration was held Sunday, December 20, 1970. Pastor Eason led the service with the assistance of Sanders and Bishop W.R. Cannon.

Work was far enough along that a part of the Christmas Eve service was held in the new building. The floor was covered with wood shavings, and it was a candlelight service. The parishioners were cautioned to be extra careful not to set fire to the new building. It was a lovely service that had its beginning in the fellowship hall and its ending in the new church. The congregation moved into the completed sanctuary January 24, 1971.

The fifty-year members of the Chesapeake Avenue Methodist Church gathered on January 26, 1969, to have this photograph taken. The minister at that time was the Reverend Robert Eason, who is standing behind the second row of members. It was not possible to name all the members seen here. However, in the first row from left to right are Axie Hayman, Hilda Starboard, unknown, Grace Wiggs, Flora Leggette, Eddie Grimes, Wilson Grimes, Lucille Grimes Miles, Mrs. Jerry G. Bray Sr., Flora Bray Howell and Joe Raper. The second row, from left to right, are unknown, Arthur Ostrander, Mrs. Wooten, Doris Powers, unknown, Courtney Grimes, Leona Kemp, Effie Grimes, Pearl Grimes and unknown. *Photo courtesy of Ben Leigh.*

This picture was taken at the ground breaking of the Chesapeake Avenue United Methodist Church on Sunday afternoon May 10, 1970. The two men are, from left to right, Norfolk District Superintendent Dr. Carl J. Sanders and the Reverend Robert H. Eason, pastor of the church. *Photo courtesy of Mark Mitchell.*

This is the new Chesapeake Avenue United Methodist Church that was constructed on the same site as the old English parish-style church, which had been built in 1920 and occupied in 1921. This modern sanctuary was completed without a steeple, but when funds became available, one was added.

When the annual conference met in 1972, the Reverend Eason was reassigned and James E. Powell Jr. became pastor of the Chesapeake Avenue United Methodist Church. James B. Grimmer replaced the Reverend Powell in 1976.

On Sunday, October 22, 1978, the members of the church administrative board authorized the trustees to secure the property behind the church at 1310 Ohio Street from Dr. Raymond Wallace. Wallace offered the property to the church with the stipulation that the members assume the remaining debt of approximately $18,000. This property was not acquired until about ten years later. At that time, it was purchased through a real estate firm for more than $60,000. Eventually the house and garage were removed, the pecan trees cut down and the lots were paved, providing parking for the church members.

A service of dedication was held November 19, 1978, at 11:00 a.m. The debt for the sanctuary, office complex and parsonage had been satisfied. Bishop W. Kenneth Goodson and District Superintendent Dr. F. Douglas Dillard Jr. assisted Pastor Grimmer in the service. A covered-dish dinner and homecoming followed the worship service. Needless to say, the church was filled to capacity and tables were set up in every available space in the fellowship hall and classrooms to accommodate the large crowd. Also the Norfolk District conference was held at 3:00 p.m. that day at the Ghent United Methodist Church at Stockley Gardens and Raleigh Avenue. For some members of the church, it was a very full day.

With all the problems of construction and the raising of large amounts of money out of the way, some of the future ministers were able to concentrate on other aspects of the church and the needs of the local community. The church continued to grow in its ministry and in 1979 sponsored a refugee family to enter the country. A meeting place was provided for the local chapter of Alcohol Anonymous and in January 1984, a preschool was started on the premises. The Society of Saint Stephen, which was established in 1995, collects, buys and distributes food to the needy of the South Norfolk community. Some members of the congregation participate in the Meals on Wheels program. A relatively new program in the church is that of Hagar Sisters. The United Methodist Men and the United Methodist Women are also very active organizations in the church.

In 1980, the Reverend James Grimmer was assigned to Chester United Methodist Church and Robert L. Morris came to serve the Chesapeake Avenue Church. Pastor Morris stayed for four years and was replaced by the Reverend Joseph G. Savinsky, who, after leaving the post in 1991, went on to serve as superintendent of the Norfolk District until his retirement at the June 2005 conference. After retiring, Joe Savinsky and his wife Carolyn made their home in nearby Smithfield, Virginia. For the first time since the Reverend Forrester served from 1939 to 1944, a minister stayed at the Chesapeake Avenue Church for more than four years. Most pastors wanted to stay longer than the allotted four years, but the previous older members of the church refused the request. The Reverend William T. Kessler, who retired after two years at the Chesapeake Avenue Church, followed Savinsky. The Reverend John M. Andrews was appointed in 1993 and remained for a record-breaking ten years. In June 2003, Dr. Louis A. Martin became the thirty-fifth minister of the church. In the year 2004, Ryan McCoy was hired to serve as a part-time youth director.

The Chesapeake Avenue United Methodist Church celebrated its centennial (1892–1992) during the ministry of the Reverend Kessler. Members of the congregation provided centennial memories, which were printed in the church bulletin throughout the year. Among the many events that took place in 1992 was an old-fashioned church ice-cream social, which was held in the courtyard on June 14. A Centennial Celebration Homecoming was held on October 4. Among the special visitors that day were Virginia Conference Bishop Thomas B. Stockton and Mrs. Stockton as well as Norfolk District Superintendent W. Dabney Walters and Mrs. Walters. On September 22, 1996, the educational building was dedicated in honor of and named for Judge Jerry G. Bray Jr. The speaker was Bishop Joe E. Pennel Jr. Other guests that morning were W. Dabney Walters, Norfolk District superintendent; Dane Mills, Norfolk District lay leader; and Darlene V. Amon, Virginia Annual Conference lay leader.

In naming the ministers since 1892, the following sources were used: *Memoirs— 200 Years! Soldiers of the Cross 1785–1987*, edited by W.D. Keene Jr., publisher and trustee; Virginia Conference Historical Society; the Reverend Reginald H. Potts III, president; local church records from 1911 to 2004; as well as the family Bible of Dr. G.N. Halstead, one of the charter members of the Liberty Street Methodist Episcopal Church, South.

Robert Tankard Waterfield	1892–1894
Edgar A. Potts (brother of R.H. Potts)*	1894–1896
Joseph G. Lennon	1896–1899
Paul Bradley	1899–1902
Samuel Summerfield Lambeth**	1902–1905
Vincent Walter Bergamin	1905–1908
Richard B. Scott	1908–1912
Cameron Eugene Pleasants	1912–1913
George William Martin Taylor	1913–1914
Robert Nelson Hartness	1914–1916
Thomas James Chandler Heath	1916–1917
James Oliver Babcock	1917–1919
Wallace Rockwell Evans	1919–1921
Charles Edward Green	1921–1924
Linton Dunn Stables	1924–1930
Lee Gary Crutchfield	1930–1932
Leonard Reid Black	1932–1936
Francis Blackwell McSparran	1936–1937
Louis Oakey Wilburn	1937–1939
George Thomas Forrester	1939–1944
Clay Williams Hillman	1944–1948
Millard Filmore Draper	1948–1952
Dewey Bert Mullins	1952–1954
Paul R. Best	1954–1958
Edward A. Plunkett	1958–1962
L.H. Youell	1962–1966
C. Reginald Walton	1966–1968
Robert H. Eason	1968–1972
James E. Powell Jr.	1972–1976
James B. Grimmer	1976–1980
Robert L. Morris	1980–1984
Joseph G. Savinsky	1984–1991
William T. Kessler	1991–1993
John M. Andrew	1993–2003
Louis A. Martin, Ph.D.	2003–Present

*Members of the Potts family have served the Virginia conference since Joseph Ezekiel Potts was received at the session in Lynchburg in October 1853. He had four sons who were members of the Virginia conference. They were the Reverends Edgar A. Potts, Eugene J. Potts, Reginald H. Potts and Thomas N. Potts. At least one past history of the Chesapeake Avenue Church listed R.H. Potts as having served the Liberty Street Church. According to *Soldiers of the Cross*, he did not serve that church; however, his brother the Reverend Edgar A. Potts did serve there for two years. Also the Halstead family Bible states that the Reverend Edgar A. Potts performed the wedding of Nicholas George Wilson to Beulah Murray Halstead on November 28, 1895, (Thanksgiving Day) at the Liberty Street Methodist Episcopal Church, South. The Reverend Joseph Potts had sons, grandsons and great-grandsons who served the Virginia conference.

** For a number of years, C.H. Lambeth was listed as the fifth minister of Liberty Street Methodist Church. Lambeth was not a minister but was an early member of the church. When the first quarterly conference met on January 25, 1911, he was a member. Lambeth served on the South Norfolk school board as early as 1932. A later historian thought that because G.H. sounded like C.H., the fifth minister must have been G.H. Lambeth. I could not find any evidence that G.H. Lambeth served the Liberty Street Church; however, according to the Halstead family Bible, his father Dr. Samuel Summerfield Lambeth was minister of the church in 1903. Dr. S.S. Lambeth performed the marriage of Samuel Norfleet Etheridge and Georgia Columbia Halstead on January 1, 1903, at the Liberty Street Methodist Episcopal Church, South.

This picturesque image, which highlights the Chesapeake Avenue Methodist Church and the brick sidewalk in the historic district, was taken by Kathy Keeney in February 2000.

South Norfolk Baptist Church

On September 9, 1891, the Berkley Avenue Baptist Church appointed Charles Blevens, C.W. Rockefellow, W.C. Meginely, H.N. Quisenberry and L.B. Allen to investigate the possibility of acquiring lots in South Norfolk for the erection of a church. On April 1, 1892, Blevens reported that Thomas H. Synon, a real-estate developer, had offered to donate lots on which to build a church. The condition being that the trustees enter into a contract to receive the lots with the understanding that construction would begin within three months and be complete within six months from the date of contract.

By July 1, 1892, the contract to build the chapel in South Norfolk had been awarded to W.J. Peel for $1,660. The structure was to be twenty feet by sixty feet. Benjamin O. Pierce of Philadelphia, Pennsylvania, drew plans for the chapel and George S. Perry of Boston, Massachusetts, provided the furniture. The total sum was approximately $2,000. The building opened on January 5, 1893, and the formal dedication took place June 11, 1893.

The South Norfolk Baptist Church began as a chapel on the corner of Chesapeake Avenue and Guerriere Street. The total cost, including furniture, was about $2,000. The original building, which was the larger part of the above structure, opened for worship on January 5, 1893. An addition was added across the back to create the sanctuary shown here. This building burned on June 13, 1914.

The Reverend C.B. Lloyd served as pastor under the guidance of the Reverend Quisenberry during those formative months. The chapel was formally organized as the South Norfolk Baptist Church, a fully constituted church on November 5, 1893, with thirty charter members.

The charter membership roll included:

J.D. Berry	Thomas Hallows	A.J. Madra
J.W. Berry	Mrs. Thomas Hallows	Miss Alice McHorney
Mrs. C.R. Brown	Charles Hallows	William McPherson
Miss Nanie Beasley	James Johnson	Miss Kate Simmons
Miss Metta Balance	Mrs. James (Julie) Johnson	Miss Mary Shultz
J.S. Barron	Miss Clara Johnson	Mrs. Annie D. Shultz
J.W. Beasley	Miss Annie Johnson	Miss Hattie Spence
Miss Naomi Beasley	Mrs. M.E. Keeter	A.W. Taylor
J.P. Downing	Timothy Keeter	Mrs. A.W. Taylor
Miss Minnie Harrell	Mrs. Susan Knox	Mrs. Annie Walker

The Reverend Lloyd resigned at the end of September to continue his education at the Southern Baptist Theological Seminary in Louisville, Kentucky. Around the middle of November, the Reverend Lloyd was stricken by a sudden illness and died.

The Reverend Charles Wright Matthews was called to be the first pastor on January 28, 1894. Before coming to South Norfolk, he had served the Lake Drummond and Mulberry Churches of the Portsmouth Baptist Association. Although the Reverend Matthews was scheduled to receive $80 per year from the church, his resignation was reported on August 1, 1894, to become effective on October 1. The Reverend Matthews accepted the pastorate of the Chincoteague Baptist Church on Chincoteague Island on the eastern shore.

The Reverend William B. Duling was called as the second pastor on May 15, 1895. He came from Louisville, Kentucky, where he had been studying at the Southern Baptist Theological Seminary. This was his first pastorate, and his salary was set at $600 per year. An ordination service was held for Pastor Duling, thus he became the first ordained minister in the history of the church. Duling served until March 27, 1898, at which time he submitted his resignation. Former Pastor Duling and his wife had continued in membership and were granted letters of dismission in January 1900. At that time, he became pastor of churches in Dinwiddie County and later served churches in Princess Anne County; Hertford, North Carolina; and Pamplin. Duling led in organizing the Pastor's Conference of the Appomattox Association. His death occurred in October 1931.

After several pastors declined the call to the South Norfolk Baptist Church, a number of people suggested a possible candidate from Washington and Tyrell Counties in North Carolina. He was Elder Joseph Tynch. Elder Tynch was a veteran of the War Between the States and had been ordained about 1873. It is believed that he was called on a trial basis and that his term as pastor expired with the trial period. Elder Tynch served from June 19, 1898, to October 9, 1898.

On February 5, 1899, the Reverend Samuel S. Robinson was elected pastor. His prior pastorate had been the London Bridge Baptist Church in Princess Anne County. He began his new pastorate on the first Sunday in March. His service of installation took place on April 9. Financial problems continued to plague the church during the pastorate of the Reverend Robinson and funds for the pastor's salary were in arrears most of the time. On February 2, 1902, Robinson submitted his resignation to take effect in three months. The resignation was accepted. After leaving South Norfolk, he served churches at Waverly, Ettrick and Victoria, and in the counties of Lunenberg, Greenville, Nelson and Northumberland.

Philip Sealey Cohoon Davis submitted his application to succeed Robinson. The Reverend Davis had studied at Wake Forest College and had been ordained in 1884. His previous pastorates were Juniper Spring Church, 1882–1883; Shady Grove, Rehoboth, Powell's Point, Poplar Branch and Roanoke Island Churches, 1885–1891; Northwest, Centerville, St. John's and Woodville Churches, 1892–1893; and Shiloh, Oak Ridge, Northwest and Bethel Churches, 1898–1902. The Reverend Davis was called on March 2, 1902. The church prospered under his leadership. During his three and a half years, three hundred members were added to the membership. On October 15, Pastor Davis resigned his pastorate, effective at the end of 1905. His last pastorate was the Belhaven Baptist Church in North Carolina. The Reverend Davis died on January 30, 1908.

On October 2, 1905, the church called the Reverend Quinton Clarence Davis, first cousin of P.S.C. Davis, as its next pastor. Q.C. Davis was born in 1863 in Elizabeth City,

North Carolina. He received his education in Elizabeth City area schools and Crozer Baptist Theological Seminary Chester in Pennsylvania. His pastorates included Elm City, North Carolina, 1892–1893; First Baptist Church, Cumberland Maryland, 1893–1899; Emanuel Baptist Church, Camden, New Jersey, 1900–1903; and First Baptist Church, Little Rock, Arkansas, 1904 as interim pastor. The Reverend Q.C. Davis has been described as a "scholarly pastor." He and his wife were parents of a daughter and three sons. His son, Dr. Hershey Davis, was a professor of Greek at Southern Seminary, Louisville, Kentucky. Another son, Q.C. Davis Jr., became judge of the Corporation Court of the City of South Norfolk. Pastor Davis's salary was raised from $12.50 to $18.00 per week in February 1906 and in February 1908, to $25.00 per week. Davis resigned May 19, 1909, and became pastor of Windsor Baptist Church in Windsor, North Carolina, where he served from 1909 to 1912. He taught Bible and philosophy classes at Chowan College from 1912 to 1913; was pastor of East Durham Baptist Church from 1914 to 1918; and was pastor of the First Baptist Church of Eustis, Florida, from 1925 to 1926. He died May 30, 1926, and was buried in Norfolk.

The Reverend Frank M. Wilson followed the Reverend Davis. Pastor and Mrs. Wilson were received by letter on November 14, 1909. They stayed a very short while, with Pastor Wilson offering his resignation on January 23, 1910. It was to take effect February 2, 1910.

The next pastor, the Reverend Edward S. Pierce, was called on June 12, 1910. The Reverend Pierce was serving Prentis Park Baptist Church in Portsmouth at the time of the call. Edward Sylvester Pierce was born on December 17, 1870, in Gates County, North Carolina. He studied at Bethel Hill Academy, Wake Forest College and the Southern Baptist Theological Seminary. He served Capron, Jerusalem, Newsome and Thomas Memorial Churches of the Portsmouth Association, and had been pastor of Ocean View before moving to Prentis Park. After a pastorate of nine months, Pierce offered his resignation, to be effective at the end of April 1912, having accepted a call to the West Durham Baptist Church of Durham, North Carolina. In February 1914, he became pastor of Chincoteague Church in Chincoteague. In 1920, he moved to Cumberland County. In 1923, he became involved in a confrontation with the Garrett brothers and was shot to death. Pierce's funeral was held on June 7, 1923, at the South Norfolk Baptist Church.

The Reverend William Madison Black came to the church on October 7, 1912. He was a native of Rockbridge County and was born in 1872. Black graduated from Richmond College with a bachelor's degree in 1912 and also earned degrees at the Colgate Rochester Theological Seminary and Colgate University.

During the pastorate of the Reverend Pierce, the South Norfolk Baptist Church facilities were inadequate. A building committee was organized and studies conducted regarding the need for a new building. On June 13, 1914, during the pastorate of the Reverend Black, the church caught fire and was completely destroyed. The church then began to meet at the WOW Hall on Twenty-second Street. At that time, the first floor of the WOW Hall housed the South Norfolk Fire Department and jail. Bids for construction of a new brick church at the corner of Chesapeake Avenue and Guerriere Street were taken. Although J.T. Jones was the low bidder, the congregation decided to use the services of James C. Johnson and his brother Albert, who were members of the church and contractors. Groundbreaking ceremonies were held on October 13, 1914. Mrs. W.C. Meginley moved the first shovel of dirt. The building cost about $22,000 and the furnishings an additional $8,000. The service of dedication was held July 5, 1915.

In November 1918, Pastor Black resigned for health reasons. His resignation became effective December 1, 1918. After a period of recuperation, the Reverend Black returned to the ministry and served several churches. He always participated in community affairs and, during his last pastorate, served as mayor of Pamplin. He died in Pamplin on March 21, 1961.

At the suggestion of Pastor Black, the church investigated the credentials of a young man by the name of Clyde Spurgeon Sawyer. The Reverend Sawyer was a native of Tyrell County, North Carolina. He graduated from Wake Forest College with a bachelor's degree in 1915 and from Crozer Theological Seminary in May 1918. He also attended Union Theological Seminary in New York City for one year. On December 1, 1918, the Reverend Sawyer was called to the pastorate of South Norfolk Baptist Church.

It was during Sawyer's pastorate that a mission of the church was begun in April 1920. C.E. Johnson was named the first superintendent. Originally thought of as a Sunday school, it was called the South Norfolk Baptist Mission. In 1954, it became the Southside Baptist Church. A parsonage was built in 1926 at a cost of $7,800. Also in 1926, Sawyer married Mable Elizabeth Davis, a public health nurse who was employed in the South Norfolk school system. They would become the parents of three children: Elizabeth, Clyde Spurgeon (Bo-Bo) and Cora Lee. The church instituted some very rigid rules and regulations during Sawyer's pastorate. The Reverend Sawyer served for twenty-eight years and retired at the end of 1946 because of ill health. Pastor Sawyer and his family continued to live in the parsonage until 1947 when they moved to Chestnut Street in Berkley. The Reverend Sawyer died on November 22, 1948. His funeral was held in the Berkley Avenue Baptist Church.

The next pastor of the South Norfolk Baptist Church was the Reverend Frank Hughes Jr., a native of Currituck County, North Carolina. His family moved to Princess Anne County, where he grew up and received his early education in local schools. The Reverend Hughes was educated at Wake Forest College and Southwestern Baptist Theological Seminary. He was ordained on July 30, 1942, by the Kempsville Baptist Church in Princess Anne County. In September 1942, he married Katherine Anne Read of Norman, Oklahoma. Katherine was also a graduate of Southwestern Baptist Seminary in Fort Worth, Texas. The Reverend Hughes's first pastorate was a mission, which he organized in Broad Creek Village in August 1943 and later became the Broad Creek Baptist Church. The Nelson Park mission was formed on January 1, 1947. Nelson Park was the western portion of Broad Creek Village. When Broad Creek Village was dismantled, the Broad Creek Baptist Church relocated and took the name of Virginia Heights Baptist Church. Its mission in Nelson Park relocated and became the Ingleside Baptist Church. The Reverend Hughes preached his first sermon at South Norfolk Baptist Church on Sunday, February 9, 1947.

Church and Sunday school membership continued its remarkable growth, and in 1952, the church joined the newly organized Norfolk Baptist Association. A church conference of August 3, 1952, voted to rent basement rooms for Sunday school from J.R. Williams of J.R.

The young people of the South Norfolk Baptist Church's Sunday school posed for this picture in 1949.

The South Norfolk Baptist Church in 1995. *Photo courtesy of the author.*

Williams Funeral Home. In December 1953, the house at 1109 Chesapeake Avenue was removed to make way for construction of the new educational building. The church had accepted a bid of $202,500 from R.R. Richardson. The occupation and dedication of the new building took place on February 13, 1955.

The church established a mission at Princess Anne Plaza Baptist Church. The Reverend Melvin Hughes became its first pastor. The church continued to grow and prosper, acquiring more property along Seaboard and Chesapeake Avenues. Frank and Katherine Hughes went on to serve the South Norfolk Baptist Church for thirty-seven years, retiring on September 30, 1984.

The Reverend Donald McCall Brunson Jr. began his pastorate at the South Norfolk Baptist Church on July 7, 1985 and served until June 21, 1992. Pastor Roger Mardis, who preached his first sermon September 12, 1993, followed the Reverend Brunson. Several other ministers have served the church since Mardis left. Dr. Scott Harris, the current minister, has served the church faithfully for several years.

South Norfolk Congregational Christian Church

In the fall of 1903, the Reverend Herbert Scholtz, who was then pastor of the First Christian Church in Berkley, organized a Sunday school, which met in the South Norfolk school on Jackson Street. The school was located behind E.M. Tilley's home and faced Jackson Street to the west between Guerriere and Ohio Streets. From its beginning, the Sunday school had a steady growth, and on May 29, 1904, the South Norfolk Christian Church was organized with sixteen charter members. The congregation worshipped in the small school building until 1905. The Reverend Scholitz then resigned, and the Reverend J.O. Cox became pastor and served for five years.

In 1906, the members of the South Norfolk Christian Church purchased land on Jackson Street and erected this small frame house of worship in November.

In 1906, the members of the church purchased land on Jackson Street near the corner of Guerriere Street, a part of which was used to erect a house of worship. This small, frame structure was formally opened in November.

In 1909, the Reverend D.A. Keys became pastor and served for five years. In 1914, the Reverend L.L. Lassister accepted a call to the church; however, because of poor health, he served only a few months. The church was then without a pastor for almost a year. During this time, many of the members became discouraged and called on the conference officials to take over the work. Colonel J.E. West, chairman of the Home Mission Committee, in cooperation with the conference officials, extended a call to young Olive Daniel Poythress, who accepted and became pastor on October 1, 1915. At that time, the streets of South Norfolk were of dirt and just a few homes had been built. The few existing sidewalks were made of boards nailed together to form boardwalks. Poythress was quoted as having said, "When he arrived in South Norfolk and got off the streetcar … he felt like he was in the middle of no where." In spite of the rough terrain, thirty-two faithful and loyal members of the church greeted him.

In 1918, the debt owing on the small house of worship was paid off and the adjoining lot was purchased.

The Reverend O.D. Poythress went on to serve the South Norfolk Congregational Christian Church for forty-three years. During that time, he married Ethel Annie Hanbury and they had six children. He was very active in the community and served on the South Norfolk School Board.

The congregation continued to worship in the small frame structure, which stood on ground that is now part of the parking lot. Ground for the new edifice was broken to the left of the frame building in October 1924, and the first brick was laid on April 10, 1925.

This photograph of the Reverend O.D. Poythress and fourteen ladies of the church was probably taken in the early years of his ministry at the South Norfolk Christian Church, *circa* 1918.

The Reverend O.D. Poythress, fifth man from the left end in the first row, and some of the men from the South Norfolk Christian Church had their picture taken in front of the house that stood next to the church on Jackson Street.

Impressive ceremonies were held April 3, 1926, to mark the laying of the cornerstone of the new South Norfolk Christian Church. A large article and several photographs appeared in the *Virginian-Pilot and Landmark* on Sunday, April 4, 1926. One of the photographs shows a corner of the old and new buildings. It appeared that there were just a few feet between the right side of the new building and the left side of the old building. The overall title was "Handsome New Church for South Norfolk." The event represented a dream come true for the congregation and marked the early completion of an edifice, which compared favorably with any other in the area. J.M. McMichael of Charlotte, North Carolina was the architect, and Albert Johnson was superintendent of construction.

Note: When interviewing Rosa Funk, a longtime member of the church, she stated that her father, Mr. Whorten, was one of the carpenters who helped build the new church. Sometime during its construction, he dropped his hammer between the walls and was not able to retrieve it. Most likely that hammer is still there and in good condition after eighty years. We will probably never know for sure.

The Reverend Poythress delivered a brief address welcoming those who came to attend the cornerstone laying and recounting the steps, which made possible the handsome new building. The Reverend J.G. Truitt, pastor of the First Christian Church of Norfolk, offered a prayer.

The Reverend Poythress explained that the building was erected through the personal labor, prayers and sacrifices of members of the congregation. The cost of the building was about $80,000; however, more than $12,000 was saved because the construction work was not on a contractual basis, but carried on week by week. The church received many gifts of material and labor. A substantial amount of the expense had already been met and the church indebtedness was very small, Poythress said.

When the congregation and other interested citizens gathered on an early spring afternoon in 1926, the new South Norfolk Christian Church was almost complete. It was modern in every respect. The auditorium and balconies contained seating space for 850. There were more than thirty Sunday-school rooms in the building, representing a systematized arrangement of a modern departmentalized Sunday school.

Members of the church building committee who participated in the service that day were G.M. Herbert, chairman; B.F. Meginley; W.F. Davis; Lennon H. Newberry; R.C. Etheridge; and Harry Seymour, secretary and treasurer. Officers of South Norfolk Lodge Number 339, A.F. & A.M., in charge of the ceremonies, were P.G. Etheridge, worshipful master; J.K. Holland, senior warden; H. P. Lane, junior warden; S. Herman Dennis, treasurer; Quimby Brewer, senior deacon and secretary; and Don F. Dickinson, tiler.

The building formally opened for worship Sunday, June 6, 1926. There were three services that day. Dr. W.H. Denison from Dayton, Ohio, delivered the morning sermon; Dr. Leon Edgar Smith, pastor of the Christian Temple in Norfolk, preached at 3:00 p.m.; and the Reverend O.D. Poythress completed the busy day with his message at 8:00 p.m. The church was beautifully decorated with flowers and other decorations donated by Elsa Seeley, the florist.

The program for the week of June 6, 1926, was as follows: at 8:00 p.m. Monday, June 7, was Christian Church Night; at 8:00 p.m. Wednesday, June 9, there was organ recital by Professor Hugh McDowald, organist from the Wells Theater in Norfolk; and 8:00 p.m. Friday, June 11, were the Education Night graduation exercises with the South Norfolk High School address given by the Reverend R.H. Crossfield, pastor of First Church Christ Disciple, Norfolk.

Church officials in June 1926 included:

Staff	Trustees
Reverend Poythress, Pastor	Joseph S. King, Chairman
Cecil E. Hollowell, Clerk	William Curling
Harry Seymour, Treasurer	Marshall M. Hall
Benjamin F. Meginley,	Eliott E. Henley
Sunday school superintendent	Raymond W. Spruill
Deacons	**Deaconesses**
Raymond W. Spruill, Chairman	Mrs. Marjorie Humphries
Lafayette Curling	Mrs. Pearl Morgan
William J. Curling	Mrs. Harry Seymour
Marshall M. Hall	Mrs. Raymond W. Spruill
Eliott E. Henley	
John J. Jones	
Lennon Newberry	
Alvah J. Peters	
Clarence L. Stewart	
Joseph S. King	

This new building, which was modern in every respect, was formally opened for worship Sunday, June 6, 1926. This photograph was taken July 21, 1926.

Many older residents of South Norfolk may still remember the lively revivals held by Poythress and Lee C. Fisher. The two sang together while Fisher played the accordion. When Fisher was in town, he held magic shows in the church basement each afternoon for the schoolchildren. Fisher, who was from Elkhart, Indiana, also held revivals at the Rosemont Christian Church in Portlock.

The debt on the church building that had been erected in 1926 was satisfied in 1945. In 1954, a parsonage was built at 1109 Decatur Street. The church continued to grow, and it was decided that an educational building was needed. Property next to the church was purchased.

After having served the South Norfolk Christian Church as its pastor for forty-three years, the Reverend Poythress retired. He continued to be active and was given the title of minister emeritus. His successor was the Reverend John Truitt Jr., who served for three years and was followed by the Reverend William Cousins. In 1965, James Rumley was called as pastor and served a short time. On May 15, 1966, the Reverend Willis Joyner began serving the church and was its pastor for nineteen years.

In 1967, an elevator was installed in the church. In 1968, the members voted to withdraw from the United Church of Christ and the church has remained an independent entity since. It was then that the name was changed to South Norfolk Congregational Christian Church.

In 1970, the pipe organ was replaced with a new Electronic Conn organ. Two years later, a much-needed educational wing was added and two new lots next door were purchased for parking. The South Norfolk Christian School was also founded in 1972. Over the next few years, the pews and paneling were refinished, a new sound system was installed and drapes were added to the choir loft. In 1979, the church acquired property in Indian River and the South Norfolk Christian School was relocated to a building that had been built on that property. The name has since been changed and is now known as Cornerstone Christian School.

The Reverend Nelson Hodges became pastor of the church in 1985. In 1990, a house on Jackson Street was purchased for use by church missionaries (it was demolished in 1998). Also in 1990, Mildred Bunch donated her home at 1417 Seaboard Avenue to be used as a mission home.

The Reverend Willis Dowling replaced Hodges in 1992. The Reverend Dowling would serve the church until 1996. It was then that the Reverend Amos Eby became pastor, and at the time of this writing, he continues his ministry at the South Norfolk Congregational Christian Church.

The Harvest Soup Kitchen Ministry was started in 1998 and on July 11, 1999, a mission home was dedicated at 1607 Jackson Street or, as it is now called, Jackson Avenue.

Hats off to two notable members of the church. Verna Stevens has attended since age seven and has been a member since 1932, which makes her the longest attending lady of the church. Be careful, Verna, you may reveal your age. The other member is Harvey Curling who has been a member since 1929. He joined when he was twelve years old and was baptized by the Reverend Poythress. He and his lovely wife are still active members. Congratulations and may God bless you both.

The South Norfolk Congregational Christian Church stands as a distinguishing landmark at the corner of Jackson and Guerriere Streets in the former city of South Norfolk. On May 22 and 23, 2004, its members celebrated the one-hundredth anniversary. I wish the congregation continued success and will be looking forward to the next celebration.

South Norfolk Church of Christ

It was in the year 1906 that the First Christian Church of Norfolk organized the South Norfolk Church of Christ. The first church had a membership of fifty-seven and was under the leadership of the Reverend C.B. Richards, the first pastor.

At that time, the Norton family home stood on the corner of Chesapeake Avenue and Poindexter Street. Joseph Herbert Norton had his house moved several lots to the south and donated the land on the corner to the church. In 1910, the Church of Christ was built on Chesapeake Avenue at the corner of Poindexter Street. The construction of the church, which was under the leadership of John W. Tyndall, president of the Industrial Christian College of Kinston, North Carolina, was completed in just one week. One feature of the South Norfolk Church of Christ was the ornamental iron fence surrounding the building. Mr. McHorney, Mr. Hand and Norton were among the early Sunday school teachers.

Chesapeake Avenue, looking South, showing Church of Christ's Desciples, built in 6 days, South Norfolk, Va.

This image of the South Norfolk Church of Christ was taken from a picture postcard. The message in the upper left corner almost says it all, but a closer look reveals that the word "disciple" has been misspelled. The church was built at the corner of Chesapeake Avenue and Poindexter Street when the streets were still dirt with streetcar tracks down the middle. The postcard, which was purchased from Preston's Pharmacy, is dated *circa* 1910.

In the course of the development of the church, there were seven pastors: S.T. Burgess, E.A. Troy, H.H. Hemple, W.A. Martin, E.A. Manly, W.A. Webster and J.H. Knibb. By September 1925, the church membership had grown to 250.

In the early 1930s, the congregation relocated to the corner of Jackson and Jefferson Streets. The building on Chesapeake Avenue was moved to a location off Campostella Road. Eventually, there was a split in the South Norfolk Church of Christ membership. One group started a new church in Brambleton and later moved to Laurel Avenue in Norfolk Highlands. This became the Laurel Avenue Church of Christ, which is located at 1126 Laurel Avenue. The remaining group maintained the original name and can be found today at 2526 Rodgers Street.

A Conoco service station was built on the property at the corner of Chesapeake Avenue and Poindexter Street.

First Presbyterian Church of South Norfolk

In the latter part of the year 1918, Dr. W.H.T. Squires, the Reverend T.H. Dimmock and Edwin Carr from the Armstrong Memorial Church in Berkley visited South Norfolk to investigate the possibility of organizing a Presbyterian Sunday school in what was then the village of South Norfolk.

The conditions were found to be favorable, and in early 1919, the services of Carrie Morris of Richmond were secured by the Norfolk Presbytery to assist in visitation of the local people. Morris stayed in the Carr home, where Edwin and his wife assisted her in her work.

After Morris and Edwin Carr completed many visits, it was announced that a Sunday school would be organized around the first of March 1919. Approximately one hundred attended a meeting where the Reverend Dimmock, Morris and Carr spoke. During this meeting, classes were organized: Mrs. Carr was appointed teacher of the beginners and primaries; Morris was to teach the juniors and intermediates; and Edwin Carr would teach all others and serve as superintendent.

Beginning in March, Sunday school services were conducted in an old store building on the north side of Mrs. F.H. Hall's home. The monthly rent was five dollars. The Sunday school continued to grow and eventually a new meeting place was needed. It was learned that John L. Jones wanted to sell the four-room house he owned at what is now Lakeside Park; however, he did not want to sell the land on which it stood. The Home Mission Committee of Norfolk Presbytery purchased the house. The Sunday school occupied the house for a period of approximately five years.

Shortly thereafter, Carrie Morris contracted influenza, which developed into pneumonia; her life was not spared to continue the work so well begun. The work continued under the sponsorship of the Armstrong Memorial Presbyterian Church, of which the Reverend Dimmock was pastor. Squires, pastor of Knox Presbyterian Church, and the Reverend John C. Ramsey, superintendent of Home Missions Committee, Norfolk Presbytery, assisted when called on and delivered short sermons after the Sunday school services. The Armstrong Memorial Presbyterian Church loaned an organ to be used in the services.

In July 1919, the Norfolk Presbytery acquired the services of Lillian Toland, superintendent of Factory Mission Work in Richmond. About this time, Dr. Squires recommended that the Sunday school be called the Geneva Presbyterian Mission. This recommendation proved acceptable, and the name was placed over the entrance of the building. The mission became the center of social and religious life for the community, remaining open day and night— except for Saturday nights. Sewing classes were conducted for the girls; handwork classes for the boys; all were taught the catechism and participated in the singing of religious songs. In these services, Mrs. Carr and her daughter Sarah were invaluable.

During the summer of 1920, Mina Amis, from the Assembly Training School in Richmond, was employed by the Norfolk Presbytery to assist Toland, who was also an Assembly Training School graduate. Vacation Bible School was held each day in South Norfolk and a Sunday school was organized at Dozier's Corner. The Vacation Bible School was the first to be held in South Norfolk and, at that time, had not become popular in many of the larger churches in the nearby areas. In late 1920, the Norfolk Presbytery sent Toland to Wachaperague.

In the beginning, the Sunday school—which held its services on the lawn of Mr. and Mrs. A.C. West—used plank benches for seats. Starting with an enrollment of twenty-five, the school increased in number to the extent that a small frame building was erected on property donated by Mrs. T.W. Butt. Dr. Squires recommended that the school be given the name Glenwood Mission. This met with favorable reactions and the school was thus named. Larry Costen, superintendent of the Armstrong Sunday school, was appointed as the first superintendent of the Glenwood Sunday school. His daughters, Louise and Myra, assisted the Geneva workers in carrying on the activities of the school.

The Geneva Presbyterian Church was organized November 1, 1920. Shortly after this the church called its first pastor, the Reverend Hugh Fitzpatrick. Fitzpatrick served the church from December 5, 1920, to December 11, 1921. All records of church activities during this period were lost and therefore cannot be included in this history. The Reverend R.W. Cousar served as pastor of the Geneva Presbyterian Church from May 14, 1922, to November 30, 1922, when he was called to become the full-time pastor of Prentiss Park Presbyterian Church in Portsmouth. During this time, Edwin Carr, A.L. Rountree and A.C. West served as ruling elders. West had taken the position left vacant when S.J. Lindley returned to the First Presbyterian Church of Norfolk. C.E. Hewitt served in the office of deacon and was the only ordained deacon until May 10, 1925. The officers of the Sunday school during this period were as follows:

Mr. C.E. Hewitt	Superintendent
Mr. Edwin Carr	Assistant Superintendent
Mr. Arthur M. Kriss	Secretary and Treasurer

The charter members accounted for at this time were as follows:

Mr. R.L. Bass	Mrs. Florence Snowden	Mrs. Ruth F. Waff
Mr. Edwin Carr	Mr. H.F. Whitfield	Mrs. W.R. Liverman
Mr. E.R. Delbridge	Mrs. J.L. Wingfield	Mr. A.L. Rountree
Mr. Raymond Fulford	Mr. A.C. West	Miss Lillian Toland
Mrs. Eva Harrell	Mrs. R.L. Bass	Mrs. H.F. Whitfield
Mrs. W.F. Gray	Mr. Cecil E. Hewitt	Mrs. A.L. Rountree
Mr. Randolph Jones	Mr. James Howlett	Mrs. A.C. West
Mr. A.M. Kriss	Mrs. L.M. Holloman	
Mr. S.J. Lindley	Mr. Earl Howlett	

The Reverend C.J. Hicks served as pastor from January 7, 1923, to December 31, 1925, when he was dismissed to the Phoebus Presbyterian Church. In November 1923, the building was moved and repaired. The congregation voted on November 5, 1923, to allocate $500 for the move and repairs. At the end of the church year—March 31, 1924—there were 3 elders, 1 deacon, 58 church members and 155 enrolled in Sunday school. The total budget was $1,319.

A congregational meeting was held on May 8, 1924, where plans for a new building and the authorization to secure a loan were approved by a vote of 29–0. Another meeting held on October 3, 1924, authorized a week of services beginning the third Sunday of October to be conducted by the Reverend Fitzpatrick. At the end of the church year—March 31, 1925—there were 3 elders, 1 deacon, 78 church members and 195 enrolled in Sunday school. The budget was $1,394.

At the congregational meeting on May 10, 1925, the congregation voted 29–0 authorizing the Geneva Presbyterian Church trustees to transfer the church property to the Presbyterian League of Norfolk Presbytery, Inc. At the same meeting, Thomas B. Ghiselin was elected ruling elder, and H.F. Whitfield and Cecil Holloman were elected deacons. A.C. West was clerk of the meeting.

At the congregational meeting held on November 29, 1925, the resignation of Pastor C.J. Hicks was read and accepted with regret by those present. At that time, a pulpit committee was appointed to find a replacement for Pastor Hicks. Forty-six were received into the church membership during the pastorate of the Reverend Hicks.

The Reverend William Thompson Baker, pastor of Prentiss Park Presbyterian Church, served at the Geneva Presbyterian Church on a part-time basis from July 18, 1926, to February 8, 1927. The Reverend R.B. Grinan, pastor of the Colley Memorial Presbyterian Church in Norfolk, served as part-time pastor from June 12, 1927, to June 1, 1928.

On October 9, 1927, a congregational meeting was held and those present approved the request of Truitt-Smith Realty Corporation that the church building be moved out of the area, which would later become Lakeside Park. The building was moved to its present location.

On May 28, 1928, Dr. Grinan resigned as supply pastor and it was proposed that J. Raymond Smith, a recent graduate of Union Theological Seminary in Richmond, be asked to serve as pastor of the Geneva church. The Reverend Smith agreed, and at the congregational meeting of January 6, 1929, a motion passed that Smith be called as pastor at a salary of $50 a month. It appears that Pastor Smith served until early 1931; the record shows that as of April 12, 1931, the church was without the services of a minister.

The Reverend S.J. Venable was moderator at the session that was held on February 24, 1932. At this session T.B. Ghiselin, one of the church elders, granted a certificate of dismissal to longtime member and elder Edwin Carr. Carr moved his membership to Armstrong Memorial Presbyterian Church.

There were no records available from March 31, 1932, to June 17, 1934.

The records from June 17, 1934, show members being received into membership, election of church officers and the granting of certificates of dismissal to other churches in the area.

On July 15, 1935, the Norfolk Presbytery granted evangelistic powers to the Reverend Thomas B. Ruff.

The church was damaged by fire on May 13, 1936. At the session held on May 20, 1936, L.W. Mann, C.E. Hewitt and the Reverend Ruff were elected as a building committee to supervise repairs.

During the church year 1936–1937, the Reverend C.J. Hollansworth and Vernon Fisher conducted revival services at the Geneva church.

On October 27, 1940, the Reverend F.G. Schriner was invited to supply the pulpit. On July 6, 1941, N.W. Blount was elected to represent the church at the Norfolk Presbytery and attempt to secure the services of the Reverend T.T. Fowler. On November 9, 1941, Dr. Minor requested that he be permitted to supply the pulpit until the end of the year. His request was granted. The Reverend F.G. Schriner reported as supply pastor on

January 11, 1942. The Reverend Curt was moderator of the session meeting, which was held on February 11, 1942. At this meeting, he gave approval for the Reverend T.K. Morrison, an African missionary, to supply the pulpit until the services of a regular pastor could be secured.

On March 1, 1942, grouping with the Park Avenue Presbyterian Church was recommended and approved. At this time, a decision was made to invite the Reverend R.W. Kirkpatrick of Accomack to preach when it was convenient for him. On May 10, 1942, the pulpit committee was authorized to secure the services of the Reverend Fowler, who served until May 1, 1943.

The Reverend Fowler was moderator of the session meeting, which took place on July 19, 1942. At this meeting, the pulpit committee recommended S.A.M. King of Kansas City, Missouri, serve as pastor of the Park Avenue and South Norfolk Presbyterian Churches (the church history does not state when the Geneva Presbyterian Church became the South Norfolk Presbyterian Church).

Fowler was moderator and N.W. Blount was clerk of the congregational meeting that was held on August 16, 1942. A motion passed that the grouping with the Park Avenue Church be dissolved. The Reverend R.W. Kirkpatrick was called to become pastor of the church. H.L. Hewitt, Margie Dillon, Alice Carr and Vernon Wilder signed the call.

At a congregational meeting held on January 31, 1943, the Reverend Fowler again served as moderator and Blount as clerk. Blount, Wilder and Alice Carr were elected to serve as trustees. The trustees were instructed by the congregation to proceed with the purchase of the manse (clergyman's residence). On February 21, 1943, the congregation approved the purchase of 1204 Park Avenue. The final cost was $4,500.

The pulpit committee presented the name of the Reverend J. Wesley Lehman at the April 18, 1943, congregational meeting and recommended that he be called as pastor of the church beginning May 1, 1943. The recommendation was unanimously adopted.

The session authorized a congregational meeting to be held September 12, 1943, to consider a location for a new church and to elect two elders and a treasurer of the building fund. Wilder and Howard Hewitt were elected to the office of ruling elder. Wilder was also elected treasurer of the building fund.

Mr. A.H. Stewart and Mr. Walter Dillon were appointed custodians of the church, and Dillon was instructed to obtain the materials necessary to build a storage house for the coal and wood. On September 28, 1943, the men of the church met to begin construction of the storage house. Apparently something went wrong because on October 18, 1943, a motion was carried to cancel building of the storage house.

At the October 18, 1943 meeting, a motion was passed to invite the Home Mission Committee of the Norfolk Presbytery to meet with the South Norfolk Church. N.J. Nolan and N.W. Blount were instructed to confer with the committee relative to obtaining financial help toward the erection of the new church building. A motion passed to request $20,000 from the Home Mission Committee toward building a new church building.

N.W. Etheridge, chairman of the Home Mission Committee, attended the congregational meeting held on October 26, 1943. Etheridge addressed the congregation on financing a new church building. Howard Hewitt was elected chairman of the building committee.

Other members included A.H. Stewart, Dorothy Lilley, C.E. Hewitt, Mrs. N.J. Nolan and Nellie Harrison.

The finance committee consisted of Chairman Vernon Wilder, N.W. Blount, Walter Dillon, Louise Waff, Alice Lee Hewitt, Margie Dillon and Hattie Pierce. On November 7, 1943, Wilder resigned as building fund treasurer. Louise Waff and C.E. Hewitt succeeded him.

Architect Thurmer Hoggard Jr. presented sketches of the new church at the November 21, 1943 congregational meeting. Hoggard answered questions and received authorization to complete the sketches.

Elder A.H. Stewart was authorized by the November 23, 1944 session to investigate the possibility of purchasing vacant lots behind and on the side of the church. At the same time, the pastor was asked to confer with Hoggard about the plans for the new church.

At the congregational meeting on May 13, 1945, M.A. Winslow and Stewart were elected to the commission in charge of erecting the new church building. The existing trustees were dismissed with thanks for a job well done and elected were Walter Dillon, Mrs. A.H. Stewart and C.E. Hewitt.

On September 18, 1945, the Reverend Lehman was authorized to purchase the lot behind the church from Mrs. J. Robert Graham for $600 and N.W. Blount was authorized to purchase the lot beside the church from the Truitt-Smith Realty Corporation for the sum of $200.

At the congregational meeting on October 26, 1947, the building committee was authorized to borrow $5,000, so that the new building might be started immediately.

On October 10, 1948, a congregational meeting was held to consider matters relating to the building of the new church. The addition of two restrooms at a cost not to exceed $800 was authorized for the existing church building. Authorization was given for payment of $1,125 to architect B.J.F. Mitchell for plans of the new church and to borrow $13,000 toward the erection of the new church building.

A joint meeting of the session and the subcommittee of the Home Mission Committee of the Norfolk Presbytery was held on October 11, 1948. At this meeting, W.E. Coley was appointed to see Oscar Smith; the Reverend Lehman was to confer with the Reverend Charles Gibboney and a committee of the Second Presbyterian Church; and A.H. Stewart was asked to contact Dr. T.B. Wood. These men were authorized to present the needs of the church and attempt to solicit funds in the amount of $3,189 to be used in the erection of the new building.

At the June 5, 1949 congregational meeting, a motion was made by Vernon Wilder and seconded by Alice Carr that the trustees proceed with the plans to borrow $13,000 from H.L. Warren. This money would be used to pay off the loan on the manse and start construction of the new church. A session meeting was held on June 22, 1949; at that time, N.W. Blount was asked to read the bids submitted for erection of the new building. A motion was passed that the bid of H.M. Lucas for the sum of $35,363 be approved, and that the contract be granted to him. On June 27, 1949, a motion was passed to add $425 to the original bid from Lucas. At the session meeting, the groundbreaking service for the new church was authorized for July 5, 1949, and the Reverend Lehman was authorized to pay the debt on the manse. The new building was dedicated in July 1950.

The Reverend Lehman requested that his relation with the First Presbyterian Church of South Norfolk be dissolved. A congregational meeting was held on March 29, 1953, and his request was granted by a vote of 42–7.

The church was without a regular pastor for the first five months of 1954. Chaplain R.W. O'Dell, of the U.S. Navy, and seven seminary students from Richmond supplied the pulpit. The old manse on Park Avenue was sold, and on March 18, 1954, a lot at 838 Wilbur Avenue was bought from A.L. Pierce and his wife to be used for construction of a new manse. The new manse was completed and ready for the Pastor John B. Rice and his family when they arrived on June 2, 1954.

In 1957, the church was again without the services of a regular pastor. One of the highlights of the year came on October 27, 1957, when Ida Gray broke ground for the new educational building. Gray observed her eightieth birthday that year. The new educational building was accepted on June 15, 1958. On May 11, 1958, a congregational meeting empowered the deacons to dispose of the old educational building. The debt on the educational building was paid off in January 1967.

On June 21, 1959, the Reverend Donald Ray Allen Jr. became pastor of the First Presbyterian Church of South Norfolk. Allen had graduated from Union Theological Seminary on May 19, 1959.

The Reverend Allen asked that a meeting of the congregation be called for July 29, 1962, where Allen requested that the pastoral relationship between him and the congregation be terminated. This would enable him to accept a call from the Presbytery of Lexington to organize a new church in the city of Harrisonburg. This request was granted, and the Allen family moved out of the manse the last of August 1962.

By unanimous vote, the Reverend G. Duane Smith was called to the pastorate on October 21, 1962. Pastor and Mrs. Smith moved into the manse on October 29, 1962. The Reverend Smith was a native of Murrysville, Pennsylvania, and was a graduate of Elizabethtown College in Elizabethtown, Pennsylvania, and Princeton Seminary in Princeton, New Jersey. He had served as a navy chaplain for two years and ten months. The service of installation was held November 25, 1962, and was followed by a reception for Pastor and Mrs. Smith. The Reverend G. Duane Smith remained at First Presbyterian Church of South Norfolk until 1965.

At the congregational meeting on December 4, 1965, the Reverend Harry Russell Goodwin was extended a call to become pastor of the church. At this time, he was serving two churches in Wallace, North Carolina. Pastor Goodwin, his wife and two children arrived January 15, 1967. Installation service for the Reverend Goodwin was held February 5, 1967, and followed by a reception for the family. A congregational meeting was held on June 20, 1982, to honor the request of the Reverend Goodwin to move to the Spring Hill Presbyterian Church in Lacoma, North Carolina. His resignation was accepted.

The Reverend Fred McCaskill-Baker was called by the congregation and confirmed by the Norfolk Presbytery. He conducted his first service on August 14, 1983, and was installed August 21, 1983. He had received his bachelor's degree from the College of William & Mary and his master of divinity degree from Duke University. The Reverend McCaskill-Baker served until April 3, 1988. The Reverend Frederick C. Sanner served as interim

The Sunday school that eventually became the First Presbyterian Church of South Norfolk was established in March 1918. The church was organized on November 1, 1920, under the name of Geneva Presbyterian Church. Church records do not indicate when the name was changed. The sanctuary seen here is located at 1605 Bainbridge Boulevard at the corner of Byrd Avenue.

pastor from June 1988 to July 14, 1991. On July 21, 1991, the congregation welcomed the Reverend James F. Giesey and his wife.

The Reverend Jan Amaimo Scully became pastor of the First Presbyterian Church of South Norfolk in 1995. Upon leaving, she went to a church in Cradock. At the time of this writing, the church has been without a regular pastor for approximately four years; however, the congregation continues to hold services each Sunday.

Southside Baptist Church

In 1920, an evangelistic meeting was held in Norfolk by the Reverend Billy Sunday. In connection with this meeting, cottage prayer services were held throughout the city and in outlying areas. As a result of these prayer meetings, and the great spiritual need in this area, South Norfolk Baptist Mission came into being. A delegation met with the pastor of the South Norfolk Baptist Church, the Reverend Clyde Sawyer, who in turn presented the matter to the Norfolk-Portsmouth Association. Through his efforts, a garage building on Bainbridge Boulevard was rented and a Sunday school mission was organized on April 20, 1920. Services were held there for approximately four years under the direction of the South Norfolk Baptist Church.

During this time, the Ladies Aid Society was organized. The group formulated plans to raise funds to purchase lots for the erection of a permanent building. When enough money had been raised, two lots on the corner of Perry and Ohio Streets were purchased. Plans were soon drawn for the erection of a building, which cost about $2,500 and was completed on September 12, 1926.

While meeting in the garage, a minister of the association held a service once a week. After the Sunday school building was completed, prayer services were held each Tuesday night. The members of the Sunday school attended church services at the mother church, the South Norfolk Baptist Church. The first Sunday school superintendent of the mission was a Mr. Chamberlain.

On October 15, 1950, the members of the South Norfolk Baptist Church voted to turn the property over to the mission. Early in 1952, it became apparent that a church was needed in that part of South Norfolk. A small group began prayer services in various homes. The services grew until it was necessary to secure larger quarters. A vacant grocery store located at the corner of Ohio Street and Bainbridge Boulevard was rented, and Arthur Harrell, a licensed minister, preached the first sermon. Services were held there until arrangements could be made to use the Sunday school building at the corner of Ohio and Perry Streets.

At a special business meeting held at the South Norfolk Baptist Church on March 12, 1952, the members voted to turn the deed of the property over to the members of the mission Sunday school. It was at that time that a new church was organized under the name Southside Baptist Church. The first pastor, W.L. Bristow, a layman, was sent by the Reverend Henry W. Tiffany, pastor of Park Place Baptist Church in Norfolk, to help. Bristow served the church for only two months, and the Reverend Andrew Johnson filled in until fall 1952. In October 1952, the Reverend Douglas E. Brawn was called as pastor and remained until July 1953. Arthur Harrell and H.H. Shiflett Sr. supplied the pulpit until January 1954. At that time, the Reverend Joseph N. Causey was called as pastor and remained until February 5, 1956. Dr. John Brown, superintendent of missions of the Norfolk association, served as supply pastor until the Reverend Billy Russ began his pastorate on March 5, 1956. Under Russ's ministry, Southside experienced tremendous growth. During his tenure, a fully graded Sunday school was formed, and by 1957, its enrollment grew to 535 members.

The training union was organized in April 1952 with Harrell as the first director and James Reed as assistant director. The church choir was formed with the beginning of the church; Mae Jernigan was the director and organist, Joseph Bright was the president and Joe Pritchard served as the song leader. The robes were made by members of the choir and donated to the church. An organ was purchased in 1952 at a cost of $1,300, and Elizabeth Smith served as organist and choir director.

A Vacation Bible School was held in 1953. June 1953 also saw the disbanding of the Ladies Aid Society, which was followed by the Women's Missionary Society. Mrs. D.E. Brawn, the pastor's wife, was the first president. When the Reverend Brawn resigned in July 1953 and moved to a new pastorate, Iola Harper became president and held the position through 1954. Marguerite Harper was the first church clerk.

The parsonage was purchased in 1952 at a cost of $8,500. An additional room and new heating system were added later. The educational building was designed and built during the pastorate of Joseph N. Causey at a cost of approximately $48,000. The dedication took place in

October 1955. Natalie Castellow, the oldest active member of the church at that time, cut the ribbon. Among other things purchased for the church were pianos for the Sunday school, at a cost of $866; chairs, at a cost of $541; and silverware for the kitchen. Furnishing the educational building was completed during the pastorate of the Reverend Russ. Also during his pastorate, the church was completely modernized. The seating capacity was doubled; a balcony was added at a cost of $1,500; pulpit furniture was bought; an addition was built on the front of the church to make space for Sunday school rooms; a steeple was added; and the exterior of the church was brick veneered and the grounds were beautified. The overall cost was $7,200.

In September 1957, a new baptistry was installed in the sanctuary. At that time, the floor was tiled and the front of the sanctuary was remodeled. A new and larger parsonage at 1004 Avalon Avenue was purchased.

Although Southside had existed as a church for just a few years, in June 1958, the members voted to start a new mission in Grassfield. The mission eventually became the Grassfield Baptist Church, which is still functioning today. Also in 1958, the property next to the church was purchased and the church members paid $8,500 for additional Sunday school rooms to be added to the church as annex I.

The Women's Missionary Union (WMU) had been successful for six years. The consensus was that the male members of the church should begin their own mission organization. As a result, in May 1959, the first brotherhood was begun.

The Sunday school was constantly growing, and again there was need for more classrooms. With that in mind, a four-family apartment house south of the church was acquired for $16,000. This became annex II.

After the busy and prosperous decade of the 1950s, the Southside Baptist Church continued to grow physically and spiritually in the 1960s. Between July 1960 and July 1962, there were at least five young men from the church who became licensed to preach. They were Nelson Odom, Edward Only, Larry Ingerman, Mike Cantrell and Frank Casper.

In February 1961, the Reverend Russell B. Cottingham became pastor of Southside church and the Grassfield Mission had grown to the point where it was ready to become a church. L.N. Howard was Grassfield's first pastor.

In 1962, Elva Owen began a long career as secretary of Southside Baptist Church. She was a dedicated employee for more than thirty-six years and retired in 1998. Well done, good and faithful servant.

Gradually more improvements were made to the church sanctuary and worship services. One improvement was the addition of an organ at a cost of $1,595.

It was on March 5, 1965, that Clark Wiseman became pastor of the church. He served faithfully for more than seven years.

On October 4, 1967, the nursery annex was sold to the Virginia State Highway Department and the proceeds were placed in the church building fund.

In 1968, Interstate 464 was built in front of the church. This had a major effect on the local community and on the church family. Three hundred and fifty homes were removed in order to accommodate the building of a right-of-way for the interstate. This project removed an entire neighborhood and changed the residential zoning to commercial and light industry. The right-of-way drastically decreased the visibility of the church complex and displaced many church families from their homes. Those families were forced to move to other parts of the city and, rather than travel to Southside, many changed their membership to churches closer to home. This project was directly responsible for a decrease in church attendance.

Three significant accomplishments were realized in 1969. First, in January, a church sign was installed on the front lawn to better identify the church to the community. Second, the church's first pictorial directory was published. Third, an important new ministry for the deaf was begun and led by William Mayes.

The beginning of the 1970s brought the beginning of yet another new ministry. In April 1970, a ministry for the mentally challenged was organized and led by Evelyn Vickers.

A new grand piano for use in the sanctuary was acquired at a cost of $1,795, and a second piano was bought for use in the fellowship hall at a cost of $800.

In 1972, Southside continued to modernize its facilities by installing air conditioners in the educational building and in a portion of the sanctuary. In August 1972, the parsonage on Avalon Avenue was sold for $17,500 and the house at 1128 Virginia Avenue was acquired for $42,500. The parsonage was then relocated to Virginia Avenue.

In May 1973, Bobbie Belcher began his ministry at Southside Church and went on to serve the members for more than five years. One of his early accomplishments was to hold Sunday evening services in Lakeside Park during the month of July.

The church members agreed to lend financial assistance to the Green Run Baptist Mission in order to assist members with their expenses. A decision was made to donate $100 per month to the mission through the year 1974. But in July 1974, the church members also undertook a mission project in the Greenbrier area of the city of Chesapeake. The financial assistance that had previously been provided to the Green Run mission was now contributed to the Greenbrier building fund.

In 1976, further changes were made to the sanctuary and grounds of the church. The annex I building was demolished. Any surplus items remaining as a result of the demolition were sold to the church members and the proceeds were contributed to the Greenbrier building fund. New carpet was installed in the front and center aisles of the sanctuary. At the same time, pew cushions were made and installed by Joe Richards. This was made possible by donations from the members of the church.

In December 1978, Harvey Myers became pastor of Southside Church and served until March 1982.

At the turn of the decade, improvements continued to the church, as carpeting was installed in the downstairs of the annex II building in September 1980.

The Greenbrier building-fund project came to an end in April 1981. Growth in Greenbrier had not materialized as was initially anticipated and a decision was made not to build a church there.

Thirteen years had passed since the first pictorial church directory had been published, so a second was printed in 1982. Also in 1982, the Reverend David Scrimshaw suggested that the members purchase a van for transportation on Sunday mornings and for special activities.

In October 1983, the church fellowship hall was named the Wiseman Hall in memory of the Reverend Clarke A. Wiseman who had served the Southside Church for more than seven years. His wife and son, Clarke, also had two stained-glass windows installed in his memory.

By vote of the church members, the land at Greenbrier was transferred to the Norfolk Baptist Association and the funds collected were donated to the association as well.

In October 1984, the Reverend Willis Switzer began a long and successful ministry at Southside. He went on to serve for eleven years—the longest pastorate of any pastor called to Southside Baptist Church. Upon retirement, he moved to Franklin.

Improvements have always been continuing at Southside, and in August 1985, new light fixtures were installed in the sanctuary. One year later, a new and improved sound system was acquired and installed at a cost of $4,200.

In April 1986, the Southside Church participated in the World Missions Conference for the first time. Another church ministry that was begun by Pastor Switzer, in August 1987, was the tape ministry for the homebound. This necessitated the purchase of a duplicator, tape player and tapes at a cost of $1,500.

In June 1988, Sunday school classes were moved from the annex II building to the educational building. The annex was not considered a sound structure and was demolished.

In May 1990, the church grounds were again improved and this time the parking lot was paved. Two hundred seventy-two new hymnals were purchased with donations made in memory or in honor of loved ones. In 1995, funds were raised and a church sign was erected on Bainbridge Boulevard at a cost of $2,800.

In July 1996, the present pastor, the Reverend Gregory Hensley, was called to serve the Southside Baptist Church. One of his first actions was to begin a new prayer breakfast. This time of prayer and fellowship is held on the first Tuesday of each month.

In January 1997, a new pictorial directory was published. Also in January, new air-conditioners were purchased for the sanctuary. During 1997 and 1998, the church constitution was revised and the sound system in the sanctuary was updated.

Many positive things were accomplished in October 1998. Southside officially joined the Church Resource Network (CRN), a local group of Chesapeake churches dedicated to meeting the needs of our community. About the same time, Southside Church began a soup kitchen. The soup kitchen, which is called Manna Ministries, is open every Wednesday.

Also in October, some changes were made to the sanctuary. The sanctuary and the fellowship hall received new carpet at a total cost of $4,647, and the woodwork in the front of the sanctuary was taken down to create more room at the altar.

The future of Southside Baptist Church looks promising. The new building committee submitted plans for a new construction to provide additional Sunday school rooms. When completed, this building will include three classrooms and a multipurpose room. At this time, the plans have been received from the architect. With the escalation in cost of materials and labor, the building may cost at least $100,000.

Southside has always been a mission-minded church, which has taken its congregation in new directions. In the summer of 2001, the church was able to send out two mission teams. A youth-mission team, led by Terri Nelson, went to South Boston, Virginia, for a week of mission work. A second team of six members traveled to Lithuania for two weeks of prayer-walking and street evangelism. In the summer of 2002, two more teams were sent out. Another youth-mission team ministered for a week in the mountains of Tennessee. Two church members returned to Lithuania to help lead a crusade. It is possible that at least one team may be able to go out from the church each summer.

Pastor Hensley has purchased a home of his own, and the former church parsonage on Virginia Avenue is currently being rented. The pastor now receives a housing allowance to assist him in making his house payments.

Two new committees have been formed: an evangelism committee will help the church members to discover new ways to reach the community, and a worship committee will look into ways of helping make the worship services more meaningful and worshipful. Also the choir director has incorporated a time for praise choruses in addition to hymns.

The ladies of the church meet every Tuesday to sew items such as quilts, hats and walker bags for those in need. Another exciting happening is that Southside is becoming more involved with other churches of the community in local ministry projects and special events. Several of the pastors in South Norfolk have begun a clergy fellowship, which has been helpful in coordinating special community activities such as Praise in the Park, a sunrise Easter service and a community Thanksgiving service.

The WMU Manna Ministry and all of the ongoing activities and ministries of the church have continued to be blessed. Southside began many years ago as an act of faith, and with full confidence, the members expect the best is yet to come. For with Christ, all things are possible.

Pastors of Southside Baptist Church:

Mr. W.L. Bristol	March 26, 1952–May 25, 1952
Rev. Andrew Johnson (interim)	June 1952–August 1952
Rev. Douglas Braun	August 28, 1952–July 5, 1953
Rev. Joseph N. Causey	November 17,1953–February 5, 1956
Rev. William Russ	March 5, 1956–February 13, 1961
Rev. Russell Cottingham	February 22, 1961–October 11, 1964
Rev. Paul Arline (interim)	November 22, 1964–December 1964
Rev. Arnold Bount (interim)	December 1964–February 1965
Rev. Clarke Wiseman	March 5, 1965–July 2, 1972
Rev. Yancey Elliott (interim)	August 1972–January 28, 1973
Rev. J.D. Seward (interim)	February 1973–April 1973
Bobbie H. Belcher	May 1, 1973–October 8, 1978
Rev. Harvey T. Myers	December 12, 1978–March 1982
Rev. William B. Pittard Jr. (interim)	March 1982–August 1982
Rev. David Scrimshaw	August 1982–February 1984
Rev. John Dearing (interim)	February 1984–October 1984
Rev. Willis H. Switzer	October 1984–December 1995
Rev. Gregory Hensley	July 1, 1996–present

When the Southside Baptist Church was duly organized in March 1952, there were sixty-four charter members, who, according to church records were as follows:

Archie Bass	Carl L. Cunningham	Wilson T. Sanders
Mrs. Anna Bass	Mrs. Lula Dailey	Mrs. Juanita Sanders
Conley Bass	Mrs. James Enson	Mrs. Beatrice Shettle
Stephen Bass	James Enson	Vernon Shettle
Charles Bright	Dolores Fischer	Mrs. Naomi Siechrist
D.C. Bright	Kermit Fischer	Ronnie Siechrist
Mrs. D.C. Bright	Mrs. Louise Fischer	George M. Smith
Mrs. Florentine Bright	Mrs. Iola Harper	J.S. Snow
Joseph Bright	Jesse W. Harper Jr.	Mrs. J.S. Snow
Susan Bright	Mrs. Marguerite Harper	E.S. Spann
Jerry Callahan	Mrs. Ella Hughes	Mrs Jean Ward
Mrs. Elsie Callahan	Mrs. Johnny Jackson	Robert Ward
Mrs. Gladys Casper	Mrs. Lettie Page	A.H. White
Mrs. Natalie Castellow	Mrs. Bernice Pillow	Mrs. Christine White
George Cornelius Sr.	Robert Pillow	Mrs Edna White
George Cornelius Jr.	Linda Pritchard	Enoch White
Mrs. Helen Cornelius	Mrs Ruth Pritchard	Jo Ann White
Ernest Lee Cowand	Mrs. Hallie Reed	Wayne White
Mrs. Grace Cowand	James Reed	W.B. White
Mrs. Nellie Cowand	Tommie Sanders Jr.	Mrs. W. B. White

Providence Christian Church

Although the old Providence Christian Church was not in South Norfolk, it was the mother church of what became the Rosemont Christian Church in August 1902.

A short history of the church was printed in the *Norfolk Ledger-Dispatch* on March 11, 1922. At that time, the old, abandoned and weather-beaten church still stood on the road leading out over the Campostella Bridge. It was one of the oldest churches in Norfolk County and its location was about four miles from Norfolk on the highway to Great Bridge. The land on which it was built was purchased with English pounds. Available information locates the sanctuary at the corner of the former Chair and Great Roads. In 1804, when the church was organized, Providence Road was referred to as Chair Road, and Campostella Road, which was the road to Great Bridge, was known as Great Road. Most likely Providence Road received its name from the church.

About the beginning of the nineteenth century, many ministers—viewing the increasing bitterness among the sects of the Christians in the state and believing it to be the result of a diversity of sentiment on doctrines of minor importance—felt seriously impressed with the idea that those troubles might be ended by an association upon principles more liberal than those hitherto pursued.

In the March 11, 1922 edition of the *Norfolk Ledger-Dispatch*, an early member of the

Providence Church wrote:

> *They contended that Christians might live in the utmost love and affection by allowing each other the privilege of thinking for themselves.*
>
> *They therefore united together under the common title Christian, which was given to the primitive Disciples at Antioch, taking for their rule of faith and practice the Holy Scriptures. Animated by the spirit of Christ, some ministers commenced laboring in St. Bride's Parish and "many found forgiveness for their complicated crimes." These, with Elder N.P. Tatem, who afterward became pastor, gave to each other the right hand of fellowship in 1804 and organized a church known as "Providence." From 1804 to 1817, records of the church conferences were not preserved.*
>
> *Delegates from the various churches of Tidewater met at Providence in May 1817 and formed a union, which became known as the Eastern Virginian Christian Conference.*
>
> *In May 1820, at a conference held at Republican Chapel, Isle of Wight County, Elder Nelson Miller, of Providence Church, was chosen a delegate to meet the brethren of the North in general conference, which was held at Windham, Connecticut, to seek to bring about a union between the brethren of the North and the South. This was accomplished and continued until the War Between the States. A conference of the churches of this section met in Portsmouth in May 1821.*

Records show that the membership of Providence Christian Church in 1821 was only thirty-six. In 1829, the membership was more than one hundred.

Pastors of the church from 1804 to 1902 were as follows:

N.P. Tatem, 1804–1829	W.H. Boykin, 1860–1862	R.A. Ricks, 1887–1890
Joshua Livesay, 1804–1829	P.S.P. Corbin, 1868–1869	J. Pressley Barrett, D.D., 1890–1896
Nelson Miller, 1804–1829	C.A. Apple, 1869–1870	W.S. Long, D.D., 1896–1898
Mills B. Barrett, 1830–1844	W.B. Wellons, 1870–1873	J.P. Barrett, D.D., 1898–1899
Joshua Livesay, 1845–1849	T.N. Manning, 1870–1873	J.W. Tickle, 1899–1900
William Tatem, 1849–1853	R.C. Tuck, 1874–1878	J.P. Barrett, 1900–1902
Nash Tatem, 1854–1855	H.H. Butler, 1878–1887	
Mills B. Barrett, 1856–1859	G.A. Beebe, 1878–1887	

Around 1900, most of the citizens of the Village of Portlock were attending the Providence Christian Church a few miles away. The roads that existed at that time were dirt, and travel was very difficult, especially in inclement weather. The local citizens began to think about how nice it would be to have a church in the community. With the organization of the Rosemont Christian Church on August 14, 1902, many of the members of the Providence Church transferred their membership to the new church in Portlock. Some of the other members of the Providence Christian Church became members of the Memorial Christian Temple at Thirty-third Street and Llewellyn Avenue in Norfolk.

Rosemont Christian Church

How did it start? In the beginning, arrangements were made to hold prayer meetings in the Portlock School, which was a one-room frame building. Sometime later, a store building owned by Charlie Tatem was rented. This structure stood across the street from the present Rosemont Church. Sunday school was held there on Sunday afternoons.

John L. Gibson offered to give a plot of ground, Edmund Christian loaned the group $560 in cash and the Rosemont Chapel was built. Adult members of the Sunday school who volunteered their services did much of the labor.

When the chapel was completed, the congregation assumed the debt due Christian. Gibson and his wife, Mary E. Gibson, gave a deed dated August 12, 1902, to the trustees of the Rosemont Chapel for a plot of ground fronting fifty feet on Bainbridge Boulevard and running one hundred feet back.

After careful consideration, it was decided that the church should unite with the Christian denomination. On August 14, 1902, the Rosemont Christian Church was organized by Dr. J. Pressley Barrett, who was pastor of the Memorial Christian Temple in Norfolk.

As is the case with most of the early churches, no one seems to know the whereabouts of the original church records. In all probability, none of the churches of that day had an office where records could be stored and, for safekeeping, a trusted member of the congregation would take them home. When the member or members died, the records were considered trash. In some cases, records were lost in moving from one church building to another. Sometimes records were destroyed in church fires, of which there many as the buildings were lighted with open flame long before electricity was discovered.

Early Members

John Luther Gibson, son of Peter Harrison and Sarah Trafton Gibson, was born at Bell Cross, North Carolina, on September 7, 1852. He was treasurer of the Sunday school before the Rosemont Christian Church was organized. He and his wife, Mary E. Gibson, donated the plot of land upon which the first church was erected. Gibson was one of the first deacons of the church. He suffered a stroke of paralysis but continued to attend church services in his wheelchair. He died on June 30, 1908, at the age of fifty-five years.

Mary Elizabeth Gibson, daughter of Francis and Elizabeth Glemming and wife of John Luther Gibson, was born in Norfolk County on May 7, 1862. Aunt Mary Lizzie was known and loved throughout the community as a friend to those in need. Whenever she heard of sickness or trouble, she went immediately to help. She found pleasure in helping wherever she could. Mary died on August 15, 1940, at the age of seventy-eight.

Gertrude Gibson Bondurant was born in Norfolk County on January 6, 1883. She was the daughter of John Luther and Mary Elizabeth Gibson. Gertrude was one of Rosemont's first members. She was faithful to her church and Sunday school, and was very active in the Woman's Missionary Society.

Elizabeth Llewellyn Gibson was born on November 15, 1853, in Norfolk, to George and

June Llewellyn. Betty was the wife of Benjamin F. Gibson. She was one of Rosemont's first members and was the first teacher of the Ladies Bible Class. The teaching of her class was her greatest joy, and she continued to teach Sunday school for more than fifty years. The Betty Gibson Bible Class was named in her memory. The cause of missions was another love of hers, and she continually prayed for them and supported them in any way she was able. Betty was dedicated to the church and played a large part spiritually and financially in every undertaking. She blessed every service with her presence until she became seriously ill. This devoted lady went to her heavenly home on November 4, 1938, just eleven days before her eighty-fifth birthday.

Laura Gibson Doughty, the daughter of Benjamin F. and Elizabeth L. Gibson, was born in Norfolk County on December 17, 1874. She became the wife of James B. Doughty. She was very interested in the building of the church and was one of its first Sunday school teachers, having taught in the "old store." The store was used as a place of worship before and during construction of the first church building. Laura died April 9, 1903, at the age of twenty-eight, less than a year after Rosemont was organized.

Benjamin Harrison Gibson, who was also known as Benjamin Harry Gibson, was born January 31, 1877, to Benjamin F. and Elizabeth L. Gibson. Benjamin Harry was very interested in organizing the church and was the one who suggested the name Rosemont. He became one of the first trustees, was a deacon of the church and held the offices of church clerk and choir director. Benjamin was involved in many activities outside the church. In 1896, he was captain of the school soldiers at the Berkley Military Institute in Berkley and later became the second mayor of the city of South Norfolk. With the exception of an eight-day span, Mayor Gibson served until his death on December 1, 1936. He lived in South Norfolk, and J.R. Williams Funeral Home on Chesapeake Avenue was in charge of his funeral arrangements. Benjamin Harrison Gibson was buried in the Portlock Cemetery.

Alice Marion Gibson was born in Norfolk County on Christmas Day 1875 to Benjamin F. and Elizabeth L. Gibson. Alice and O.S. Mills were married in the Rosemont Church on March 25, 1908. Dr. W.D. Howard performed the service. Alice was very interested in the church and worked in its Sunday school when it met in the "old store." She was the church's first organist and participated in choir work, which she enjoyed very much. In 1912, she helped organize the Woman's Missionary Society and served as its president for eight years. Later she was elected president again and served another eight years. Another of her church accomplishments was the organization of the Junior Missionary Society and she served as its sponsor for a number of years. In 1942, Alice's health began to fail and she was forced to give up many of her church activities.

Oliver Stanley Mills was born in Mount Morris, Michigan, on August 31, 1875. He was the son of James L. and Alice Stanley Mills. Oliver worked in the prayer meetings and the Sunday school that preceded the organization of the church. He was active in soliciting funds and materials for construction of the first church building. On March 25, 1908, he became the husband of Alice Marion Gibson. He worked with the church choir for forty years, taught the Sunday school primary class for about twenty-five years and served as a teacher for other classes. Oliver was one of the first trustees of the church and later became one of its deacons.

Benjamin Franklin Gibson was born on December 22, 1847, at Bell Cross, North Carolina. He served as a deacon in the Providence Christian Church for many years. When Rosemont Church was organized, he transferred his membership and became one of its first deacons. His health began to fail, and he was not able to be as active at Rosemont as he had been at the Providence Church. In spite of his poor health, he was deeply interested in the progress of the new church and helped support it financially. It was said that his greatest contribution was his fine Christian character. This rare gentleman died on February 19, 1910, at the age of sixty-two.

John Robert Morrison Sr., the son of Mary F. and Thomas Morrison, was born in Portsmouth on December 5, 1858. John was one of the original members of Rosemont and was the first Sunday school superintendent. He was also the first teacher of the Men's Bible Class. In later years, this class would become the John Morrison Bible Class in his honor. He was a senior deacon and trustee of the church from its beginning. He was faithful in his church attendance and consistent in his stewardship, performing his duties as God directed. John went to his heavenly home on November 7, 1941, at the age of eighty-two.

Nannie Rowland Morrison was born in Norfolk on May 19, 1859. She was the daughter of Fannie Bernard and J. Hamilton Rowland. She became the wife of John R. Morrison Sr. She was one of the original members of Rosemont and was interested in all phases of the church work. Nannie was totally deaf but attended church every Sunday with her husband and six children. Nannie died April 27, 1922.

Thomas O. Morrison was born in Norfolk County on January 1, 1883, to Nannie Rowland and John R. Morrison Sr. He was one of the original members of Rosemont and served faithfully for a number of years. When he married, he moved to New York.

Maude McCloud was one of the early members of Rosemont Church; however, because of ill health, she was unable to work in the church very long.

Sallye Rowland Morrison was born September 24, 1881, in Norfolk County. She was among the original members of the Rosemont Church who worshiped in the old schoolhouse and taught in the store building. Sallye was married to Harry E. Roane in the first church during the pastorate of J. William Barrett (1905–1907). The couple then moved to Norfolk for a number of years. Later, she returned to Rosemont Church and resumed her activities. After twenty-nine years of teaching in the Sunday school, the class was named the Sallye Roane Bible Class in her honor. She was active in and supported the Missionary Society. She served as its president for two years and was in charge of missionary programs in the Sunday school for a while.

Mary F. Morrison, the daughter of Nancy Culpepper and John Cotton, was born in Portsmouth on March 29, 1839. She was one of the original members of the Rosemont Church and was one of its first Sunday school teachers. Her class of boys held her in high esteem. Mary was a member of the Missionary Society. It was said that her testimonies at prayer meetings were full of love for God and the church. She died July 25, 1922. Her descendants continued to worship at Rosemont Church through the 1940s.

Pastors and Facts of History

Dr. J. Pressley Barrett organized the Rosemont Christian Church on August 14, 1902. He was pastor of the Memorial Christian Temple, Norfolk.

Fannie Maria Martineau assisted Barrett with his work at the temple and was interested in having a church organized in this community. She held prayer meetings in the homes of the members. When permission was obtained to hold prayer meetings in the schoolhouse, she helped with the work there.

John W. Harrell, son of Elkanah and Lula Harrell, was born in Whaleyville on October 18, 1870. He attended Elon College and Duke University. He was Rosemont's first pastor, giving part-time service. He was pastor of the First Christian Church, Portsmouth, at the same time. He served Rosemont from 1902 to 1905.

J. William Barrett, son of John William and Mary Holland Barrett, was born in Windsor on May 5, 1862. He received his theological training at Graham College and Berea College. He was Rosemont's second part-time pastor, preaching on Sunday afternoons. He was pastor at the Old Zion Christian Church at the same time. He served Rosemont from 1905 to 1907. He died on May 17, 1939.

William Daniel Harward, son of George W. and Margaret Harward, was born in Durham County, North Carolina, on December 7, 1870. He received his theological training at Elon College and the University of North Carolina. He was Rosemont's third pastor, giving part-time service. He served the church during 1907 and 1908.

Christopher C. Ryan (1908–1910), son of Shadrick M. and Mary Ann Ryan, was born in Anglaize County, Ohio, on February 3, 1875. He was Rosemont's fourth pastor. He gave part-time service, preaching on Sunday afternoons from April 1908 to November 1910. At that time, he was the full-time pastor at Memorial Christian Temple in Norfolk and did extension work for the Navy YMCA.

McDaniel Howsare, son of Joshua and Sara Elizabeth Howsare, was born in Chaneysville, Pennsylvania, on April 5, 1869. He received his theological training at Dickenson Seminary and Antioch College. He was Rosemont's fifth pastor, giving part-time service, while serving as pastor of the Memorial Christian Temple in Norfolk. He served Rosemont from 1910 to 1912.

The Reverend D.A. Keys was Rosemont's sixth pastor. He preached on Sunday afternoons from 1912 to 1914. At that time, he was pastor of the South Norfolk Christian Church. In 1914, he became Rosemont's first full-time pastor, serving until 1916. It was during his pastorate that the second church was built.

Warren H. Denison, son of Leonard A. and Alida J. Cook Denison, was born in Hunter's Land, New York, on June 18, 1870. He attended Starkey Seminary and Antioch College. He received his bachelor of arts in 1896 and his master of arts in 1897 from Antioch College. In 1908, he received an honorary degree of doctor of divinity from Elon College. He was Rosemont's seventh pastor, giving part-time service, while serving as pastor of the Memorial Christian Temple in Norfolk. He served Rosemont from 1916 to 1917.

G.O. Lankford was the son of John Wesley and Sarah Lane Lankford. He was born in Chipley, Georgia, on March 13, 1883. He received his bachelor of arts from Elon College in 1907. He was awarded his master of arts from Elon in 1909. He became Rosemont's eighth pastor, beginning his pastorate on March 18, 1917, and closing it on March 27, 1921. The first parsonage, located on McKinley Avenue, was purchased during his second year. The church ceased to receive missionary aid and became self-supporting. The membership of the church and Sunday school more than doubled during his pastorate.

Walter C. Hook graduated from Elon College in June 1921. Immediately after graduation he became Rosemont's ninth pastor. The Reverend Hook had served the church for only a short time when his physician informed him that he needed to move to a higher altitude. Citing his health, he resigned around October 1, 1922.

Benjamin Franklin Black was Rosemont's tenth pastor. He was the son of Charles and Joanna Black and was born in Keezletown, Virginia on January 24, 1871. He received bachelor and master of arts degrees from Elon College. The Reverend Black enlisted in the army as a chaplain in World War I. He went to France in September 1917 and returned to the United States in July 1918. He served Rosemont from 1922 to 1925. He died September 19, 1925, at the age of fifty-four.

Joseph Franklin Morgan was the eleventh pastor at Rosemont and served the church for nineteen years, from 1925 to 1944. He was the son of Joseph P. and Sarah Ann Morgan and was born in Moore County, North Carolina, on June 16, 1885. During the Reverend Morgan's ministry at Rosemont, he received 485 members and performed 290 marriages, an average of 16 per year.

In 1930 peanuts were sold to help raise money for a new church building. Oscar F. Smith, chairman of the building committee, guaranteed $8,000 and agreed to ask the conference to help. The third church building was erected in 1931. In 1936, Smith donated a new organ to the Rosemont Church. The following year, sidewalks were installed on the west side of the church and curbing on the north side at a cost of $178. In July 1939, a new brick parsonage was completed beside the church on Bainbridge Boulevard. It appears that the church prospered during the nineteen years that the Reverend Morgan served as its pastor.

Howard Scott Hardcastle became the twelfth pastor of the church on January 1, 1945. The Reverend Hardcastle was the son of William Scott and Mary Jones Hardcastle and was born in Cheswold, Delaware, on August 30, 1891. He received an artium baccalaureatus from Elon College in 1919 and a bachelor of divinity from Yale Divinity School in 1922. He was later awarded a doctor of divinity from Elon College. After serving Rosemont from 1945 to 1947, he accepted a call to become pastor of the First Congregational Christian Church in Newport News, Virginia.

Herbert George Councill was Rosemont's thirteenth minister. He was the son of Herbert George and Mary Davidson Councill and was born in Franklin on January 19, 1915. He was a graduate of the College of William and Mary, Class of 1936, and received a bachelor of divinity from Yale Divinity School in 1939. He served Rosemont from 1947 to 1951.

The Reverend Melvin Dollar became Rosemont's fourteenth pastor in 1952 and served until 1958. The fourth church building and Sunday school addition were completed in 1952. In 1954, the brick wall was added around the property.

Walstein Snyder served as Rosemont's fifteenth pastor from 1952 to 1960.

The Reverend Carroll Wayne Lewis, who arrived on March 1, 1961, became

Rosemont's sixteenth pastor. The Reverend Lewis was from Illinois and had served the Methodist churches. He received an artium baccalaureatus from Greenville College, in Greenville, Illinois, and a bachelor of divinity from the School of Theology at Emory University, Atlanta, Georgia, in March 1960. The Reverend Lewis served Methodist churches in Illinois for eight years and the Congregational Christian Church in Langdale, Alabama, for four years. He served at Rosemont until 1967.

Richard Prince served as Rosemont's seventeenth minister from 1968 to 1969.

Dr. Harold Harris was Rosemont's eighteenth pastor, arriving in 1969. When Dr. Harris resigned on October 26, 1971, Lieutenant Thomas served as interim pastor.

In 1974, Oscar Smith's son-in-law, Roy Charles, gave the last gift from the Oscar F. Smith Foundation. The amount of $2,000 was donated toward the purchase of buses. Also in 1974, the glass in all the sanctuary windows was removed and replaced with colored glass.

The Reverend Carroll Lewis returned to Rosemont to become its nineteenth pastor. He resigned in 1977. Don Chick then served as interim pastor.

In 1977, the church property on Franklin Street was purchased for $8,000.

In 1978, the Goodwin house was purchased and became the Rosemont Mission House. The cost of the property was $20,000.

In 1980, Rosemont withdrew from the Virginia Christian Church Fellowship.

Wallace Gabel came from Wisconsin in 1978 to become the church's twentieth minister. He resigned in 1981. It was also in 1981 that the church split. After that a large number of members went to Greenbrier and formed the Greenbrier Congregational Christian Church.

In 1981, Jim Hunnewell became the twenty-first minister. He resigned in 1983, preaching his last sermon on May 22.

Dr. Matthews served as interim pastor during the summer of 1983 and was then relieved by the Reverend Kello another interim pastor. During the cold winter of 1984, the parsonage was vacant and as a result of this the water pipes froze and burst, causing considerable damage to the property.

Also in 1984, the Reverend Carroll Lewis returned to Rosemont for the third time. He became the twenty-second pastor and served until February 1988.

In 1986, property was bought from the Viginian Railroad. In earlier years, railroad tracks connecting the Virginian Railroad to the Norfolk & Western Railroad ran through the area where the parking lot is today.

After the Reverend Lewis resigned, Don Chick served as interim pastor until the Reverend Mark B. Musser arrived in September 1988, to become the twenty-third minister of the church. He served until August 30, 1993.

The Reverend Henry Napier served as interim pastor until May 7, 1994, when the Reverend Robert Harrell arrived to become Rosemont's twenty-fourth pastor. The Reverends Harrell and Napier coauthored a book titled *Anniversary Devotions*. It was in 1997 that Rosemont Christian Church celebrated its ninety-fifth anniversary and Raleigh Heights Baptist Church celebrated its one hundredth anniversary. The Reverend Harrell resigned

The cow in this May 1926 picture is grazing in the field in front of the second Rosemont Christian Church. *Photo courtesy of Edna Weaver.*

The Rosemont Christian Church was organized on August 14, 1902. Most of the original congregation had been members of the old Providence Christian Church, which was about four miles from Norfolk on the road to Great Bridge. This is the third church building, which was constructed in 1931 during the ministry of the Reverend Joseph Franklin Morgan.

This picture shows Rosemont's fourth church building. It was constructed in 1953 at a cost of approximately $112,000.

in October 1997, and the Reverend Napier once again became interim pastor.

On June 1, 1998, the Reverend James Dunn became the twenty-fifth pastor of the church. He served until September 2000, when the Reverend Napier served as interim pastor for the third time.

On October 12, 2001, Dr. John T. Cornette became the twenty-sixth minister of Rosemont Christian Church. He was pastor when Rosemont celebrated its one hundredth anniversary in 2002 but has since resigned. At Rosemont's anniversary celebrations on August 11, 2002, the Reverend Carroll Lewis, who served the church on three occasions, was the guest speaker.

At the time of this writing, the Reverend Jerry Kilyk was serving the Rosemont Church.

The church has a long and colorful past, and throughout the years, its growth has coincided with that of the local community. A more in-depth history of Rosemont Church can be found by reading the *History of Rosemont Christian Church Celebrating 100 Years 1902–2002*.

Raleigh Heights Baptist Church

This history of Raleigh Heights Baptist Church is due to the efforts of the Reverend Henry V. Napier who was called to the church in November 1963. Napier served faithfully until his retirement in December 1988. After his retirement, he served both Raleigh Heights and Rosemont Churches as interim pastor and holds the title of interim pastor emeritus of the Rosemont Christian Church.

As is the case with many of the early churches, the records of Raleigh Heights Baptist

Church from its beginning until 1922 were destroyed by fire. In this case, the fire was at the home of a Mr. Jones. As a result of this tragedy, much of the history and facts about the early church and its pastors came from people who have since passed on to their reward.

Several pastors and supply pastors served the church between 1912 and 1922. The only name that has not slipped into the past is that of Pastor Ramsey. All the others remain buried in that part of the brain that is filled with cobwebs.

According to Norfolk County Common Law book 17, page 153, the church's official beginning was November 10, 1897. Although it is quite possible that around 1895 a group of men living in the Dozier's Corner community began to think about a church closer to their homes. Most of them were members of the new Baptist church in the village of South Norfolk, which was about three miles away. The road to the church was not much more than a dirt path, and the only available transportation was the family horse and wagon. Under normal circumstances, the trip was rough, but it became even more so during inclement weather.

Samuel O'Neal, Benjamin Phillips, Bill Berry and R. McClain met to discuss the matter. They came to the conclusion that there would be at least fourteen families interested in the formation of a new church. As with every new project or program, there were questions that needed to be answered. The two most important were: where would they meet and where would they find a preacher? Someone suggested contacting Pastor Lancaster down in Gilmerton. Norman Dozier owned an old log barn that he was not using and offered it as meeting place.

The barn was cleaned and a wood-burning stove was installed. Log benches were brought in for the parishioners to use for seating. A.J. Truitt gave a table and a Mr. Gleming donated a desk to be used by the preacher. All this having been accomplished, the Broadway Baptist Mission School came into existence. W.J. Berry, Benjamin Phillips and Samuel O'Neal were appointed to serve as its trustees.

In 1897, A.J. and Julia Truitt offered a piece of land for use by the church so long as it was used for a church. When the land was no longer used for a church, it was to revert back to the Truitts; church members would have the right to remove any buildings that they may have built on the property. The deed was recorded in the Circuit Court of Norfolk County on December 10, 1897.

In the spring of 1898 a church raising was held and a one-room building was erected. The Sunday after its completion, it was dedicated with about forty-five people present.

Pastor Lancaster who had been serving the congregation announced that he could not continue. At that time, the church called Pastor Robertson, who promised to supply until the church members could find a regular minister. He and other supply speakers kept the church going until the Reverend Quinton Clarence Davis Sr. was called in 1901. Mr. Davis remained until 1906.

It was about this time that a new road to Portlock was built and land in the village became available for development. Because of its closeness to industrial Money Point and the shipping lanes, small businesses began to thrive. People began to leave Dozier's Corner and move to Portlock so they could be near their businesses and places of work. As they moved, they wanted to take their church with them. A place to meet was needed, and the old one-room Portlock School was made available to the church. The Reverend William M. Black of the South Norfolk Baptist Church assisted in getting the congregation settled in the school. Many of the members wanted to change the church name to Portlock Baptist Church, but these efforts failed.

In 1912, there were not enough members at Dozier's Corner to continue operating the church. The entire membership was moved and the Broadway Baptist Mission School became the Broadway Church of Portlock. The land given by the Truitts reverted back to them, and the one-room building was removed to the Dozier home.

With the steady growth in attendance, it became apparent that a proper building was needed. The members were asked to help find a suitable location to erect a church.

According to information passed down through the years, J.W. Leafe—pastor of the Court Street Baptist Church, in Portsmouth and father of Nellie Day—was riding around Portlock looking at property. As a real-estate agent and preacher, Leafe was interested in the area north of Freeman Avenue and west of Bainbridge Boulevard. For some reason, he made the statement that a good name for the area would be Raleigh Heights. The name caught on, and the area became known as Raleigh Heights and for many of us it still is known as Raleigh Heights.

Several builders were responsible for developing the area. Among them were Elmer Gordon and Simeon Leary, who had been longtime residents of Portlock. They would eventually develop other parts of the village. Negotiations were soon begun by the church members to purchase a lot at the corner of First Street (later named Miles Street) and Crowell Avenue. On December 29, 1916, a deed was recorded conveying property from the Raleigh Heights Development Corporation to E.S. Leary, R.B. Dozier and Emmett McClain, trustees of the Broadway Church. The property is described as being in the Washington Magisterial District of Norfolk County, Virginia.

A building was completed and dedicated in 1918. It consisted of a sanctuary with two rooms across the back. Curtains were used to divide the sanctuary for use as classrooms. W.S. O'Neal was elected the first Sunday school director, and his daughter Violet, became the pianist for the Sunday school and church. Mr. Burfoot ministered in the new building until J.W. Byrum was called in April 1922. Byrum stayed until September of that year.

The ladies of the church formed the Ladies Aide Society in 1917. Their meetings were held in Mrs. W.S. O'Neal's home, which was located at the southwest corner of Bainbridge Boulevard and Freeman Avenue (where Hardee's stands today). Eleanor Wilson, a member of the Berkley Avenue Baptist Church, helped the ladies to organize the society. Among those present were Mrs. O'Neal, Florrie Gordon, Gladys Leary, Mrs. Riggs and Carrie Edmonds. Mrs. O'Neal was the first president, and Mrs. Gordon was secretary.

The Ladies Aide Society held bake sales, suppers, etc. to help furnish the new church building. With this money, the ladies bought hymnbooks, carpet and other furnishings.

After J.W. Byrum left as pastor in September 1922, Thomas E. Boarde served from May 1923 until May 1926. The next pastor was C.E. Anderson, who came in June 1926 and stayed until April 1930.

For several years, the members felt that the name Broadway Baptist Church did not reflect the area in which the church was located. As the building was in the Raleigh Heights residential area, it was decided that the church should take the name of the community. After submitting the proper application, the name of the church was changed to Raleigh Heights Baptist Church. The new name became effective March 7, 1928, and the court appointed W.M. Edmonds and J.Y. Jones trustees.

The Reverend Ira Harrell was called in July 1930. He agreed to serve with the understanding that he would be preaching in other churches as the occasion arose. It was the beginning of the Great Depression, and the church was feeling the financial pinch. On July 2, 1932, the members voted to notify the Reverend Harrell that they could no longer afford to pay him. Upon receiving this notification and needing to earn a living, he packed his belongings and left in August. On Sundays, from then until 1934, supply preachers filled in when one was available. A preacher by the name of Everett agreed to supply for $10 per Sunday. On August 12, 1934, because of a lack of funds, it was decided to discontinue services. When finances improved, the Reverend R. Gerald Moore from Lake Drummond Baptist Church was called. He served until 1935.

On June 3, 1937, the Reverend Guy Foster was installed as pastor of the church. He remained until 1947. The Reverend Ivan Hart was called in 1947. He became very active in community affairs, especially the Portlock Volunteer Fire Department. His work with the fire department led at least one member of the church to remark that if he was going to be a fireman, let him stop preaching. He resigned in 1950. (Note: If my memory serves me correctly, I think Pastor Hart enlisted in the U.S. Army Chaplain Corp).

It was in 1950 that the Reverend Junis Foster Sr. was called (he was not related to the Reverend Guy Foster who served from 1937 to 1947). The Reverend Junis Foster had been active in the establishment of the DeBaum Baptist Church. This church is located just a few blocks from where the Broadway Mission School began in 1895. Foster saw Chester Phelps, a longtime resident, enter the ministry and ordained him in 1958. The Reverend Foster remained until April 1963.

The City of South Norfolk annexed the town of Portlock in 1951, and when South Norfolk merged with Norfolk County in 1963, the area became a part of the City of Chesapeake. The Reverend Junis Foster Sr. was the last minister of Raleigh Heights Baptist Church before the merger took place on January 1, 1963.

In November 1963, the Reverend Henry V. Napier was called and served the Raleigh Heights Church until December 1988. After twenty-five years at Raleigh Heights, the Reverend Napier retired.

In August 1989, after several months of supply preaching by the Reverend Paul Moore, the Reverend Paul Menard came to Raleigh Heights from Knotts Island, North Carolina. Menard served for about three years before resigning. Once again the pulpit was filled with supply pastors until the Reverend Penny Wilson arrived. The current pastor is the Reverend James (Jim) Thompson.

Portlock United Methodist Church

According to records, the official beginning of Raleigh Heights Baptist Church was on November 10, 1897. It is most probable, however, that about fifteen families began holding Bible study at I.R. Dozier's old log barn in 1895. On December 29, 1916, a deed was recorded that conveyed property from the Raleigh Heights Development Corporation to the trustees of the church. A building was completed on that property and was dedicated in 1918.

The Portlock United Methodist Church had its beginning in 1923 under the ministry of W. Farley Powers. Its first meeting place was the Portlock School on Bainbridge Boulevard. About two years later, a building was constructed on Edgewood Avenue. The first service in the new church was conducted May 3, 1925, and two weeks later— on May 17, 1925—the first revival meetings began. The revival lasted two weeks, and during that time, seventeen of the nineteen charter members joined the church. Mr. and Mrs. S.H. Johnston requested that the books remain open until they made a decision whether to move their membership. They wanted to become charter members but were afraid the new church might not stand. They finally decided to risk it and become members.

When plans were made to build the first sanctuary, money was in short supply and there wasn't any collateral available for a loan. Mr. and Mrs. John Pearce mortgaged their home so the church could receive construction money. Daniel B. Rishel donated a large amount of the materials that went into the church. The pews from the old Gilmerton Methodist Church were brought to Portlock to help furnish it.

In 1941, during the ministry of the Reverend Eugene Rawlings, the church building was remodeled and necessary repairs were accomplished. Five Sunday-school classrooms were provided. In 1947, additional improvements were made. The Women's Society

The building now occupied by the Bible Baptist Church was, at one time, the home of Portlock United Methodist Church. The Methodist church moved to a new sanctuary in 1969.

The Portlock United Methodist Church had its start in 1923 under the ministry of W. Farley Powers. The congregation met in a four-room schoolhouse on Bainbridge Boulevard, until the church building was constructed on Edgewood Avenue. The first service in the little building was conducted May 3, 1925. In 1968, ground was broken for the building in this picture. A service of consecration was held on September 7, 1969.

of Christian Service furnished the new kitchen, and two restrooms were added. The heating facilities were improved, a kneeling pad was added and a Hammond Spinet organ was installed.

In 1950, during the ministry of the Reverend Henry T. Logsdon, a parsonage was purchased on the adjacent property. Once again the Women's Society of Christian Service came to the rescue and furnished the parsonage. In 1954, the church was redecorated inside and improvements were made to the outside. It was about this time that property on Bainbridge Boulevard was purchased. The Reverend William N. Colton Jr., the first full-time pastor, was then minister of the church.

In 1958, during the ministry of the Reverend Raymond Carson, an educational building that contained six classrooms and a pastor's study was erected. Two years later, ground was broken for a new brick parsonage on Redstart Avenue and members of the church did most of the work. In 1968, ground was broken at the property on Bainbridge Boulevard for a sanctuary and educational building. The educational building included eight classrooms and a study for the minister. A service of consecration was held September 7, 1969. The construction of the sanctuary and educational building on Bainbridge Boulevard was accomplished during the ministry of Pastor James B. Grimmer. Additional work to the interior of the educational building was completed in 1974.

The Portlock Methodist Church celebrated its fiftieth anniversary on May 4, 1975. There were seven surviving charter members and six were able to attend—William F. Edwards, Sarah Edwards Parker, Roxie Fentress, Mattie Pearce Voliva, Ada Pearce Sawyer and Annie Pearce Sawyer. Lois Odell Downing was not able to attend. Each charter member was presented with a certificate commemorating the occasion. The Reverend W. Farley Powers, the church's first minister, spoke about the church and its beginning. Dr. Harry W. Backhus III, Norfolk District superintendent, delivered the sermon.

Throughout the years, several organizations have been established in the church and although they have gone through periods of change in name and character, most still exist today. Among them is the Ladies Aid Society, which became the Women's Missionary Society, then the Women's Society of Christian Service and now it is the United Methodist Women. What was the Epworth League is now known as the United Methodist Youth Fellowship.

Cub Scout Pack 460 was organized in 1966. In 1968, Boy Scout Troop 460 was established and in 1971, Girl Scout Troop 48 was formed. It was in 1976 that final steps were taken to complete the Scout building, which is located on a lot behind the church. Recently, because of a lack of membership and attendance, the Boy Scout troop was disbanded. A church fellowship hall has been built on the property.

The original nineteen members of Portlock United Methodist Church were:

Mr. John Wesley Pearce	Mrs. S.H. Johnston
Mrs. John Wesley Pearce (Mary)	Mrs. Earl Sawyer (Annie)
Mrs. W.C. Voliva (Mattie)	Mrs. R.O. Sawyer (Ada)
Mr. J.J. Brown	Mr. William M. Edwards
Mrs. A.L. Fentress (Roxie)	Mrs. William M. Edwards
Mr. William F. Edwards	Mrs. Winslow Downing (Lois)
Mrs. Winona Blanchard	Mr. Frank C. Odell
Mr. Daniel B. Rishel	Mrs. Frank C. Odell
Mrs. Robert I. Evans Sr. (Maude)	Mrs. Sarah Parker
Mr. S.H. Johnston	

Pastors of Portlock Methodist Church (1925–2004)

W. Farley Powers, 1925–1927

M.S. Forbes, 1927–1928

C.J. Pair, 1928–1930

J.R. Timberlake, 1930–1931

J.E. Brooks, 1931–1932

W.H. Hantzmon, 1932–1938

G.C. Flora (student), 1938 (2 months)

J. William Hough (student), 1938 (4 months)

Henry T. Logsdon, 1938–1940

Eugene W. Rawlings, 1940–1941

John W. Hobbs, 1941–1946

Leroy W. Davis, 1946–1950

Henry T. Logsdon (second time), 1950–1954

William N. Colton Jr., 1954–1958

Raymond P. Carson, 1958–1959

W. Ware Trent, 1959–1960

Irwin G. Cough, 1960–1964

Lewis H. Morgan, 1964–1965

Malcome L. Yaple, 1965–1967

James B. Grimmer, 1967–1970

Robert F. Cofield Jr., 1970–1978

Samuel S. Cole, 1978–1979

John B. Morris,1979–1981

John M. Andrews, 1981–1984

Albert L. Crockett, 1984–1989

Robert H. Woodfin, 1989–1991

Art Myers, 1991–1993

Ellen Comstock, 1993–1998

John Hayes, 1998–2002

Robert M. Pihlcrantz, 2002–present

Bethel Assembly of God

In July 1926, Myrtle Chambers, an evangelist, held services in a tent on the northeast corner of Bainbridge Boulevard and Poindexter Street. As a result of those meetings, the South Norfolk Assembly of God was born. Its first place of worship was Mrs. W.D. Todd's vacant building, which had served as an automobile repair shop. The location was across the street from where the tent meetings had been held. Delk Todd was faithful to the church and contributed many hours to its upkeep. In the winter

Members of the South Norfolk Assembly of God met in this converted garage at the intersection of Bainbridge Boulevard and Poindexter Street in 1930 with their pastor, J.M. Oliver. The church later became the Bethel Assembly of God, and is now located at the corner of Decatur and Grady Streets. *Photo courtesy of Ray White.*

months, he could be relied upon to build the fire in order that the building would be comfortable for the services. The Reverend O.M. Hilburn was pastor of the church in its formative years.

The congregation met on Bainbridge Boulevard for almost five years. During this time, plans were made to obtain property suitable for construction of a church building. Ira Johnson of the Tunis-Johnson Lumber Company, owned most of the land bounded by B Street, Poindexter Street, Bainbridge Boulevard and the Belt Line Railroad. Johnson agreed to donate lots on the northwest corner of Decatur and Grady Streets with the stipulation that they be used for the erection of a church. Soon after the agreement had been signed, construction began. Most of the building materials were donated. Arthur Dowdy, a charter member, approached the proper authorities at the Norfolk Navy Yard, and as a result of his efforts, bricks from a demolished smokestack were donated. The bricks were collected and cleaned by the men, women and children of the church. The lumber was donated by a mission in Portsmouth, and the church members and other friendly citizens of South Norfolk furnished the labor. Eventually the church was completed at a cost of $15,000, which was $10,000 less than the original estimated cost. It was about this time that the name was changed to the Bethel Assembly of God. A picture of the original building taken in 1930 shows a sign over the entrance designating it as the South Norfolk Assembly of God and J.M. Oliver as its pastor.

On March 29, 1931, the congregation of 164 met at the building on Bainbridge Boulevard where the Reverend Oliver led them in prayer. After a brief meeting, the members reportedly lined up four abreast and marched to the new church while singing, "We're Marching to Zion" and "Jesus Never Fails." Pastor Oliver's first sermon in the

This is the Bethel Assembly of God at the corner of Decatur and Grady Streets. In this image the church does not have a steeple and the education building has a flat roof. *Photo courtesy of Richard Spratley.*

new church was taken from Judges, chapter 17. The offerings on that first Sunday were Sunday school $10.58, the morning worship $40 and the evening service $8.34—for a total of $58.92.

April 5, 1931, was dedication Sunday; the sermon was delivered by the Reverend Harry V. Schaeffer, secretary of the Potomac District Council of the Assemblies of God, Washington, D.C. The offering that day totaled $103.64—the largest offering of the year. The membership continued to grow, and sometime before 1944, dormers were added to make space for Sunday-school classes. During the ministry of Pastor Wigfield—which ran from 1944 to August 1956—the dormers were removed and an addition was added on the rear of the church. In 1958 during the ministry of the Reverend Hugh Mason—from August 8, 1956 to April 12, 1972—a second addition was constructed and the church was remodeled.

In its more than seventy-eight years, Bethel has contributed to the organization and building of churches in Suffolk, Virginia Beach, Franklin and Great Bridge. The church has also produced many Christian workers and missionaries.

According to church records, the following people are considered to be charter members:

R.C. Ashley	Mr. and Mrs. Jesse Hilburn
Mr. and Mrs. George Baker	Rachel Hogshire
Maggie Balance	S.E. Hollowell
Ruby Boyce	Mr. and Mrs. William L. Johnson
Mr. and Mrs. John Burden	Blanch Lawton (White)
Sarah Burges	Louise Marshall (Evangelist)
A.B. Carlye	Mr. and Mrs. Jesse McCloud
Mr. and Mrs. E.F. Cartwright	M.C. Parker
Laura Casper	Della Robertson
Louise Castello (Evangelist)	Mr. and Mrs. Rodgerson
Rosa Cooper	Mr. and Mrs. L.C. Sawyer
Hattie Dale	Daisy Singleton
J. Emma Dale	Bennie Smith
Mr. and Mrs. Arthur Dowdy	Mr. and Mrs. David Smith
F.C. Dowdy	Sarah Elizabeth Snow
Sister Dunlow	Mae Todd
J.W. Evans	J.W. Trueblood
Mr. and Mrs. J.E. Gwyn	Jodie White
Tommie Harrell	Mr. and Mrs. R.M. White
Minnie Hebberbe	Mr. and Mrs. B.B. Young

Among the early children of the church were:

Mildred, Blanch and
Mahala Baker (Higginbotham)
Helen and Aleene Dowdy

Mildred and Naomi Dowdy
Dorothy Gwynn (Beiler)
T.E. Gwynn Jr.

Marion White
Rudolph and Ray White
Thelma White (Hardesty)

The ministers who have served the South Norfolk/Bethel Assembly of God since 1926 are as follows:

O.M. Hilburn	
H.O. Chestnut	
J.M. Oliver	
John Slye	Superintendent of North Carolina District
Stanley Berg	1937–summer of 1938
Augustus Kramer	October 1938–January 1939
E. Welford	1939–August 1943
T. H. Spence	August 1943–September 1944 (Superindentent of Alabama District)
Kelly Wigfield	September 1944–August 1956 (Superindentent of Potomic District)
Hugh Mason	August 8, 1956–April 12, 1972
Orville K. Thomas	July 6, 1972–March 1, 1977
Daniel Hare	August 1, 1977–December 1978
Hugh Mullen	January 1979–October 1982
Joel Mathisen	January 1, 1983–June 1986
George C. Colston	July 1986–August 1988
David Hargis	September 1988–February 1990
Stanley Turnbull	May 1990–June 1994
Kenneth Cates	December 1, 1994–June 30, 1995
Arthur Slye*	October 1, 1995–served about three years
Rev. Todd Hodges	Current pastor

South Norfolk Pentecostal Holiness Church

*He was the grandson of the Reverend John Slye who served as the fourth pastor of the church.

In October 1912, the South Norfolk Pentecostal Holiness Church was organized with twenty-six charter members. The Reverend F.W. Gammon conducted a tent meeting on property near the corner of Liberty and Commerce Streets. He then organized the church and became its first pastor. Information has it that the congregation met in a fish house where scrubbed fish boxes were used for seats. Another version has the congregation worshipping in a store building until 1913, at which time members began meeting in a frame tabernacle that had been erected on the same land where the tent meeting had taken place. In 1933, the tabernacle was replaced by a frame building, which became the first unit of the structure that eventually occupied the

This later image shows the building as it was in the year 2002. At that time the steeple was a recent addition and the leaky flat roof on the education building had been replaced with a slanted one. *Photo courtesy of Richard Spratley.*

land at the corner of Liberty and Commerce Streets. Additional room for expansion was provided in 1947 with the purchase of the corner lot adjoining the church. In 1949, the sanctuary was enlarged and an ell was added for an educational building. The entrance and steeple were remodeled and the entire building was brick-veneered in 1956.

The church remained at 1608 Liberty Street until the 1970s. It was then that a new complex was built at 1313 Burns Street and the South Norfolk Pentecostal Holiness Church became the Chesapeake First Pentecostal Holiness Church.

In the early years of the church, baptisms were carried out in the Southern Branch of the Elizabeth River, near the Ford Motor Company plant. The church also had an orchestra that performed for the congregation; Claude McPherson was the bandmaster.

In 1957, there were four charter members still in the church: Herbert Niles, H.A. Tarkenton Sr., Della Robeson and J.C. Brothers.

The South Norfolk/First Chesapeake Pentecostal Holiness Church is now more than ninety-two years old. In that period of time, it has had seventeen pastors. In reviewing the histories of the early churches of South Norfolk, that is some kind of record. It seems that many of the local churches changed pastors every two or three years.

The known ministers of the church were:

F.W. Gammon, 1912–1917

J.F. Epps

W.J. Noble

O.M. Hilburn

H.T. Spence

Bishop J.A. Synon, served two years

W.L. Butler

H.B. Johnson

J.H. Mashburn

Arthur D. Beacham

Harry E. Wood, served 16 years

Douglas Young

Pastor Mayor, served 13 years

Wayne Sawyer

Hauns Hess

Tim Minor

Larry Lane, present pastor

CHAPTER VI

LOCAL CEMETERIES

THROUGHOUT THE EARLY YEARS WHEN most of the area was farmland, there were family cemeteries. Usually a section of the farm was reserved as a final resting place for members of the family. Some churchyards also served as burial grounds. A few of those early graves have been moved to large city cemeteries. The number of most unlikely places where tombstones have been found is quite surprising. For example, there are tombstones in the woods behind Rutgers Avenue—this land was owned by Nathaniel Portlock (1773–1841) and later by his son Tapely Portlock (1809–1862). There were additional graves in the wooded area behind Joseph Avenue. Today a housing development called Varsity Estates is sitting on that land. Some of the local citizens speak of having seen graves on Edgewood Avenue and Monticello Street.

On July 21,1954, a deed of gift was made between the City of South Norfolk and the Commonwealth of Virginia, Department of Military Affairs. This gift was a five-and-a-half acre parcel of land to be used for construction of the armory on Bainbridge Boulevard. The land included one acre that had never been laid off or surveyed. On this piece of land was a family cemetery, which measured fifteen feet by twenty feet. This cemetery was vacated, and the remains were transferred from the site. This may have been the George family burying ground. The graves on the Franklin Street property in Portlock, which once belonged to the Spain family, may be those of children.

It was around 1918 that the young daughter of the Dean family died from severe burns. The family was living in what would become the 1000 block of Jackson Street. She was buried in the front yard; however, a city ordinance eventually required that the remains be moved from the residential area. Available information states that the body was removed to the Riverside Cemetery on Indian River Road.

The Massenburg Cemetery was relocated to make way for the extension of Rodgers Street and the construction of the Oscar F. Smith School campus. The South Norfolk City Council adopted a resolution on December 17, 1953, authorizing the abandonment, removal or transfer of an unused and neglected burying ground in the City of South Norfolk. The property had been acquired by the City of South Norfolk on April 4, 1950, from the Commonwealth of Virginia by deed. Apparently when the last member of the Massenburg family died, there wasn't a will and the property reverted to the state. A description of the property reads as follows: Parcel No.1 containing 13.23 acres more or less, being duly recorded in deed book 984, page 399 in the clerk's office of the Circuit Court of Norfolk county (now located in the City of Chesapeake).

Other local cemeteries of historical importance are the Portlock Cemetery, which dates to the year 1747, and the Gibson Family Cemetery, which was originated in 1905. There are two other cemeteries in the Portlock area: one is located at the corner of Franklin Street and Kay Avenue, and the other is the Workmen's Circle, a Jewish cemetery on Railroad Avenue.

Massenburg Cemetery: 1731–

The Massenburg Cemetery was located in a section remembered by longtime residents of the South Norfolk and Portlock areas as Big Hill. The original site of the eighteenth-century cemetery was in the vicinity of the Rodgers Street entrance to the Oscar F. Smith High School athletic field. In my youth, there wasn't a railroad crossing at what later became an extension of Rodgers Street; instead, there was a crossing at Jackson Street. Sunday afternoons required a bicycle trip in the woods and a visit to the Massenburg Cemetery at Big Hill. This was a real must in early December for the trees were full of mistletoe, which was gathered by either climbing the trees or shooting the commodity down. Mistletoe brought a fair price at the Norfolk City Market. Other residents out for a Sunday afternoon walk would visit the cemetery, talk about the mysterious past and share stories of buried treasures; there was one story about the grave of a giant, but we were never able to find it.

Throughout the years, the tombstones became weather beaten and broken. Others were uprooted by horses and cows; it seems that the local farmers used the tombstones as hitching posts. In early 1955, the remains of the long-dead southsiders were boxed and moved to another site, about three hundred yards due east to make possible the continuation of Rodgers Street and construction of the Oscar F. Smith stadium. The area in the vicinity of the new site had, in earlier times, served as the city dump. The land was later filled and leveled.

The City of South Norfolk hired the Francis A. Gay Funeral Home to remove the remains and inter them again in the new graves. Many of the original graves were almost two hundred years old, and the dig yielded only a few bones and small pieces of wood that may have been the remains of a coffin or coffins. By that time, there were only five tombstones remaining in the cemetery. The new burying ground was originally set up using the individual stones. These were later replaced with a single marker. One side of the marker reads:

Massenburgh Cemetery, Interments at This Location During Period 1731 – 1859, Bodies Interred Here Include:

Mary Whiddon, 1739 – 1818
Elizabeth M. Peters, dates unknown
Elizabeth Whiddon, 1737 – 1757
W. Cunningham, 1786 – 1807
Elizabeth Corprew, 1722 – 1799

When the Massenburg Cemetery was moved from its original location, there were only five tombstones remaining, and the information was engraved on this side of the marker. (picture left) The Massenburg Cemetery was located in a section remembered by longtime residents of the South Norfolk and Portlock areas as Big Hill. During my youth, it was the final resting place of approximately two dozen early citizens of the area. The information on this side of the marker (pictured right) states that the cemetery was abandoned during the Civil War, but this is not accurate. William H. Etheridge, Elton Williamson and Thomas Williamson signed Anne Frances Tatem's last will and testament on July 18, 1867. Anne lived another nine years, died on August 16, 1876, and was buried in the Massenburg Cemetery. The Civil War ended eleven years before her death, so apparently the cemetery was abandoned sometime after 1876. It was probably in use from 1731 until that time.

The reverse side inscription states:

THIS IS THE SITE OF
THE OLD MASSENBURGH CEMETERY,
ONE OF THE OLDEST CEMETERIES IN THE AREA.
THE SITE WAS ABANDONED DURING THE CIVIL WAR.

ERECTED BY THE
SOUTH NORFOLK CITY
SCHOOL BOARD

Some of the inscription information above is in error. Anne Frances Tatem's last will and testament was signed and witnessed by William H. Etheridge, Elton Williamson and Thomas Williamson on July 18, 1867. Anne lived another nine years. She died on August 16, 1876, and was buried in the Massenburg Cemetery. The Civil War had ended more than eleven years before her death. Apparently, the cemetery was abandoned sometime after 1876—not during the Civil War. With this in mind, it is difficult to determine the correct period of interments.

The following is a listing of known burials that were in the Massenburg Cemetery. Most likely there were others but to my knowledge, this is the only existing list.

John Whiddon / Born September 19, 1730 / Died April 14, 1796 / Age 66 years, 5 mos. 3 days

Elizabeth Whiddon / Wife of John Whiddon / Born 1737 / Died 1767 [The stone marker at the new site indicates that Elizabeth died in 1757 instead of 1767. One thing for certain is that her life was very short.]

Mary Whiddon / Who departed this life / The 13th of January 1818 / Age 78

Abigail Whiddon / Died 1774 / Age 13 months

Joshus Corprew Whiddon / Born 1775 / Age 13 months

Thomas W. Gatewood/ Born 1758 / Died 1810

In memory of John Peters / Who departed this life / Oct. 7, 1796 / Age 35 years

In memory of Martha C. Camp / Daughter of John Camp & Anne / his wife / Died Oct. 12, 1816 / Age 17 years

To the memory of Mrs. / Elizabeth Corprew / who was born the 10th / Day of June 1722 and / Departed this life the 7th day of Oct. 1799

Here lies the remains / Of Susanna Whiddon / Died 1776 Age 18 mos.

Thomas Gatewood Candish / who departed this life / on the 22nd day of July / 1819 – 23 mos.

In memory of / Elizabeth Tucker Peters / Daughter of John & Anne / Peters who departed / this life on the 23rd day of Sept. 1795 / Age 9 years & 2 months

Sacred to the memory of / Mrs. Anna Camp, wife of / John Camp and daughter / Of John & Mary Whiddon / who departed this life / the 31st day of May 1816 / Age 27 years

William W. Cunningham / died July 29, 1807 / Age 21 years

Sacred to the memory of / Elizabeth Cunningham / Relict of the late Capt. / William Cunningham, who / was born Nov. 30, 1758 / and died May 31, 1831 / Age 73 years / Blessed are the dead / who died in the Lord

John W. Massenburgh / Born July 12, 1789 / Died Jan. 23, 1825

Anne F. Tatem / Born May 5, 1805 / Died Aug. 16, 1876

In memory of / Alexander M. Etheridge / who departed this life October 17, 1846

A. Wilson

W.C. Wilson

Frank L. Portlock Jr., recorded the above inscriptions during the early years of the twentieth century. It was through his generosity that the information was made available to me for use in the first history of South Norfolk. A close reading of the inscriptions indicates that John Whiddon may have married Mary after Elizabeth died. Further reading of the inscriptions brings forth the question: was John Camp's wife Anne or Anna? Martha C. Camp, daughter of John and Anne Camp, died October 12, 1816, at the age of seventeen. Another inscription states Anna Camp, wife of John Camp, departed this life May 31, 1816, at the age of twenty-seven. If Anne and Anna were the same person, then the difference between mother and daughter's ages was only ten years.

The name W.C. Wilson is listed, but there wasn't any information available. It is possible that W.C. Wilson was William Wilson who was clerk of the Norfolk County Court in 1828.

The name Massenburg can be found today on the deeds of property owners in the vicinity of the Oscar F. Smith school campus. The properties are described as being a part of the Massenburg tract. The Massenburg family owned a large amount of land in the area that eventually became part of South Norfolk.

Some of those buried in the Massenburg Cemetery were born before the Revolutionary War and survived the surrender at Yorktown. It is quite possible that a few members of the family participated in the battle at Great Bridge on December 9, 1775.

Portlock Cemetery: 1747–

The Portlock Cemetery is located on Franklin Street on part of the property that was once owned by Nathaniel Portlock (1773–1841) and later by his son Tapley Portlock (1809–1862). The land has had several owners since. In the early 1950s, Franklin L. Portlock

Jr. purchased eighteen gravesites in Forest Lawn Cemetery on Granby Street in Norfolk. In 1954, he had ten members of his immediate family moved to that cemetery; however, the original tombstones or grave markers were left in the Portlock Cemetery. Franklin L. Portlock Jr. died May 10, 2003, and was buried in Forest Lawn Cemetery. For a number of years, there has been one gravesite left in the Portlock Cemetery. Most likely it will never be used.

The following is a listing of those family members buried in the Portlock Cemetery. An asterisk identifies those who were re-interred in Forest Lawn:

Mother / Margaret E. Spain / 1856-1902

Emma J. Spain / 1852-1894

Etta Jackson Swain / Aug. 5, 1879 / Feb. 27, 1952

Mother / Laura Gibson Doughty / Dec. 17, 1874 / April 9, 1903 / Jesus Save Me, Thou / In Whom I Trust

Charles Llewellyn Gibson/ 1884–1961

Ruth Monell Gibson / 1893–1974

Father / Benjamin Franklin Gibson / December 22, 1847 / February 19, 1910

Mother / Elizabeth Llewellyn Gibson / November 15, 1853 / November 4, 1938

Alice Gibson Mills / Dec. 25, 1878 / Jan. 7, 1953 / At Rest

Oliver Stanley Mills / Aug. 31, 1875 / Feb. 1, 1958 / At Rest

Stanley Gibson Mills / May 10, 1916 / Oct. 11, 1947 / At Rest

Father / Benjamin Harry Gibson / 1877–1936

George P. Llewellyn / 1818–1873

Virginia F. Gibson / 1836–1893

Peter H. Gibson / 1819–1896

In Memory of / Virginia W. Rawls / Daughter of Henry & Fanny Keeling / And Widow of / Benjamin B. Rawls / Born Nov. 2, 1826 / Died Jan. 28, 1885

[There is a small tombstone beside that of Virginia W. Rawls. The inscription is not readable. There is a lamb engraved near the top of the stone, which possibly indicates that it is the grave of a child.]

*Bettie / Daughter of Franklin and Eugenia H. Portlock / Born Sept. 2, 1861 / Died July 26, 1864 / Re-interred Forest Lawn Cemetery / 1954

*In Memory of / Franklin Portlock / of Norfolk County / Born January 18, 1826 / Died April 6, 1896 / Re-interred Forest Lawn Cemetery / 1954

*Sacred To the Memory of / Eugenia H. Portlock / Widow of The Late Franklin / Portlock & Daughter of Dr. / William & Anne Eugenia Tatem / Born April 7, 1832 / Died February 8, 1918 / The Lord is my Shepherd / I Shall Not Want / Re-interred / Forest Lawn Cemetery / 1954

In Memory of / Frank Portlock / Son of Mary Lane & J.Q. Hewlett / Born March 25, 1885 / Died October 29, 1896

*William N. Portlock / Son of / Franklin And Eugenia H. Portlock / Born May 7, 1854 / Died June 17, 1910 / Re-interred / Forest Lawn Cemetery / 1954

*In Memory of / Emmie A. Portlock / Daughter of Franklin / And Eugenia H. Portlock / Dec. 22, 1855 / Jan. 24, 1925 / Love / Loyalty / Fidelity / Devotion / Re-interred / Forest Lawn Cemetery / 1954

*In Memory of / Bettie F. Young / Wife of Charles L. Young / Daughter of Franklin / And Eugenia H. Portlock / Born July 21, 1867 / Died Jan. 20, 1925 / Asleep in Jesus / Blessed Sleep / Re-interred Forest Lawn Cemetery / 1954

*In Memory of / Charles Lew Young / Born in Mamaroneck, N.Y. / July 23, 1864 / Died in Norfolk, Va. / December 25, 1921 / Re-interred / Forest Lawn Cemetery / 1954

*In Memory of / Thomas Webb Butt / Son of Henry Butt / And Mary A. Butt / Born February 14, 1848 / Died June 6, 1921 / Father In Thy Gracious / Keeping, Leave We Now Thy / Servant Sleeping / Re-interred / Forest Lawn Cemetery / 1954

*In Memory of / Franklin L. Portlock / Son of Franklin Portlock and / Eugenia Herbert Portlock / Born at Knell's Ridge, Norfolk / County / September 6, 1859 / Died January 9, 1932 / "Sleep on Beloved, Sleep / And Take Thy Rest." / Re-interred / Forest Lawn Cemetery / 1954

*In Memory of / Mrs. Mary Eliza Hall / Daughter of Henry And / Mary A. Butt / Born February 25, 1840 / Died June 24, 1900 / Asleep in Jesus / Re-interred / Forest Lawn Cemetery / 1954

Ira Armstrong / 1841–1909

Martha A. Armstrong, / Wife of Ira Armstrong / Born / Feb. 20, 1839 / Died Feb. 18, 1900 / At Rest

Mary E. Williamson / Wife of / James E. Armstrong / 1827–1905

Franklin P. Williamson / 1857–1926

Laura Armstrong Williamson / 1862–1936

Barbara A. Williamson / Wife of Henry Williamson And / Daughter of Nathaniel And Nancy Portlock / Born Feb. 10, 1823 / Died Oct. 12, 1860

Ida Williamson / Born May 23, 1851 / Died December 22, 1922

John H. And Mariah Hodges, Sr. / Son and Wife / George T. And Herbert Lively Hodges / Parents of / Nannie Hodges Baker Pritchard

Tapely Portlock / Son of / Nathaniel Portlock And Barbara / Carson Portlock / 1809–1862

Margaret Hodges Portlock / Wife of Tapley Portlock / 1819–1853

Arthur Barle Newby / Born Jan. 11, 1872 / In Norfolk Co., Va. / Died Sept. 21, 1905 / In Columbus, Miss.

Henrietta B. Newby / July 16, 1848 / June 7, 1916 / In His Holy Keeping

James Newby / Born / Perquimans Co, N.C. / Aug. 10, 1847 / Died Portsmouth, Va. / Dec. 23, 1914 / Asleep in Jesus

In Loving Memory / Alvah Tapley Portlock / Son of / Tapley II And Emma S. Wise / Portlock / November 26, 1877 / May 15, 1906

In Loving Memory / Emma Scarburgh Wise / Portlock / Wife of Tapley Portlock II / 1855–1930

In Memory of Tapley Portlock II, Husband of Emma S. Wise, 1849-1933

Nathaniel Portlock, Born Oct. 14, 1814, Died June 9, 1863

In Memory of / Mary Emily B. Portlock / Daughter of William And Anne Tatem / Born April 23, 1833 / Died February 16, 1859 / The Lord is My Shepherd

Nancy Portlock / Born April 9, 1782 / Died Oct. 3, 1863

Nathaniel Portlock / Born May 9, 1773 / Died April 15, 1841

There is a fence that divides the cemetery into two sections. The entrance to the first section is by way of the main or front gate. Another gate at the back of the first section leads to the area where the older graves are located. In the middle of the back section lies a large, flat granite marker with the following inscription:

PORTLOCK
BURIAL GROUND
FOR
SEVEN GENERATIONS
1747 TO 19-—

This photograph of Judge William Nathaniel Portlock's grave and the Portlock Cemetery was taken soon after his funeral. The judge died June 17, 1910. A close look at the surrounding area beyond the fence reveals how sparsely the area was settled at that time. A note of interest to the history enthusiast: the dark, sharp, pointed fence posts are still standing in 2005. *Photo courtesy of Frank L. Portlock Jr.*

Here are six tombstones in the Portlock Cemetery. The remains of ten members of the immediate family of Frank L. Portlock Jr. were removed to Forest Lawn Cemetery in 1954; however, the grave markers were left in place. *Photo courtesy of Frank L. Portlock Jr.*

With the death of Frank L. Portlock Jr. on May 10, 2003, there aren't any remaining trustees of this cemetery.

Gibson Family Cemetery—Originated 1905

The Gibson Family Cemetery is located in Portlock adjacent to the Rosemont Christian Church. It is enclosed by a chain-link fence and has two entrances. A double gate faces the parking lot, and a single gate allows entrance from Rosemont Avenue. I accompanied Hazel Rhodes and Effie Bondurant in revisiting the cemetery after about eleven years and carefully checked the inscription on all grave markers. Effie Bondurant pointed out an area where at least two unmarked graves are located. One of the unmarked graves is that of Elizabeth Gleming. There is a large monument in the center of the cemetery inscribed with "Gibson Family Cemetery – Originated 1905." At its base and on the front side is the grave of infant Luther Harrison Gibson and the date 1919.

Beginning at the row of grave markers nearest to Bainbridge Boulevard and working back to the markers near the parking lot, the following information was recorded.

[First row]

    John H. Fleming, 1882–1939

    Mamie Gibson Fleming Sawyer, 1887–1969

    Nicholas T. Fleming, 1912–1961

    Lina M. Gibson

    John Ben Gibson Jr. / Died / July 6, 2001

    Gertrude P. / "Princess" Gibson / Died / Apr. 10, 1984

    John Ben Gibson Sr. / Died / Mar. 13, 1978

    Luther H. Gibson / 1893–1921

[Second row]

    Jesse McCloud / July 1, 1866 / October 1, 1952

    John Nolan / son of / J. & A.J. McCloud / 1909–1911

    Mother / Annie J. Gibson / wife of Jesse McCloud / 1866–1910

    Jennie Manson / daughter of / J.H. & B. McCloud / 1919–1923

[Third row]

    Alton P. Cofield / 1904–1976

    Elizabeth Cofield / 1915–

    Dyton Dooris / Johnston / Oct. 9, / 1890 / Oct. 20, / 1969

    Grace Gibson Johnston / Sept. 2, / 1896 / Dec. 8, / 1955

    Mary E. Gibson / 1862–1940

    John L. Gibson /1852–1908

    Sarah E. Gibson / 1889–1896

    Callie G. Burden / 1906–1907

    John C. Burden / 1877–1905

    Linwood G. Burden / 1904–1905

[Fourth row]

    Dooris Gibson Johnston / U.S. Army / World War II / Jun 30, 1913–May 15, 1987

    John Luther Gibson / Virginia / PFC U.S. Army / World War II / Nov 16,1925–Nov 7, 1973

    Howard L. Gibson, Sr. / Sept. 9, 1900–March 8, 1974

    Myrtle Chillson / Gibson / Mar. 28, 1901 / May 5, 1978

    Mary Gifford / 1836–1919

    Husband / Herbert Louis / Bondurant / Oct. 2, 1883 / Sept. 7, 1960 / In Loving Memory

    Wife / Gertrude Gibson / Bondurant / Jan. 6, 1883 / July 15, 1952 / In Loving Memory

[Fifth row]

    Alphes "Buck" Weaver / 1915–1988

    Edna J. Weaver / 1916–

    John L. Gleming / 1884–1915

    Lois Fay Bondurant / Nov. 9, 1928–

Maury Nelson Bondurant / May 9, 1927 / Aug. 11, 1997
Nathaniel Bondurant / Browning / Oct 4 1974 / Feb 20 1975

[Sixth row]
Ralph Leon Gibson, Sr. / Jan. 31, 1933 / Mar. 3, / 1979
Brian David / Gibson / 1955–1955

In one corner of the cemetery near the fence and parking lot is the above-ground final resting place of the Morgans. The backside has the word Morgan in very large letters. The front reads as follows:

IN LOVING MEMORY
MORGAN

Mattie Levert / Bondurant / Sept. 29, 1916 / Aug. 24, 1993
Richard Fleming / "Billy" / April 5, 1912 / Dec. 7, 2001

Cemetery at the Corner of Franklin Street and Kay Avenue

In this cemetery, visitors will find graves that are unmarked, sunken and completely caved in. There are homemade markers and some graves are covered with slabs of concrete, both of which may have been manufactured on site. Most of the graves are not very old, the most recent being 1992. Until recent years, the cemetery was totally neglected. In the spring and summer, it was completely hidden by weeds, small trees and bushes. Today its care and upkeep is performed by one of the local organizations. It is my belief that this is an African American cemetery and is known only by its location. Listed below is the information from the tombstones that are legible:

George E. Wilson / May 7, 1918 / May 25, 1992
Catherine A. Wilson / July 1, 1918 / June 20, 1961
Ananias A. Anderson / Virgina Pvt. / 563 Casual Co. / World War I / September 23, 1895 / July 2, 1960
Henrietta Anderson Skinner / 1914–1943
James E. Anderson, Sr. / August 17, 1912 / July 6, 1969
Ivebella J. Anderson / May 4, 1915 / August 1, 1987
E.W. Cuffee/ Died November 18, 1945 / Age 60
Howard Butts / Virginia / Pvt OMC / World War I / October 25, 1897 / February 24, 1949
Martin V. Butts / March 22, 1887 / October 14, 1946
Martha Hall / [Unreadable homemade marker]
Lafayette Armstrong [A well preserved or possibly a new stone that had sunken to the point where the inscription could not be read]

Workmen's Circle Cemetery

The Workmen's Circle is a Jewish cemetery located on Railroad Avenue a short distance from Portlock Road. The gate remains locked, making it impossible to enter. There are approximately 255 gravesites.

CHAPTER VII

TRANSPORTATION

O_{NE OF THE AREA'S EARLY} forms of transportation was the local ferry. There were numerous branches and creeks that emptied into the Elizabeth River. The waterways divided Norfolk County into three sections, making public ferries necessary from the time of the earliest settlement.

By 1636, Norfolk County was the proud owner of a ferry system. Captain Adam Thorowgood set up the first ferry using a hand-rowed skiff to replace the log canoes used by American Indians. By 1637, there were three regularly established ferries in lower Norfolk County. They were supported by a levy of six pounds of tobacco on each tithable person. There were small boats for foot passengers as well as scows for horses and the vehicles they pulled. In August 1702, the General Assembly of Virginia enacted legislation requiring the ferries to be kept at designated places. At that time, the fare from Norfolk Towne to Sawyer's Point or Lovitt's Plantation (Portsmouth's site) was six pence for a man and one shilling for a man and a horse.

The first steam ferry, the *Gosport*, was built in Portsmouth and outfitted with engines in Philadelphia, Pennsylvania. She made her first trip across the harbor between Norfolk and Portsmouth in 1832. The approximate time was five minutes. Another early steam ferry (probably the third one) was the *Union*, so named because it served as a link uniting the "Twin Cities by the Sea." Captain William Chiles remained its engineer for many years.

During the War Between the States from 1862 to 1865, the Federal forces operated the ferries. At the turn of the century (1800s to 1900s) the ferry rates were: foot-passengers, a single ticket was three cents; two or more tickets were two and one-half cents each; man-and-horse, a single ticket was eight cents, two or more tickets were seven and one-half-cents each; bicycle and rider, all tickets were five cents. During my youth, a ferry ride from Norfolk to Portsmouth (foot passenger) was five cents.

The *Rockaway*, *City of Norfolk* and *City of Portsmouth* were side-wheel ferryboats that ran from Berkley and Portsmouth to Commercial Place in downtown Norfolk. The ferries were a connecting link between Berkley, Norfolk, and Portsmouth for almost 250 years. The maiden voyage of the *Gosport* established a tradition of regular service that terminated 123 years later on August 31, 1955 when the new bridge-tunnel complex went into operation. A few years later, the midtown tunnel from Hampton Boulevard to Portsmouth was built. It was in the 1990s that a ferry once again plowed the waves between Norfolk and Portsmouth.

As early as 1636, Norfolk County had a ferry system. By 1637, there were three established ferries in lower Norfolk County. This *circa* 1920 picture is of the *Rockaway*, one of the ferries that operated between Norfolk, Portsmouth and Berkley. *Photo courtesy of Hardy Forbes.*

It was about 1892 that David West operated the Berkley Express seen here. It appears that he has two passengers who would like a ride from Sam Wilson's store on Liberty in South Norfolk to Berkley. The church in the left background is the Liberty Street Methodist Episcopal Church, South. *Photo courtesy of Richard Womack.*

By that time, Commercial Place no longer existed and the ferry began operation between Waterside in Norfolk to Portside in Portsmouth.

In 1869, the Norfolk City Railroad Company began laying streetcar tracks, and in August 1870, Norfolk received its first five streetcars. They were tiny four-wheeled vehicles with narrow front and back platforms, and were equipped with hard benches for the passengers. They had a maximum capacity of eight passengers. These first horse-driven cars were placed in service on August 12, 1870. It was not long before the population became accustomed to the clang of the bell and the clickety-clack of the horse's hoofs on the cobblestone street.

The city council stipulated that the upkeep between the rails and two feet on either side was the company's responsibility. In the winter months, straw was spread on the floor of each car in an attempt to help keep the passenger's feet warm. The driver was exposed to the elements at all times.

It was around 1873 that James McNeal attempted to establish passenger service between McCloud's store and the village of Berkley. The establishment of J. Alonzo McCloud and Son was located on what would become Liberty Street in South Norfolk. The area was very sparsely populated, and McNeal's venture failed for lack of passengers. His service was a little premature.

A standard-gauge horse-car line began operation in Berkley on February 3, 1888. The route was from the Berkley Ferry to the Norfolk and Portsmouth Belt Line Railroad. Shortly thereafter, the line was extended to South Norfolk. The first streetcars served the residents of Berkley and South Norfolk over several miles of single track. In 1893, the Berkley Street

The horse-drawn streetcar shown here ran over several miles of single track from the ferry wharf on Chestnut Street in Berkley to the park on Holly Street in South Norfolk. In 1893, the Berkley Street Railway Company owned twenty head of horses and mules as well as seven streetcars.

Railway Company consisted of twenty head of horses and mules as well as seven cars. The stables were behind the South Norfolk Baptist Church. The cars that were used between South Norfolk and the Berkley Ferry wharf could be identified by a large sign that read "So Norfolk Park & Ferries." In 1894, the streetcars were electrified, enabling them to be propelled by a trolley that was attached to an overhead wire.

In the beginning, the streetcar ran from the limits of Berkley, which was at the Belt Line Railroad to the intersection of Chesapeake Avenue and Guerriere Street. By 1900, the Berkley Street Railway Company extended the line to the limit of South Norfolk and on to Money Point in the village of Portlock.

Money Point was a heavy industrialized area at the end of Freeman Avenue and along the Southern Branch of the Elizabeth River. The streetcar provided transportation for most of the work force. The route traveled from Money Point to the junction on Berkley Avenue included Freeman Avenue to Portlock Station on Bainbridge Boulevard where there was a passenger-waiting station. The streetcar continued its run along Bainbridge Boulevard, crossed the Virginian Railroad tracks (this was before construction of the Portlock overpass) and arrived at Jones's Switch.

The streetcar switch allowed cars to pass when approaching from opposite directions. After the streetcars were electrified, the company installed signal lights on a pole at each switch location. If there was a green light, the motorman could continue on through the switch to the single track leading to his destination. If the signal was red, he would wait in the switch until the car coming from the opposite direction arrived. Occasionally the light would malfunction, exhibiting a green light instead of a red one. Such an occurrence would usually lead to a heated discussion between the motormen involved, because one of them would have to back up. This would also cause the passengers to fume and fuss.

Jones's Switch received its name from William Jones, who operated a small grocery store at that part of Bainbridge Boulevard. The residents of several surrounding streets always included Jones's Switch as part of their mailing address. Jones owned a considerable amount of land in the vicinity, and a creek that ran into the Elizabeth River was also named for him.

After leaving Jones's Switch, the next stop was Barnes Station at the corner of Barnes Road and Bainbridge Boulevard. The E.H. Barnes Company was at the foot of Barnes Road near the Southern Branch. Continuing along Bainbridge Boulevard, the streetcar soon arrived at the corner of Holly Street and Bainbridge Boulevard, known as Knitting Mill Curve. This was a passenger stop that was used frequently by employees of the Elizabeth Knitting Mill. The route continued along Holly Street to Chesapeake Avenue where there was another switch in the 1300 block. After passing through the switch, the streetcar continued along Chesapeake Avenue to the intersection with Poindexter Street. The streetcar then followed Poindexter Street for one block before turning left on Liberty Street. From there, the track followed Liberty Street to Main Street in Berkley. There was a junction on Berkley Avenue where two routes were available. The northern route was from Berkley Avenue to Chestnut Street and then down to the ferry wharf. The ferry went to Portsmouth or to Commercial Place in downtown Norfolk.

By 1900, the Berkley Street Railway Company had extended their line to the industrial area of Money Point in the village of Portlock. A part of the track can be seen here on what is now Bainbridge Boulevard. Ms. Hassell and the family dog posed for this picture around 1930. The streetcars ran to Portlock until the overpass was built in 1937 and they were replaced by buses.

This 1902 photograph of Emmie Argyle Portlock and two-year-old Marion Hunter Portlock was taken at the Portlock Station where a passenger-waiting room was provided. *Photo courtesy of Frank L. Portlock Jr.*

On September 21, 1936, Captain Mac, the motorman, drove streetcar number 700 to the end of the line on Holly Street in South Norfolk. Red Hewitt, who was at one time employed as a motorman by the Virginia Electric and Power Company, met him. At that time, Virginia Electric and Power Company provided streetcar services to Norfolk and vicinity. *Photo courtesy of Richard Spratley.*

The southern route originated at Berkley Avenue and crossed the Norfolk & Western and Belt Line Railroad tracks by way of a viaduct to Albertson's Corner at Wilson Road. Wilson Road was followed to Campostella Road, which the streetcar ran along before crossing the bridge to Brambleton Avenue and then to Granby Street. This stop was referred to as Uptown Norfolk.

Albertson's Corner was named because a Mr. Albertson operated a grocery store there. Mr. Grimes and then Mr. Allen later operated the store, and there may have been other owners.

Many people may ask, "Where did the name Campostella came from?" It has been said that it was possibly named for a Mr. Camp and his daughter Stella. There are likely other explanations for such an unusual name.

When the Portlock overpass was built, streetcar tracks were not included in the construction. So after the overpass opened in 1937, the streetcar could no longer travel to Portlock. The corner of Holly Street and Bainbridge Boulevard then became the end of the streetcar line. Passengers needing to go to Portlock had to transfer to a bus.

When arriving at the end of the line, just how was the streetcar able to travel the opposite way over a single track? There was no such thing as a turntable for a car to enter and change direction. The streetcars had two trolleys, two motors, two sets of control handles and two doors. At the end of the line the motorman walked through the car and flipped the back of each seat. He would then pull one trolley down, secure it, release and connect the other trolley to the overhead cable. The next step was to remove the brake handle and the crank used to control the speed of the car. These he carried to the opposite end of the streetcar and reconnected them. The motorman was then able to drive the car in the opposite direction.

Eventually a switch was installed on D Street between Twenty-first and Twentieth Streets. At that time, the route to Berkley was changed. The streetcar no longer ran along the 1400 block of Poindexter Street; instead, when it left Chesapeake Avenue, it traveled the 900 block of B Street, turned at Twenty-second Street and then turned on to D Street to the switch. After exiting the switch, the car ran the length of D Street, crossed the Belt Line Railroad tracks and turned on to Thirteenth Street. At the corner of Thirteenth and Liberty Streets, there was another switch. Upon leaving the switch, the streetcar turned left on Liberty Street and continued to South Main Street in Berkley. The route continued along South Main Street and crossed the old Berkley Bridge to Union Station at the foot of East Main Street in Norfolk. After traveling East Main and Bank Streets, the car soon arrived at the end of the line, which was City Hall Avenue in downtown Norfolk. Passengers with final destinations in another part of Norfolk asked the motorman for a transfer and boarded another streetcar or bus. There was no extra charge for the transfer.

In earlier years, the end of the line, or transfer point at City Hall Avenue, was Town Back Creek. That area east of Bank and old Catherine Streets was filled in 1839. So after a heavy rain, it flooded and passengers stepping off the streetcar might step in water up to their knees. After streetcar service to Campostella was discontinued, it was necessary to transfer from the streetcar to a bus at City Hall Avenue to reach Chesterfield Heights, Campostella Heights and Newton Park.

The old Berkley Bridge was built in 1916 and was privately owned until the City of Norfolk purchased it in 1946. For each streetcar heading to Norfolk and returning to Berkley from Norfolk, a toll collector boarded to collect two cents from each passenger. The driver of each automobile, truck or other vehicles crossing the bridge had to stop at the tollbooth on the bridge and pay the required toll. Once the City of Norfolk purchased the bridge, the toll was removed. During World War II and at other times, the toll collectors were badly abused by members of the military and others. Many times those who refused to pay were pulled off the streetcar by a policeman and thrown in jail. They ended up paying a lot more than two cents.

Several of the toll collectors lived in South Norfolk. Those who come to mind are Dewberry, Sawyer and Harry Seymour. Leroy Smith, whom the bad boys of South Norfolk called "Slew Foot," also worked as a toll collector.

On May 7, 1948, it was all aboard for the last streetcar ride out of South Norfolk. Mayor Clarence E. Forehand of South Norfolk, Mayor Richard D. Cooke of Norfolk, other city and company officials as well as their guests climbed on board the last streetcar to be driven out of South Norfolk. Joseph K. Forbes, veteran motorman and South Norfolk resident, rattled the bell and all forty passengers prepared themselves for the ride. Buses then replaced the streetcars. Some of the tracks in South Norfolk were removed, and others were covered over with asphalt.

In May 1948, the streetcars were replaced by buses. This picture was taken at the corner of Liberty and Twentieth Streets. *Photo courtesy of Linwood L. Briggs Jr.*

The Berkley Bridge, which was built in 1916, extended from South Main Street in Berkley to East Main Street in Norfolk. In 1952, a new bridge-tunnel complex went into operation, and shortly thereafter this old bridge was removed.

The Norfolk newspapers reported that when the last streetcar in Norfolk had almost finished its run, the remaining passengers literally tore the car apart. It was further reported that it had to be towed to the car barn.

In May 1952, a new $23 million Norfolk–Portsmouth tunnel and bridge complex was opened to traffic. Eventually the old Berkley Bridge at the end of South Main Street was removed.

Throughout the history of streetcars, the name of the company providing service changed several times. Beginning on February 3, 1888, the provider was the Berkley Street Railway Company, then in 1906 it became the Norfolk and Portsmouth Traction Company. On June 29, 1909, the Virginia Railway and Power Company was incorporated. It provided service locally as well as other areas in the state. Virginia Railway and Power operated until October 27, 1925, when the Virginia Electric and Power Company (VEPCO) became the supplier of public transportation. Around the mid-1940s, VEPCO—which controlled the gas, electric and transportation—was forced to give up its transportation company amid monopoly fears. It was then that the Virginia Transit Company took over the business of public transportation. It later operated as the Tidewater Regional Transit.

At the end of the 1800s, a number of people with interest in the Berkley Street Railway Company lived in South Norfolk. Thomas H. Synon, president of the line, resided in South Norfolk before moving to Norfolk. Joseph Herbert Norton, foreman of the line, lived on Chesapeake Avenue. William Tilley, secretary-treasurer, lived at 17 Ohio Street. A number of people who worked for the streetcar company moved to South Norfolk. Eugene Hodges, a conductor, lived on B Street. John Sturges and George Vellines, motormen, lived on Chesapeake Avenue, and John Howell, another motorman, lived on Jackson Street. Vellines owned the house at 1030 Chesapeake. Other residents of South Norfolk who worked for the streetcar companies were Messrs. Chapman, Dowdy, Forbes, Harris, Hatfield, Mansfield, Massey, McGlaughon, McHorney, Phelps and Trevathan as well as others who may have unintentionally slipped out of an aging memory.

The streetcar came along and solved the problem of overcrowding; for if a man did not own a horse and carriage, he was forced to live no more than a mile from his place of employment. But with the advent of the streetcar, he was able to live some distance from the crowded downtown area.

The region's infant railroads before the Civil War were the Seaboard and Roanoke to the south and the Norfolk and Petersburg to the west. Both became casualties of the war.

At the end of the Civil War, General William Mahone resumed running the Norfolk and Petersburg. In 1867, he pushed a bill through the General Assembly of Virginia to consolidate the Norfolk and Petersburg; the Southside Railroad, which ran from Petersburg to Lynchburg; and the Virginia and Tennessee Railroad (running from Lynchburg to Bristol). The consolidated company was called the Atlantic, Mississippi and Ohio (AM&O). The AM&O was forced into receivership in 1876 and was bought by interests in Philadelphia, Pennsylvania. It was then reorganized as the Norfolk & Western Railroad Company. After another reorganization in 1895, it became the Norfolk and Western Railway.

The Norfolk and Western Railroad station was located on Seaboard Avenue at Guerriere Street. The station, which dated back to *circa* 1886, was torn down shortly after March 1962. During my youth, the station was operated by John Sutherland who lived on Ohio Street in South Norfolk. The station was mostly for freight, but occasionally passenger trains would stop. During World War II, draftees boarded the train to Richmond, where they received induction physicals. *Photo courtesy of Linwood L. Briggs Jr.*

Eventually passenger trains became a thing of the past. After a while, a group of railroad employees and former employees formed a club and sponsored trips to places such as Petersburg and Lynchburg. The trips were one day long, and most of the passengers carried a picnic lunch. On September 12, 1982, the Norfolk and Western 611 made such a trip. By that time, the sight of a passenger train was such a novelty that people gathered at crossings just to catch a glimpse. This picture was taken at the Liberty Street crossing in South Norfolk. *Photo by the Reverend Doctor Robert Morris.*

Other railroads that arrived in the area were the Chesapeake and Ohio in Newport News and in 1881, the Elizabeth City and Norfolk Railroad, which became the Norfolk and Southern.

In 1898, A.J. Cassatt built the Norfolk and Portsmouth Belt Line Railroad, which linked other rail lines in Tidewater. In 2005, most of the local railroads are now owned and operated by Norfolk and Southern.

CHAPTER VIII

GOVERNMENT AND POLITICS

ORIGINALLY SOUTH NORFOLK WAS A village in the Washington Magisterial District of Norfolk County. It was around 1908 that Leroy Nichols was the supervisor who represented South Norfolk on the Norfolk County Board of Supervisors. The board held monthly meetings at the Norfolk County courthouse in Portsmouth.

Q.C. Davis Jr. was a member of the House of Delegates from Norfolk County and South Norfolk. After having met with and receiving approval from the citizens of South Norfolk, he introduced a bill at the special session of the General Assembly of Virginia in 1919 to incorporate the town of South Norfolk. This was enacted and became law on September 11, 1919. The town government came into existence and began to function as a municipality on September 19, 1919.

The town government consisted of a mayor, nine councilmen, a town treasurer, a clerk of the common council and a town sergeant. The mayor possessed all the power and jurisdiction of a justice of the peace. The first councilmen named in the charter were J.H. Duncan Jr., V.L. Sykes and H.M. Chillson from the first ward; S.W. Wilson, H.P. Lane and H.H. Rountrey from the second ward; and O.M. Lynch, A.A. Morse and Edward L. Harper from the third ward. At their first meeting, the councilors elected Q.C. Davis Jr. as mayor, S.H. Dennis as treasurer, A.L. Grimstead as clerk of the council and Sergent W.H. Taylor. One year later, George L. Grimes replaced Councilman Sykes in the first ward and O.O. Boykins replaced Taylor as sergeant.

By December 22, 1920, South Norfolk had met the population requirement to become a city of the second class. Mayor Davis prepared the petition, and on January 1, 1921, South Norfolk became a city of the second class. F.L. Rowland became the mayor; Q.C. Davis Jr. was the first city attorney; W.T. Madrin served as clerk; P.M. Warden was the city sergeant; S.H. Dennis the treasurer and E.H. Branch became commissioner of the revenue.

Floyd L. Rowland had defeated Thomas Black to become mayor of the new second-class city. A few days after Rowland's victory, an election contest was filed. It was charged that the successful candidate had been illegally registered and therefore was ineligible. It was also asserted that forty-four voters were disqualified through improper registration. W.C. Meginley and others filed the contest with James G. Martin and Q.C. Davis Jr. as counsel. George Pilcher and Lawrence Brooks represented Rowland and filed a demurrer to the charge. Judge Charles W. Coleman of Norfolk County Circuit Court

COUNCILMEN :

PRESIDENT
EDWIN L. HARPER

1ST WARD
J. H. DUNCAN
GEO. L. GRIMES
H. B. CHILLSON

2ND WARD
S. W. WILSON
H. P. LANE
H. H. ROUNTREY

3RD WARD
O. M. LYNCH
A. A. MORSE
EDWIN L. HARPER

MAYOR
Q. C. DAVIS, JR.

CLERK OF COUNCIL
A. L. GRIMSTEAD

TREASURER
S. H. DENNIS

SERGEANT
O. O. BOYKINS

Town of South Norfolk

VIRGINIA

OFFICE OF MAYOR

This is the letterhead on the stationery used in the mayor's office of the new Town of South Norfolk. All the town officials are listed here, *circa* 1919. *Photo courtesy of Stuart Smith.*

overruled the demurrer but decided in Rowland's favor on the grounds that if there had been any fault in the registration, the blame rested upon the registrar. Evidence that Rowland had previously legally qualified as a voter in Norfolk was introduced. A transfer, it was ruled, was all that Rowland required to qualify as a voter in the South Norfolk election. The blame for registering Rowland instead of transferring him to the poll books was placed on Registrar V.L. Smith of Washington District, whose action was arbitrary, as far as the voter was concerned. Therefore, Judge Coleman declared Rowland duly elected.

No decision was rendered on the charge that forty-four voters had been ineligible for the election, the case being settled on the demurrer dismissal. There wasn't any evidence to show how any of the forty-four had voted, whether for Rowland or Black. Rowland, after being awarded a certificate of election, qualified before Clerk G. Taylor Gwathmey.

As a second-class city, South Norfolk's administration and government was vested in the mayor and five councilmen, who constituted the common council. The mayor was the chief executive officer of the city and his duties, among other things, were to see that the bylaws and ordinances were fully executed. He was president of the common council but didn't have a vote except in case of a tie. The police force was under the control of the mayor for the purpose of enforcing peace and order as well as for executing the laws of the state and the ordinances of the city.

Other municipal officers of the city were the treasurer, commissioner of the revenue, city sergeant, clerk of the common council and city attorney. There was a trial justice, who was also judge of the Juvenile and Domestic Relations Court. The city charter also provided for the office of street commissioner and sanitary inspector. South Norfolk was divided into three wards, and each had its own justice of the peace.

Beginning in 1921, city and state taxes were collected by the treasurer, located at 144 Liberty Street.

Benjamin Harrison Gibson, also known as Benjamin Harry Gibson, became the second mayor of the city of South Norfolk. During his administration, a $300,000 bond issue was floated to build concrete streets. When he became mayor, the streets were dirt and the sidewalks were wooden boardwalks. There was one mile of sewerage lines, which were privately owned.

In June 1929, there was a three-man race for mayor. Gibson was running for re-election, and S. Herman Dennis Sr. and C.L. Williams were opposing him. Dennis won and died eight days later. His passing ended a remarkable career in the history of South Norfolk. Alvah H. Martin, clerk of the court of Norfolk County, appointed Sampson Herman Dennis to his first office as sanitary inspector of South Norfolk. In 1919 when South Norfolk was incorporated as a town, Dennis was chosen as its first treasurer and was holding the office at the time of his death. Dennis was born in Salisbury, Maryland, on February 15, 1883, and came to South Norfolk around 1904. He entered into the lumber business, becoming a partner and holding an executive position with D.W. Raper and Son Lumber Company. He was a director of the Chesapeake Building Association and the Bank of South Norfolk, which was merged with the Merchants and Planters Bank. Dennis was chief of the South Norfolk Volunteer Fire Department at the time of his death.

Judge Charles W. Coleman of the Circuit Court of Norfolk County appointed Benjamin Harrison Gibson to continue as mayor. It was also up to the court to appoint someone to fill Dennis's unexpired term as city treasurer. A number of city bills could not be paid until an interim treasurer was appointed. C.L. Williams was appointed to fill the position until the general election was held.

Gibson died in 1936, and J. James Davis was appointed to fill his unexpired term as mayor. Gibson had directed the military classes at the Berkley Military Institute in Berkley. After his death, his remains were brought to the J.R. Williams Funeral Home on Chesapeake Avenue in South Norfolk. Mayor Gibson was buried in the Portlock Cemetery in Portlock.

The structure on the right was the new City Hall that was built *circa* 1930. The city offices were located on the second floor, and the first floor served as the fire department's third fire station. *Photo courtesy of Linwood L. Briggs Jr.*

The three buildings seen here are, from left to right, the fire station, the new courthouse and the municipal building on Liberty Street as they appeared in March 1957. A close look reveals the controversial parking meters; citizens banded together and forced the meters' removal. Also, it is obvious from the many window units that the municipal building did not have central air conditioning. *Photo courtesy of Linwood L. Briggs Jr.*

After filling Mayor Gibson's unexpired term, J. James Davis ran for election against his cousin Q.C. Davis Jr., defeated him and went on to serve as mayor until 1947.

The following is a listing of offices and employees of the City of South Norfolk from 1937 until the merger with Norfolk County in 1963.

In 1937, the members of city council were C.F. Abbott, C.W. Davis, J.B. Dean, E.E. Henley and W.B. Smith. Clerk of the common council was W.T. Madrin. Other employees of the city included city attorney, W.F. Whitley; trial justice, Herman White; director of public works, C.H. Hughes; superintendent of public welfare, Frances Carter Smith; department of health, Dr. I.L. Chapman; chief of police, E.L. Boyce; chief of the volunteer fire department, L.H. Newberry; city treasurer, W.M. Townsend; commissioner of the revenue, H.P. Lane; city sergeant, E.S. Overman; justices of the peace, C.E. Ansell, M.D. Hobbs and G.E. Williams.

In 1938, the changes in city positions were as follows: A.B. (Bus) Howell replaced J.B. Dean on the city council, Frances Carter Smith became Frances Carter Bratten and Bryan W. Holloman replaced M.D. Hobbs as one of the justices of the peace.

By 1939, H.E. Winston had replaced W.B. Smith on the city council and S.H. Dennis Jr. became chief of the fire department. In 1940, Margaret Brooks West replaced Frances Carter Bratten as superintendent of public welfare.

In 1941, the members of the city council included J.F. Forehand, J.M. Meginley, A.B. Howell, E.E. Henley and H.E. Winston. There weren't any other changes in city positions.

In 1942, N.H. Morse became the city's fourth justice of the peace. The other city offices remained as they were in 1941. The only change in 1943 was the return to three justices of the peace. They were C.E. Ansell, G.E. Williams and N.H. Morse. There was one change in 1944: Thelma S. Edwards replaced West as superintendent of public welfare.

By 1945, C. Edward Meginley had replaced W.T. Madrin as clerk of the common council and Henry L. Scheuerman had replaced Edward L. Boyce as chief of the police department. The changes in 1946 were J.C. Bagley, city sergeant; W.L. Nicolas, fire chief; and E.S. Overman and G.A. Peebles, justices of the peace.

Before his separation from the navy, Commander Jerry G. Bray Jr. submitted his application for city attorney. The city council voted 3–2 to retain C. F. Whitley for an additional two years. Councilmen Meginley and Howell voted in favor of Bray.

At the same meeting of council, a petition signed by thirty-five Avalon citizens complained about the keeping of cows in the vicinity.

In 1947, the newly formed Junior Chamber of Commerce supported by Jerry G. Bray Jr. petitioned the city fathers to change the form of government from the mayor-council to the city-manager form. A referendum was held on April 1, 1947, and the vote was 669–501. The new form of government went into effect September 1, 1947. It comprised a city manager and five members of council. The new governing body was made up of many departments: police, fire, recreation, public works, welfare and health. There was also a planning commission.

In 1947, Clarence Edward Forehand was elected to the South Norfolk City Council. He was also elected by the other members of council to serve as the first mayor under the city-manager form of government. Forehand served eight years on the council and was mayor for six of those years.

In the early years of the manager-council form of government, the position of city manager was very transitory. There were several acting appointments, and those managers who were hired, for one reason or another, did not remain in South Norfolk very long. The first man to fill the position was Irving W. Dunning. He was appointed acting city manager until the position could be filled. Dunning's regular job was that of city engineer. The first man hired as city manager was R.L. VanNoaker. He assumed office April 15, 1948, and by October, he was out.

B.R. Fuller was hired and filled the position on October 21, 1948. It was during Fuller's tenure that South Norfolk won its bid for annexation of the town of Portlock. The October 14, 1949 *Norfolk-Virginian Pilot* reported that as a result of the annexation, South Norfolk would triple in size and double in population. The article also stated that the annexed areas included Riverdale; the entire town of Portlock, with its industrial area of Money Point; as well as the communities of Providence Terrace, Providence Grove Annex, Edmonds Corner and West Munden. This was a lot more than South Norfolk bargained for. City leaders wanted only Portlock and Money Point but were told by the court that the other sections would have to be included.

The court suggested July 1, 1950, as the effective date of the decree. The judges assigned to the case by Chief Justice Edward W. Hudgins of the state Supreme Court of Appeal were Judge Edward L. Oast, of the Circuit Court of Norfolk County; Judge Floyd E. Kellam, of Princess Anne and the Circuit Court of the Twenty-eighth Judicial District; and Judge J. Jorden Temple, of Petersburg and the Circuit Court of the Third Judicial District.

Apparently Fuller held the city-manager position for two years because James S. Hughes became acting manager on November 16, 1950. Walter Freeman was the next man hired to fill the position. The date of his appointment could not be verified; however, according to minutes of the city council, he resigned February 15, 1952.

City council meetings are usually interesting, especially those of the smaller cities. There is always that down-home flavor and familiarity. The regular meeting of the Common Council of the City of South Norfolk was held at 8:00 p.m. December 6, 1951, in the municipal building. The Reverend Frank Hughes Jr. offered the invocation before the council proceeded with its business. The meeting was called to order by Mayor Forehand. The clerk called the roll, and Councilmen Mahlon K. Hassell, J. Preston McClain, W. Joseph White and Elliott E. Henley as well as Mayor Forehand were present. City Attorney R.E. Gibson and City Manager W.R. Freeman Jr. were also present.

The minutes of the previous meeting were read and approved. The first citizen to speak was O.G. Hairston, who requested that street improvements be accomplished on Partridge Avenue. The mayor stated that no agreement existed between the developer of the Cloverdale project and the city for street improvements.

The next two men to speak were William J. Lassiter Jr. and John B. Gibson Jr. Lassiter represented the South Norfok Jaycees, and Gibson represented the Portlock Athletic Association. The men stated that their respective organizations were planning to sell Christmas trees for charitable purposes during the Christmas season and requested that the usual license tax fee of $20 be waived. Mayor Forehand advised that should the fee be waived, it would be necessary that all proceeds from the sales be used for charitable purposes. Both requests were approved, and the police department was notified of the action.

Ovie Yensen reported that Christmas carols would be sung at the Portlock Fire Station, the municipal building and the Riverdale Community Center on December 13, by a group of eighty schoolchildren.

The city attorney read the following resolution: A resolution requesting the United States Government through and by the Secretary of the Army and the United States Engineers to permit the City of South Norfolk to pump water from the Dismal Swamp Canal and the waters of Lake Drumond. This would be for the purpose of furnishing water to itself and to its inhabitants and to acquire the necessary easements and rights therefore, subject to the terms and conditions as required by law for such cases made and provided. The resolution was adopted as read.

Several requests for building permits were read by the clerk and acted on by the council. Mayor Forehand appointed the following members to the library committee: Mrs. W.J. White, Mrs. C.E. Forehand, Mrs. W.Y.E. Davis, Mrs. D.P. Whitfield, Miss Aurelia Leigh and City Manager W.R. Freeman Jr., an ex-officio member. A list of city bills amounting to

$10,747.50 was read. It was moved and carried that the bills be paid. It was also mentioned that inquiries had been made relative to hunting in the city.

The motion was made and unanimously carried to adjourn. These were just a few actions that came before council that December evening more than a half century ago.

Irving W. Dunning was again appointed acting city manager on December 6, 1951. Shortly thereafter, he submitted his resignation to become effective March 24, 1952. C.W. Holdzskom became acting city manager on March 10, 1952, and also succeeded Dunning as city engineer.

The fifth head executive of South Norfolk was William J. Ganster. He took office on April 1, 1952. The city council minutes of September 8, 1953, included a resolution requesting the resignation of City Manager Ganster. H.D. Hamner Jr. was appointed acting city manager, effective September 8, 1953.

The next city manager was Philip W. Ansell, whose appointment became effective October 1953. The city council—meeting on Friday October 29, 1954—requested Ansell's removal, citing differences between the council and the city manager. The minutes also contained a resolution appointing Philip P. Davis acting city manager retroactive to September 30, 1954. Not to be outdone, Ansell brought court proceedings to stay his removal. The decision of the city fathers prevailed; Ansell resigned December 2, 1954—the same date Philip P. Davis became acting city manager.

Earnest L. Thacker became city manager on September 20, 1955, and served until he resigned August 31, 1957. C.W. Holdzskom was again appointed acting city manager effective August 15, 1957. Philip P. Davis became city manager in 1961.

Clarence E. Forehand served as mayor from 1947 to 1953 and remained on the city council for an additional two years. In 1952, the other members of council were Mahlon K. Hassell, J. Preston McClain, W. Joseph White and Elliott E. Henley. William J. Ganster was city manager; Robert Gibson served as city attorney; C.W. Holdzskom held the position of city engineer. Jerry G. Bray Jr. became the next city attorney and eventually filled the position of commonwealth attorney of South Norfolk.

In February 1953, South Norfolk got its own corporation court and Q.C. Davis Jr. became the first judge. Davis had received his law degree from the University of Richmond in 1912 and practiced in New Jersey before relocating to South Norfolk in 1914. After Davis died on August 31, 1954, Jerry G. Bray Jr. became the second judge of the South Norfolk Corporation Court. Justice Herman White continued to run the Civil and Police Court. Edwin Jones served as clerk of the Civil and Police Court from January 20, 1953, to October 1, 1955.

Corporation-court cases were tried in the civil and police courtroom in the municipal building until the new corporation courthouse was built. The courtroom was also used as chambers for the city council.

The new corporation courthouse was constructed between the municipal building and the fire/police station on Liberty Street. The structure is of colonial style, built of brick with white trim and is one story high. It is seventy-four feet by sixty-eight feet, and at the time of construction, there was a seven-foot walkway between the courthouse and the fire/police station and a twenty-foot alleyway between it and the city hall. Of the three buildings, the

Marion White Nichols, Lil Holloman and Julian Raper check construction of the South Norfolk Corporation Court building on November 30, 1953. An unidentified gentleman stands on the right. Holloman, who later became Mrs. Norman Hart, retired in 2003 as clerk of the circuit court for the City of Chesapeake. *Photo courtesy of Ms. Lilly Hart.*

courthouse is the only one still remaining today. It is currently occupied by the W.B. Dawley & Company Insurance offices.

The courtroom seated seventy-eight people. The building contained a record room, a clerk's work room, a jury room, judge's chambers, a judge's conference room, a room for the city sergeant, a boiler room and rest rooms. A. Ray Pentecost Jr. was the architect.

In 1953, N.J. Babb became the seventh mayor of South Norfolk and served until 1957. It was during his administration that the first Oscar F. Smith High School was built on Rodgers Street. It now serves as a middle school.

Linwood L. Briggs Jr. was elected as a member of city council in 1953 and became mayor in 1957. He served until 1961. Other members of council were Jesse McCloud, Osmond Evans, Charles L. Richardson and Daniel W. Lindsey Jr.; Philip P. Davis was city manager; Vernon T. Forehand held the position of city attorney; Raymond Spence was city clerk.

One of the headlines in the October 17, 1957 *Norfolk Virginian-Pilot* was "Tax Rate Cut Promised On Southside." The article stated that the battle of the budget was shaping up along the familiar 3–2 council split. The original budget, which had been voted on in June 1957, was $2,416,202. Mayor Briggs, Vice Mayor McCloud and Councilman Evans were the majority. Councilmen in minority were Charles L. Richardson and Daniel W. Lindsey Jr. Briggs stated that the people were going to see a tax reduction, new capital improvements and a rise in the city's contingency fund. He further stated that city employee salaries would not be cut and the school budget would not be touched.

On January 7, 1958, the South Norfolk Planning Commission met to consider the rezoning request of contractor Woodrow W. Ford, who wanted to build South Norfolk's first shopping center. His request was to rezone a ten-acre tract of land bounded by the Bainbridge Boulevard overpass, Swain Avenue and the Virginian Railroad tracks from one family residential to general commercial. The contractor stated that if the planning commission and the city council approved the request, he would proceed with plans to build a twelve- to fourteen-store shopping center costing between $750,000 and $1 million.

Ford's construction company, which had dealt primarily with piling and foundation work, had been located on the proposed site for a number of years. It had been classified as a nonconforming property because the company was in business before the establishment of zoning regulations. Ford reported that his company would be moving elsewhere, probably to a location along Military Highway, later that year.

An anticipated point of controversy was the traffic at the base of the overpass. It was thought that cars heading south on Bainbridge Boulevard would have to make a left turn across the busy thoroughfare in order to enter the shopping center. Locating the entrance immediately north of Swain Avenue solved this problem.

Plans for the shopping-center parking included spaces for between 260 and 280 vehicles. As with most shopping centers, it was felt that a supermarket would form the nucleus for the operation. Ford received the go-ahead from the planning commission and city council, and the Southgate Plaza Shopping Center was built.

During Brigg's administration, the tax rate was lowered by eight cents, more than a mile of curbing was installed in Portlock, the new shopping center was built in Portlock, new voting machines were brought to the city, two new community centers were built and

The construction on the left is that of the new South Norfolk Health Center in the late 1950s. The white building near the left top is Rawl's South Norfolk Furniture Company on Liberty Street. St. James Street ran behind the furniture store. The large water tower in Berkley can be seen at the top right of the photograph. The shacks near the center were removed in the slum clearance program of 1957–1961. *Photo courtesy of Linwood L. Briggs Jr.*

This picture, which was taken from the South Norfolk overpass, shows the new welfare building under construction on the left and construction of the health center on the right. Soon after this photograph was taken, a new police station was constructed to the left of the welfare building. A large parking lot was built in front of the buildings. When completed, all three structures were debt free. *Photo courtesy of Linwood L. Briggs Jr.*

In early 1958, South Norfolk became the possessor of its first and only city flag. This photograph depicts the city seal on a field of royal-blue silk. Oil paints were used to paint the seal on the banner.

an aerial ladder was bought for the fire department. Also built were the South Norfolk Memorial Library as well as a new health center, welfare center and police station.

In early 1958, South Norfolk became the proud possessor of its first and only city flag. Betty Miles, president of the Future Homemakers of America, presented it to Mayor Briggs. The idea of designing a city flag originated from a conversation between the mayor and assistant principal of Oscar F. Smith High School, E.E. Brickell. Peggy L. Spruill, home economics teacher and sponsor of the Future Homemakers of America, assisted the students in making the flag. It depicts the city seal on a silk, royal blue field. Oil paints were used to paint the seal on the banner. The school's art students, under the leadership of Gloria Harper, accomplished the painting of the seal.

Two other flags were presented to the mayor that day. The American flag was presented by W. Henry Rawls, national legislative committeeman of the Woodmen of the World, on behalf of Berkley Camp number 46 of the WOW. Buddy Rodgers, president of the Key Club at the Oscar F. Smith High School, also gave a Virginia State flag to the city. Wooden flagstaff stands for the three flags were built under the direction of Edward R. Radke in the wood shop at the Oscar Smith School. The three flags added a bit of color to the newly renovated office of the mayor.

What happened to the city flag after the merger? No one seems to know. Most likely it went home with a politician and, after his death, was thrown away. In 1997, Paula Jones operated Norfolk Flag on Bainbridge Boulevard across from Lakeside Park. Jones contacted me about the design of the South Norfolk flag. After receiving the above information, she made a few flags and sold them for about $25 each.

At a public rally held June 16, 1960, the South Norfolk Business, Professional and Industrial Association voted to pursue a change of the city name. One week later, the association asked the citizens of South Norfolk to send in suggestions. On July 14, the name Delata was chosen by the Business, Professional and Industrial Association as a new name for South Norfolk. Action on this proposal was tabled, and on August 11, in a compromise move, the association decided to ask that the city be referred to as the "City of South Norfolk" rather than just South Norfolk. It was decided this move would be best.

A letter from the Virginia Municipal League dated February 15, 1961, and signed by Harold I. Baumes, executive secretary, stated that South Norfolk had the third-lowest per capita total net debt of all the first-class cities of Virginia. Another letter, this one from Milton McPherson, certified public accountant, dated March 1, 1961, informed City Manager Philip P. Davis that the City of South Norfolk's surplus was greater than it had been in the previous four years and that the city was in good financial condition.

For more than forty years, a false rumor has been floating around that South Norfolk was deep in debt and city leaders had begged Norfolk County to come to their rescue. I hope the two letters presented here will shed light on the truth. To quote McPherson's letter, "[T]he city was in good financial condition." All the new buildings listed above were free of debt upon completion.

Future plans for the city included a multimillion-dollar shopping center, a new downtown office building and a Broad Street housing project for those persons who would be displaced by clearance of the Liberty Street slums.

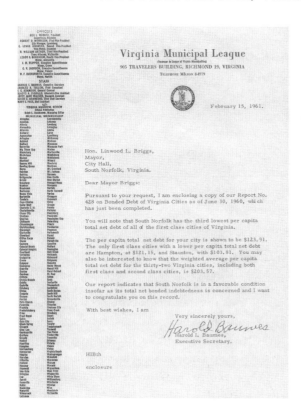

This letter from the executive secretary of the Virginia Municipal League dated February 15, 1961, stated that the City of South Norfolk had the third-lowest per capita total net debt of all the first-class cities in Virginia. *Courtesy of Mayor Linwood L. Briggs.*

Milton L. McPherson, certified public accountant, wrote this letter to City Manager Philip P. Davis on March 1, 1961. It was in response to a request from council as to the financial condition of the city of South Norfolk. In McPherson's opinion, relative to his latest audit report, the city was in good financial condition. *Courtesy of Mayor Linwood L. Briggs.*

This is part of a booklet titled *Rebirth of a City* that was printed and distributed to the citizens of South Norfolk. It was to let the residents know the completed new construction had been paid for as well as to inform them of future plans for the city. *Courtesy of Mayor Linwood L. Briggs.*

This is a continuation of the *Rebirth of a City* booklet. It addresses other accomplishments as well as plans to rid the city of existing slums, replace downtown slums with a multimillion-dollar shopping center and construct a high-rise office building in downtown South Norfolk. *Courtesy of Mayor Linwood L. Briggs.*

The Past And The Present Through Redevelopement

LIBERTY STREET SLUMS

LIBERTY STREET SLUMS

LIBERTY STREET SLUMS - BROAD STREET HOUSING PROJECT FOR THOSE DISPLACED FROM LIBERTY STREET SLUMS

This part of the *Rebirth of a City* booklet concentrates on the Liberty Street slums and the Broad Street housing project planned for residents displaced by removal of the slums. The slums were removed between 1957 and 1961, but the planned improvements never materialized. The election in 1961 saw the positive majority on city council replaced by three new members who sided with those who fought against all the previous improvements to the city. Within one month they began merger talks with Norfolk County and, as has been said before, the rest is history. *Courtesy of Mayor Linwood L. Briggs.*

This photograph shows the new buildings for the health, welfare and police departments. These buildings were completed in June 1961. Upon completion, all three were debt free. *Photo courtesy of Mayor Linwood L. Briggs.*

In September 1961, Charles Richardson became the last mayor of South Norfolk. Four members of the new council were from the annexed area of the city. In October, meetings with Norfolk County politicians began and merger was discussed. By December 22, 1961, a consolidation agreement for the City of South Norfolk and Norfolk County had been drawn up. This agreement covered all aspects of the merger, including that the new city would consist of South Norfolk and the five magisterial districts of Norfolk County. The boroughs would be South Norfolk, Butts Road, Deep Creek, Pleasant Grove, Washington and Western Branch.

The *Virginia-Carolina News* of Thursday, January 25, 1962, reported a merger meeting that was held at the B.M. Williams School. The panel of representatives included Charles Cross Jr., clerk of court; R. H. Waldo, commissioner of revenue; J.A. Hodges, sheriff of Norfolk County; A.O. Lynch, treasurer; Peter M. Axson, commonwealth attorney; and Eugene Wadsworth, supervisor of Washington District. Their primary concern was the loss of Norfolk County citizens and taxes because of annexation. From 1951 to 1962, the county lost thirty-three square miles by annexation.

South Norfolk Corporation Court Judge Jerry G. Bray Jr. and Norfolk County Circuit Court Judge Major M. Hillard set the date for the merger referendum, which was held on Tuesday, February 13, 1962.

The citizens of the annexed area turned out in record numbers and, according to the election board secretary, voted almost entirely for the merger. His count was 6,648–3,432 in favor of consolidation. The next step was to be granted a charter by the Virginia General Assembly.

The voting machines were new, and the story that has been talked about for years is that by using a screwdriver, anyone could change the count—an act that supposedly was responsible for the win. The only person or persons who know for sure died years ago. One thing for sure is that the promerger politicians had rented Carl Parker's Restaurant for a victory party long before the election took place.

After receiving approval from the general assembly, it was decided that a name for the new city would be chosen in a later referendum. A total of twelve names appeared on the ballot. The choices were:

Bridgeport	Great Bridge
Chesapeake	Norcova
Churchland	Port Elizabeth
Glendale	Sunray
Glennville	Virginia City
Gosport	Woodford

Chesapeake received 3,130 votes, and the next highest was Great Bridge with 1,883. All this accomplished, the City of Chesapeake came into being on January 1, 1963.

South Norfolk, from the time of its incorporation as a town until the merger went into effect, was served by many dedicated citizens. The nine mayors have already been named, as have the three men who held the position of treasurer. N. Duval Flora became treasurer of South Norfolk in 1950 and was the first treasurer of the City of Chesapeake. He served a total of thirty-nine years and retired from Chesapeake in 1989.

E.H. (Mike) Smith, an early citizen of South Norfolk, held the position of deputy clerk of the Norfolk County Circuit Court. Around 1953, he became deputy city treasurer of South Norfolk. After H.P. Lane retired, Smith ran for and was elected commissioner of revenue. He also was South Norfolk's first real-estate assessor. After the merger, Smith became deputy commissioner of revenue for the City of Chesapeake.

Raymond Spence served as city clerk for twenty-five years, beginning with the City of South Norfolk and retiring from the City of Chesapeake. Julian R. Raper held the position of clerk of the Corporation Court for the City of South Norfolk.

The last councilmen serving the City of South Norfolk were Charles L. Richardson, mayor; Dan Lindsey; Howard McPherson; H.S. Boyette; and Floyd Allen. They all served the City of Chesapeake after the merger.

Portlock

It all began with Chapter 329—an act to provide a charter for and incorporate the town of Portlock, to authorize the taking of a census and the effect thereof. The act reads as follows:

> 1. *Be it enacted by the General Assembly of Virginia:*
> *Section 1. The territory hereinafter set forth and described in section two of this act is a thickly settled community within the State, lying wholly within the County of Norfolk, and it is now and since time immemorial has been known as Portlock, and the number of inhabitants thereof exceeds two hundred and does not exceed five thousand, and it will be to the interest of the inhabitants of the territory that it be incorporated as a town, and the area of land designed to be embraced within the town is not excessive.*
> *Section 2. The description of the territory according to the metes and bounds thereof is as follows:*
> *Beginning at a point where the western line of the right of way of Norfolk and Western Railway Company intersects the southeastern line of the right of way of the Virginian Railway Company to its intersection with the Port Warden's line of the Southern Branch of the Elizabeth River. Thence in a southwesterly and southerly direction up to the Port Warden's line of the Southern Branch of the Elizabeth River to its intersection with the northern line of the right of way of U. S. Route thirteen—thence easterly and northeasterly along the northern right of way line of U. S. Route thirteen and the northern right of way line of the outer loop of the northwest quadrant of the interchange to a point on U. S. Route four hundred sixty north of the limits of the interchange, thence in an easterly direction to the northern right of way of the Norfolk and Western Railway Company and in a northeasterly and northerly direction along the northern and western line of the right of way of the Norfolk and Western Railway Company to the point of beginning aforesaid.*
> *Section 3. The territory and inhabitants thereof are hereby incorporated as a town to be known as Portlock. The town and its officers shall have all the powers and privileges and*

be subject to all the restrictions provided by the general laws of this commonwealth for the existence of a body corporate and politic, and for the government of towns and the powers of officers of towns.

Section 4. The first election of town officers shall be held on the second Tuesday in June, nineteen hundred forty-eight, at a place in the town designated by the electoral board of the County of Norfolk. The electoral board of Norfolk County shall, not less than fifteen days before the election, designate one registrar and three judges of election who shall also act as Commissioners of election and such officers of election shall conform to the requirements of section twenty-nine hundred ninety-five of the code of Virginia, and the conduct of such election shall conform in all respects to the requirements of the general law regarding the holding of elections in towns, so far as applicable. The election shall be held and the vote counted, canvassed and certified, but officers elected at the election shall only hold office until the next regular election of town officers to be held as provided for by general law.

Section 5. Until the regular election held on the second Tuesday in June, nineteen hundred forty-eight, the following shall constitute the council of such town: Simeon Leary, mayor; A. L. Cofield, H. S. Boyette, M. K. Hassell, C. L. Richarson, and W. P. Nothnagel, councilmen. The town council shall appoint a recorder and a town sergeant.

Section 6. The council as soon as may be shall proceed to have a census taken of the town at the expense thereof.

2. An emergency exists and this act is in force from its passage.

The General Assembly of Virginia enacted the above document on March 18, 1948. Governor William Tuck appointed the interim mayor and councilmen who served the town of Portlock from March 18, 1948, until the second Tuesday in June, which was June 8, 1948.

Mayor (vote for one)

H.S. Boyette	367
C.R. Fentress	176

Councilmen (vote for five)	
Mahlon K. Hassell	398
Larry L. Milteer	396
William P. Nothnagel	361
Charles L. Richardson	356
William E. Todd	327
H.D. Curtis	234
M.A. Hogan	230
W.R. Capehart	198
C.D. Dunn	136
R.W. Capps	130

H.S. Boyette was elected mayor; Mahlon Hassell, Larry L. Milteer, William P. Nothnagel, Charles L. Richardson and William E. Todd were the elected councilmen.

After annexation, Boyette, Hassell and Richardson served on the South Norfolk City Council. Richardson was the last mayor of South Norfolk. When the merger became effective on January 1, 1963, he became the first vice mayor of the City of Chesapeake and served on the council until August 31, 1970. Boyette served as a Chesapeake councilman from January 1, 1963, to August 31, 1965.

CHAPTER IX

SOUTH NORFOLK
FIRE DEPARTMENT

In 1892, Captain George Funk, S.W. Wilson Sr., E.H. Whitehurst, L.M. Nicholas, H.L. Nicholas, J.F. Hutchins, W. Giarid, J.C. Garrett, Henry Clark and R.D. Haley organized a volunteer fire department in the village of South Norfolk. Captain Funk was elected chief. The first equipment acquired by the department was an old hand-drawn reel and a few hundred feet of hose, both of which were stored in an old building behind J.T. Lane's Drug Store on Liberty Street.

South Norfolk's first fire department was located in a house on the corner of Twenty-second and A Streets. In earlier years, the home had been the residence of the White family. After the South Norfolk School was built, the house was in a corner of the schoolyard. Beginning in the early 1920s, the house served as a classroom for the domestic science (home economics) class. It was later used by the welfare department, as a voting precinct, as a workshop for the boy's club and as a meeting place for the Boy Scouts.

The department eventually became inactive; however, reorganization took place in 1909 and Captain Funk was again elected to the position of chief.

In 1910, the South Norfolk Fire Department received a state charter. The members listed at that time were L.M. Nicholas, S.W. Wilson Sr., W.F. Gray, W.M. Poyner and J.F. Hutchins.

In 1911, a horse-drawn hose reel was obtained from the Berkley Fire Department, which received it from the fire department in Jamestown. The reel and wagon were pulled by any available horse (usually Mr. Sherman's big white horse) when the alarm was sounded. In 1915, Ira Johnson of the Greenleaf Johnson Lumber Company donated a mule to the department. As soon as possible, the department traded the mule for a horse. Unfortunately, the horse ate itself out a job and had to be sold to pay the feed bill. After that, D.W. Draper and Son Lumber Company on Wilson Road donated the services of its horse to pull the equipment.

In 1915, members of the fire department constructed a new building on Twenty-second Street, across from its previous headquarters. When the construction note came due, the department was unable to pay and the building was sold to the Woodmen of the World Lodge. The building then became known as the WOW Hall. Early photographs of the WOW Hall show the first fire engine in front of the large, sliding front door. It appears that the department continued to use at least part of the building after selling it to the lodge.

In 1915, members of the South Norfolk Volunteer Fire Department constructed this building on Twenty-second Street. It was to serve as the second fire station, but when the note came due, the department was unable to raise the necessary funds and had to sell the building. It was acquired by the Woodmen of the World (WOW) lodge. On March 10, 1920, the WOW Hall, as it became known, burned. When it was repaired, the bell tower was removed. During its existence, the hall served as the home for the police station, court, town hall, election headquarters, boys club, Junior Chamber of Commerce and possibly others. *Photo courtesy of Linwood L. Briggs Jr.*

This is South Norfolk Fire Department's first motorized fire engine in front of the second fire station. When this picture was taken, the building was the property of the Woodmen of the World lodge. As can be seen, the large door was still on the front of the building. This gives the impression that perhaps the fire department was allowed to continue using the ground floor until the station on Liberty Street was built. *Photo courtesy of Hardy Forbes.*

This is South Norfolk's first motorized fire engine, shown after extinguishing a major conflagration *circa* 1917. *Photo courtesy of Linwood L. Briggs Jr.*

This American LaFrance fire engine, which was manufactured in Elmira, New York, became South Norfolk Volunteer Fire Department's second engine.

S. Herman Dennis Sr. became the second fire chief, and in 1917 under his leadership, the department completely updated its equipment. An American LaFrance fire engine was purchased—bringing a capacity of five hundred gallons per minute—and a Ford truck chassis was converted to a hose wagon. The new equipment was paid for within two years.

Around 1926, a new American LaFrance pumper with a capacity of one thousand gallons per minute (GPM) was purchased. Donations from the citizens and businesses of South Norfolk paid all but $6,000 of the debt. When Chief Dennis died in 1928, the equipment was conveyed to South Norfolk and the remaining debt was paid by the city.

In the early 1930s, a city hall was built on Liberty Street and the fire headquarters was moved to the first floor. There was a double house next to the city hall. The Humphries and Winfield families occupied the house. This was the third fire station. At that time, W.F.

This photograph of the South Norfolk Volunteer Fire Department was taken in 1916 on the grounds of the South Norfolk Grammar School on B Street. The members are, from left to right, Harvey Bunch, P.G. Etheridge, T.R. Keller (sitting in the fire engine), L.H. Newberry, A.M. Spivey, H.A. Stewart, Ralph Stewart, S.H. Dennis Sr. (chief), D.E. Gregory (seated beside the chief), Jack Brown, R.G. Reber, Richard (Billy) Morgan (mascot), M. Parron, Russell Garrett, C.L. Sykes, F.L. Rowland and W.F. Morgan. The engines are, from left to right, a 1914 Model T Ford and an American LaFrance pumper with a capacity of five hundred gallons per minute. *Photo courtesy of Ben Newberry.*

South Norfolk's third fire station was located on the first floor of the new city hall building at 13 Liberty Street. *Photo courtesy of Linwood L. Briggs Jr.*

The members of the volunteer fire department dressed in their new uniforms to have this picture taken in 1936. The stone steps of the grammar school building provided the background for many pictures. The members are, from left to right, (first row) Howard Jones, Cecil Gregory, Forest Williams, L.H. Newberry, Winston Dunning and Jack Brown; (second row) John Humphries, Billy Morgan, R.G. Reber, Aubrey Harrell and D.E. Gregory; (back row) Harvey Bunch, Herman Powers, Herbert VanVleek, John Jernigan (who would lose his life in an accident at the corner of Park Avenue and Bainbridge Boulevard in 1938), A.M. Kriss, William Nicholas, Harry Stewart and Churchill Brown. *Photograph by Atlantic Photo Studios in Norfolk and courtesy of Ben Newberry.*

Morgan was elected chief and held the position until 1934 when D.R. Gregory succeeded him. Chief Gregory held the office for one year and then retired.

In 1935, L.H. Newberry was elected chief and the position of deputy chief was created. Forest G. Williams was selected to fill the office. Chief Newberry was an effective leader and his accomplishments were many. The Ladies Auxiliary was formed to help the department with its social affairs and promote department morale. A chemical hose wagon was purchased in 1935, and the members received new dress uniforms.

The consensus of the members was that ambulance services were needed in the city, and by 1937, the fire department was operating the first ambulance in the South Norfolk and Norfolk County areas. Members of the department went door to door and held fund-raising events to pay for the unit. This new service was available free of charge, twenty-four hours per day to residents of South Norfolk, Portlock and surrounding areas.

Around the latter part of 1937, S. Herman Dennis Jr., son of former chief S. Herman Dennis Sr., followed L.H. Newberry as fire chief. At that time, the South Norfolk Fire Department was the best-equipped volunteer unit in the state. Its inventory included one

The members of the South Norfolk Volunteer Fire Department are pictured here in their new clothing in 1936. The department reached its peak in number and performance between 1936 and 1945. Thanks to the efficiency of the fire department, the city received an excellent rating from the National Board of Fire Underwriters. *Photo courtesy of Ben Newberry.*

The officers of the volunteer fire department in 1936 are, from left to right, Captain D.E. Gregory, Assistant Chief Forest Williams, Chief L.H. Newberry and Captain Winston Dunning. This picture was taken on the grounds of the South Norfolk Grammar School. The houses and buildings in the background are on Liberty Street. *Photo courtesy of Ben Newberry.*

South Norfolk's first ambulance was parked at Blanchard Motor Company, a Packard dealer on Liberty Street. This ambulance was probably purchased, as were several others, with contributions from the citizens of South Norfolk. *Photo courtesy of Linwood L. Briggs Jr.*

The fourth fire station was built on the corner of Liberty and Twentieth Streets around 1938. Before the construction of this station, the corner was occupied by Blanchard Motor Company. *Photo courtesy of Linwood L. Briggs Jr.*

500 GPM and one 1,000 GPM American LaFrance pumpers, a chemical wagon and an ambulance. There were thirty members in the department, and they were paid by the hour while fighting fire. The average number of calls per month was ten.

It was an evening in 1938 when tragedy struck the department. A Norfolk and Southern jitney was in South Norfolk picking up workers when it collided with the one-thousand-gallons-per-minute pumper at the corner of Bainbridge Boulevard and Park Avenue. The pumper was totaled, and John Jernigan was killed. Three other firemen were seriously injured but recovered. The wrecked pumper was stored in the building that had been Gregory's Blacksmith Shop at 700 Liberty Street. A new pumper was ordered from American LaFrance.

The next fire station was built around 1938 at the corner of Liberty and Twentieth Streets on property that had been vacated by a Mr. Miles. This location was across the street from Gregory's Blacksmith Shop.

A new Cadillac ambulance was purchased around 1941 at a cost of $4,000. The purchase was financed as the other ambulance had been—by donations from the citizens, businesses and industrial plants. The ambulance was an asset for all the many industries along the Southern Branch of the Elizabeth River.

In 1944, a 750-gallon-per-minute LaFrance was purchased at a cost of $14,000. When it arrived, firefighters discovered the truck was too large for the streets of South Norfolk. No one had thought to check the size of the engine or the streets before ordering. As luck would have it, Norfolk was able to use the pumper at the Ocean View Station and South Norfolk was able to recoup $10,000 of its investment.

In 1945, the fire siren that had been mounted on a pole at Park Avenue and Jackson Street was removed by the city. This action resulted in a serious disagreement between the fire department and the city government. As a result, the majority of the department resigned and the Ladies Auxiliary was disbanded. The city immediately filled the vacancies and appointed W.L. Nicholas fire chief.

When the City of South Norfolk changed to the city manager form of government in 1947, the fire department was again reorganized. At that time, R.D. Wallace was elected

Chief of the Fire Prevention Bureau Ovie Yenson is shown here with a group of schoolchildren. After Portlock became a part of South Norfolk on January 1, 1951, Yenson was assigned the full-time position of fire inspector.

chief with F.G. Williams as deputy chief and T.J. VanVleek, J.W. Dunning and D.S. Ford as assistant chiefs. The Fire Prevention Bureau was also established with Ovie Yenson appointed chief. This was the first Fire Prevention Bureau established in the region. Chief Yenson was dedicated and made every effort possible to remove fire hazards from the city and to instruct the citizens about fire prevention and safety. At the same time, VanVleek implemented a training program for all members of the department. When the City of Chesapeake was formed in 1963, VanVleek became its first fire marshal.

In September 1949, Chief Wallace resigned and the city manager appointed Forest Williams to fill the position. It was also in 1949 that legal proceedings began for the annexation of the town of Portlock.

When Portlock became a part of South Norfolk on January 1, 1951, the city hired its first full-time employees to serve on the fire department. W.H. (Wink) Evans and John Ben Gibson Sr. were appointed deputy chiefs; Maxie Chappell, Vernon Eure, Stanley VanVleek, Peter Hollowell, Tom Sawyer and George Gwynn were hired to operate the equipment. A

This picture, which was taken after South Norfolk annexed Portlock, shows John Ben Gibson Sr., the first full-time fire chief, and some other members of the fire department looking at what appears to be drawings. The men around the tables are, from left to right, John Ben Gibson Jr., possibly Vernon Eure, Chief Gibson and Robert Bagely. Ovie Yenson is standing beside Robert Bagley. In the back row, from left to right, are William Cartwright, unknown, Charlie Wiliford, unknown and Maxie Chappell.

This old house at 701 St. James Street behind the fire/police station at one time served as the welfare department. In May 1942, the Office of Price Administration opened local board number 65-4 on the first floor of the house. That was where War Rationing Books were issued to the families of South Norfolk. At that time, the second floor was the meeting place for Boy Scouts Troop 54. After a full-time fire department became a reality, the house became the sleeping quarters for the firemen on duty. The sign on the porch read "Police and Fire Recreation members only." This picture was taken in 1959. The house became a part of the slum clearance program of 1957–1961. *Photo courtesy of Linwood L. Briggs Jr.*

In November 1960, the South Norfolk Fire Department answered a call for assistance on nearby St. James Street.

In this February 1962 photograph, the fire station is shown on the corner of Twentieth and Liberty Streets. The corporation court and municipal buildings stand next to it.

More than a dozen chiefs watch three braves connect a fire hose to the hydrant. The man second from the left with his hands in his hip pockets is Chief John Ben Gibson Sr. Some of the other recognizable men in the picture are a Mr. Wood standing next to Chief Gibson, Tommy VanVleek, Milburn Hines, Maxie Chappell and possibly Jack Twine.

Left: This photograph, taken on March 10, 1920, shows several brave firemen climbing a tall ladder to fight the fire at the WOW Hall on Twenty-second Street. *Photo courtesy of Hardy Forbes.*

Right: Also on March 10, 1920, the fire at the WOW Hall spread to and ignited this two-story house. The side near the rear of the WOW Hall can be seen in the background. This leads me to believe the house was located on B Street.

This 1941 model Peter Pirsch fire truck was top of the line, and two were ordered in October 1941. When the United States entered World War II, production for civilian use was soon terminated; however, one truck was delivered to the Portlock volunteers in May 1942. South Norfolk did not receive its fire truck until after the war ended and production for civilian use began again. This fire truck went on to serve Chesapeake.

short time later, Ovie Yenson was assigned to the full-time position of fire inspector. Forest Williams, a volunteer, remained fire chief. The position of volunteer fire chief carried a salary of $100 per year.

Chief Williams died in 1953 and T.J. VanVleek was appointed to fill the vacancy. When Chief VanVleek resigned in 1954, John Ben Gibson Sr. became the first full-time fire chief. A second-battalion chief position was created in 1958; Robert G. Bagley, who in later years would become the second chief of the Chesapeake Fire Department, was appointed.

In 1963, when the City of South Norfolk merged with Norfolk County to form the new City of Chesapeake, John Ben Gibson Sr. was appointed to the position of fire chief.

The present fire station, which is designated as station number 1, was built in the 1200 block of Twentieth Street. It is the fifth fire station constructed in South Norfolk.

South Norfolk's early fire department consisted mainly of volunteers. The department was an important part of their lives: they spent many hours soliciting funds to purchase needed equipment and then used their knowledge and ingenuity to keep it operational.

Listed below are some early members of the South Norfolk Fire Department. Most likely some names have been left out. This is not intentional, for a high percentage of the male population served the fire department at one time or another. If your name does not appear, please forgive me because I, too, am getting old.

Robert G. Bagley	George Gwynn	R.G. Reber
Jack Brown	R.D. Haley	R.M. Rich
Harvey Bunch	Peter Hollowell	J.R. Rock
Maxie Chappell	J.F. Hutchins	F.L. Rowland
Henry Clark	J.J. Inman	Tom Sawyer
Roy Cuthrell	John W. Jernigan	A.M. Spivey
S. Herman Dennis Sr.	T.R. Keller	H.A. Stewart
S. Herman Dennis Jr.	W.C. Keller	Ralph Stewart
C.L. Dowdy	Dutch Kriss	C.L. Sykes
J.W. Dunning	C.L. Lee	Paul Sykes
P.G. Etheridge	Richard Morgan	R.D. Wallace
Vernon Eure	W.F. Morgan, Captain Billy	E.H. Whitehurst
W.H. (Wink) Evans	Norman Morse	Forest Wiliams
J.C. Garrett	L.H. Newberry	Hunter Williams
Russell Garrett	L.M. Nicholas	Herbert Van Vleek
W. Giarid	H.L. Nicholas	Stanley Van Vleek
John Ben Gibson Sr.	W.L. Nichols	T.J. Van Vleek
W.F. Gray	M. Parron	S.W. Wilson Sr.
Cecil Gregory	M. Pollard	Ovie Yenson
D.E. Gregory	W.M. Poyner	Austin Zimmer

CHAPTER X

PORTLOCK VOLUNTEER
FIRE DEPARTMENT

Nestled just south of South Norfolk was the small village of Portlock. Citizens of the small but active community were concerned about the need for effective fire protection. A meeting was held in K.C. Karnegay's garage in November 1923 to address the issue. G.B. Downing, A. Gallop, S.S. Leary, W.S. O'Neal, D.B. Wood, Howard Gibson and John Ben Gibson were some of the more vocal attendees. It was unimaginable at the time that some forty years later, John Ben Gibson, one of the youngest men at the meeting, would become fire chief of a new city, many times the size of tiny Portlock. During the meeting, the Portlock Volunteer Fire Department was organized. Gallop was elected chief of the department, and O'Neal was elected president of the organization. A monthly meeting schedule was established with the meetings being held at Gallop's garage, the headquarters for the department.

The department's first piece of apparatus was an old hand reel with two hundred feet of hose, donated by County Supervisor Charlie Olds from the Deep Creek District of Norfolk County. A large bell was mounted on the roof of the garage, and when a fire call came in, it sounded for several minutes to alert the volunteers. Upon hearing the bell, they would report to the garage to pick up the reel and hose before responding to the fire.

The Gibson garage gave the young department its first fire truck in 1925. The 1924 Model-T Ford was used to tow the hand reel to the fire scene. In 1926, Sheriff A.A. Wendel, of Norfolk County, gave the department a Buick automobile. Members converted this car into a truck and equipped it with additional hose, back tanks and fire extinguishers.

Plans for a new fire station began to take shape in 1928. The Norfolk County School Board granted the department permission to build a station on the corner of school property at Freeman Avenue and Bainbridge Boulevard. Through a public appeal, funds were obtained and building materials were purchased. The members built the small station themselves. The bell that was previously mounted on Gallop's garage was replaced with a siren that could be heard from a much greater distance. Also at that time, membership in the organization began to increase.

The year 1930 was important for the Portlock Volunteer Fire Department. Through the efforts of D.B. Wood, a county supervisor, a Chevrolet fire truck was obtained. The new truck was equipped with a front-mounted pump and five hundred feet of new hose. Because of its size, the acquisition required a larger housing space. This was the department's opportunity

Although Mr. and Mrs. Bruce Hassell were important and respected citizens of the small village of Portlock, the background in this photograph is also of importance in telling the story of Portlock's small but effective volunteer fire department. The old tin garage that served as the first fire station can be seen here on Bainbridge Boulevard near the corner of Freeman Avenue. The small house to the left of the station was used as the health department. This two-room house was moved to Lakeside Park in 1952 and, on August 20, became South Norfolk's first library. *Photo courtesy of the Hassell family collection.*

This picture of the old tin garage that served as the Portlock fire station was taken in April 1944. Portlock became part of South Norfolk in 1951. At that time, the two fire departments became one paid, full-time department.

Plans for a new and larger fire station began to take shape in 1928. The Norfolk County School Board granted the department permission to build a station on part of the unused land acquired from the Shea family in the later 1800s. As the department added new and larger equipment to its inventory, it became necessary to remodel and enlarge the station. In 1930, a second bay was added. Again in 1942, additional equipment made it essential to construct a new and larger fire station. This photograph shows large stacks of cinder blocks and other materials used in the construction of a new station beside the old tin garage.

to remodel and enlarge its small station. During the renovation, a second bay was added with a meeting hall in the rear.

Chief Gallop died in 1932, and E.H. Cuthrell was appointed to fill the vacancy. C. Glemming was elected president; after serving in the position for one year, he was succeeded by J.H. McCloud, who also served one year.

In 1934, Cuthrell was again appointed to the position of chief and began to receive a small salary from the department for maintenance of the equipment. A.L. Capps was appointed as assistant chief. One of these two men was always on duty.

John Ben Gibson Sr. became fire chief in 1935. Under his leadership, the department continued to grow. Raincoats, boots, etc. were added to the equipment list and purchased with county funds.

In 1938, Oscar F. Smith, president of Smith Douglas Fertilizer Corporation, donated a 1930 Packard, which became the department's first ambulance. Most of the fire department members received first-aid training, and in January 1939, the department's first emergency medical unit was placed in service. The importance of offering ambulance service to the community was soon apparent, and the department began to solicit donations to purchase a 1938 Cadillac to replace the Packard. Following a successful fund drive, the Cadillac was purchased and put into service in 1941. As true then as it is today, the Portlock ambulance

This picture was taken at the dedication of the new fire station in August 1944. It had four bays, a workshop, an office, a meeting hall and bedrooms upstairs. The original bell and the siren the department acquired later were both installed on the roof. This was a tremendous accomplishment for a village the size of Portlock, and many citizens turned out to support the department. Chief John Ben Gibson Sr. is wearing the white cap in front of the first bay on the left. A part of the Portlock High School building can be seen in the left background.

had the reputation for being a busy unit. By 1945, the ambulance averaged one call per day, which according to a publication, was "quite a record."

In 1942, a 1941 GMC truck with a front-mounted pump was obtained for use as a second-run piece with a new 750-gallon-per-minute Peter Pirsch pumper. The pumper carried two thousand feet of hose, two hundred gallons of water and other small equipment. Again, the fire station was too small for the new equipment and plans were put in motion for construction of a new and more elaborate fire station. The station would have four bays, a workshop, an office, a meeting hall and bedrooms. Wilson Paxson, county supervisor at the time, secured an appropriation of funds for the new building. It was built and dedication took place in August 1944.

Following the opening of the new fire station, the chief and the assistant chief became full-time, salaried employees of the Portlock Fire Department. In addition, two full-time firemen were hired. The paid department in 1945 consisted of Chief John Ben Gibson Sr., Assistant Chief A.L. Capps, Chief Engineer E.O. Spruill and Assistant Engineer R.L. Halstead. Two men were on duty at all times. The Portlock Volunteer Fire Department

After South Norfolk annexed Portlock in 1951, the fire station on Liberty Street in South Norfolk was designated as station number 1 and the Portlock station became known as South Norfolk Fire Station 2. This attractive night photograph may have been taken during the 1951 Christmas season. As can be seen, the large puddle of water in front of the station produced a reflection of the holiday lights.

served the areas of what is now Indian River, Greenbrier and Great Bridge as well as the area south to the North Carolina line. The farthest response within their first run area was some twenty-five miles from the station.

Gibson continued to serve as fire chief until Portlock was annexed by South Norfolk in 1951. In 1954, he became the first full-time chief of the South Norfolk Fire Department.

On the evening of December 31, 1962, as local residents prepared to ring in the new year, firefighters of the South Norfolk and Norfolk County fire stations anxiously watched the clock, awaiting something more. An important era of the fire service was about to fade into the past and a new chapter was about to unfold. With the arrival of the New Year came the merger of South Norfolk and Norfolk County. With this merger, the Chesapeake Fire Department was born.

INDEX

Y

About the Author

Author and historian Raymond L. Harper is a lifelong resident of South Norfolk, and has served the old city of South Norfolk and the city of Chesapeake in several capacities, including president of the Chesapeake Museum's Board of Directors and as a commissioner on the South Norfolk revitalization commission. He received his formal education from The College of William and Mary, Virginia Tech, Old Dominion University and Weber State.

He has authored or co-authored seven books about the city of South Norfolk, Norfolk County and the city of Chesapeake, including *South Norfolk: Then and Now*, *Norfolk County (Images of America)* and *Chesapeake, Virginia (The Making of America)*. He and his wife of fifty-seven years, Emma, still live in the borough of South Norfolk, which is now part of the city of Chesapeake.

SOUTH NORFOLK
VIRGINIA
1661–2005

A DEFINITIVE HISTORY
VOLUME II

RAYMOND L. HARPER

SOUTH NORFOLK VIRGINIA
1661–2005
A DEFINITIVE HISTORY
VOLUME TWO
RAYMOND L. HARPER

From the introduction of volume two:

With the settlement in the Elizabeth River Parish, around 1649 to 1651, it became necessary to build additional "chapels of ease" to accommodate those who lived a great distance from the parish church. The first chapel is evidenced by a grant of 1653 to Richard Pinner on the Western Branch. The second chapel was the Tanner's Creek Chapel, which was built between 1659 and 1661 on a branch of Mason Creek on land in present-day Norfolk near the naval air station. The third chapel of the Elizabeth River Parish was the Southern Branch Chapel. This land was on the east side of the branch between what is now called Scuffletown Creek and Jones Creek.

Before September 19, 1919, South Norfolk was a small flourishing community in the Washington Magisterial District of Norfolk County. It was a five-mile by seven-mile area nestled to the south of Berkley, which by that time had been annexed by the city of Norfolk. The magistrate's office and other local government offices were located in the Flatiron building near the Belt Line Railroad crossing on Liberty Street.

After South Norfolk became a second-class city on September 19, 1919, citizens formed their own police force. The early officers didn't receive any formal training and some took advantage of the fact that they wore a badge and carried a gun. In other words, shoot first and ask questions later. The Woodmen of the World (WOW) Hall on Twenty-second Street became the police, fire, court and election headquarters. Many court cases were heard at night. Court cases and differences of opinion that occurred at election time sometimes led to old-fashioned shootouts. It was like the Old West: If you had a gun, you could carry it.

The downtown or shopping district of early South Norfolk was centered mostly around three blocks of Liberty Street, two blocks of Poindexter Street, one block of Chesapeake Avenue and, before 1938, a part of St. James Street. In 1873, J. Alonzo McCloud operated the only store in what was then known as McCloudtown. By 1888, S.W. Wilson's grocery business was situated in a small frame house on Liberty Street.

The growth of South Norfolk continued at a rapid pace. New homes, schools and churches were built. The shopping areas were expanding with new businesses opening almost daily. One thing that the prosperous town lacked was entertainment on a continuing basis. That void would be filled with the opening of the Grand Theatre in 1919. In addition to the

Grand Theatre, the citizens of South Norfolk saw the construction of the Preston Building and the Chesapeake Pharmacy in 1919.

New construction continued throughout the 1920s and 1930s. The 1920s saw a period of national prosperity. C.M. Jordan, W.P. Jordan, and Associates financed construction of the Norfolk-Portsmouth (Jordan) Bridge. Permission to build the bridge was secured from the Sixty-ninth Congress on May 22, 1926.

In the early years, there were many street vendors using their horse-drawn wagons. Among them were produce and fish peddlers. They usually came in late spring, summer and early fall. Each August, there were many vendors with wagons filled with homegrown watermelons. These melons could be purchased for 10, 15 or 25 cents each. In the winter months, deliveries of wood and coal were made by horse-drawn carts, carrying several tons of coal or cords of wood. The same companies made summer deliveries of ice.

South Norfolk was a community of sports enthusiasts. There were high school, amateur and eventually community league teams. Some teams were organized and played full schedules in the early 1900s. The South Norfolk Athletic Association was formed in 1924. Early history of amateur athletics in South Norfolk was said to have been divided into two periods—the earlier period was represented by the Panthers and the second period was represented by the Aces. Apparently the Panthers' last season was in 1929. Sunday afternoons in the 1930s attracted many local citizens to Johnson's Park, Baker's Field or Cascade Park to watch the Aces play either football or baseball. The 1940s brought World War II, and most able-bodied men either enlisted or were drafted into the military.

After the war ended and life began to settle down for those who were fortunate enough to return home, several projects of interest began to surface. Clarence Forehand's individual campaign to bring an armory to South Norfolk began as early as 1948 when he was mayor of the city. After much planning and politicking, ground breaking for the structure took place in November 1955. About the same time the population of the city of South Norfolk began to take an interest in the finer things, such as reading and libraries. The first library was a two-room house that was moved from the lot next to the fire station in Portlock to Lakeside Park in South Norfolk. On August 20, 1952, it officially became the city's first library. The program was a huge success and the library soon required larger quarters. A store building on Chesapeake Avenue was rented and a temporary move was made until construction of the memorial library on Poindexter Street could be accomplished in 1958.

While Berkley was not a part of South Norfolk, its citizens played a large and important part in the founding of the community immediately to its south. The years after the Civil War through the end of World War I were mostly prosperous for Berkley. Everything began going down hill after the city of Norfolk annexed the area on January 1, 1906. A few years later, Prohibition came and the very successful Garrett Winery closed in 1916, putting approximately five hundred people out of work. Much of the forest had been cleared, causing the lumber and other businesses to move out of the area. As if this wasn't enough, the day before Good Friday in April 1922, most of Berkley was destroyed by fire

The history of Berkley is one of great interest and should be recognized as such. I have never seen a book devoted entirely to the history of that community.

As I did in my original history of South Norfolk some ten years ago, I have devoted space to short biographies of some of our founding fathers. Some did more than others, but all should be recognized for their many good deeds.

When all has been said and done, and the correct information is made known, it can be truthfully stated that the merger to create the city of Chesapeake was the biggest mistake of the past century. South Norfolk—a perfectly sound city with a bright future—died because of it, and the area is still trying to recover. It may never be revitalized, and if it is, the financial cost will be out of this world.

The future of South Norfolk…just where do we begin? On October 10, 2000, a Chesapeake City Council work session was held with Professor Bradford Grant, the head of the Architectural Department of Hampton University, and several of his senior students. They were asked to make a study of conditions in South Norfolk and come up with recommendations for its revitalization. The group met with various civic organizations and the South Norfolk Revitalization Commission, and after an in-depth study, produced a list of suggestions. After completion of this study, the City of Chesapeake entered into a contract with Urban Design Associates from Pittsburgh, Pennsylvania. The firm accomplished its task in three very in-depth phases and as a result the plans for revitalization of South Norfolk are built around five initiatives, which are covered in Chapter 20 of volume two.

Some projects that lend themselves to the revitalization of South Norfolk have already been completed, and others are in the works. Revitalization will not take place overnight. It could possibly take twenty years to accomplish what is planned. A few young families have acquired old homes in the historic district and are in the process of restoring them to the beauty that they once enjoyed. Steps need to be taken now to ensure that plans from all the previous studies will come to fruition. The city fathers should take a few steps backward and remember that without South Norfolk, there wouldn't be the city of Chesapeake or the positions that they enjoy.

There were many individuals and families who figured in the early years of South Norfolk. How wonderful it would have been to have known them all. Some were well known and made it big, while others, whose names were less familiar, contributed in their own way to the world around them and to future generations. It is to them that I would like to devote the final chapter of this volume. As an added treat, a few additional photographs have been included. I hope you enjoy them.

"Small-town USA" all but disappeared during the past century. Many communities have been annexed by larger surrounding cities or have merged with other towns or counties to avoid the loss of land, population and tax dollars. South Norfolk's population increased until it became a first-class city, yet even after this growth, its small-town flavor survived and neighbors remained friends—not just people to tolerate. Many of the pictures in this volume will help us step back in time when life was slower and much simpler, visit some of the prospering businesses and admire some of the old homes (many of which are still standing today). This volume contains images from the 1880s through 2004. It is my hope that people will not just look at the pictures but will also read the text, for I feel that there is a lot of worthwhile information between the two covers.